The Senior Volunteer

The Senior Volunteer

Where and How Retired Americans Can Give Back

CHARLES C. SHARPE

McFarland & Company, Inc., Publishers
Jefferson, North Carolina, and London

LIBRARY OF CONGRESS CATALOGUING-IN-PUBLICATION DATA

Sharpe, Charles C., 1935–
The senior volunteer : where and how retired Americans
can give back / Charles C. Sharpe.
p.   cm.
Includes bibliographical references and index.

ISBN 0-7864-2144-4 (softcover : 50# alkaline paper) ∞

1. Voluntarism—United States.   2. Older volunteers—United States.
3. Retirees—United States.   I. Title
HN90.V64S43 2005   302'.14—dc22   2005011463

British Library cataloguing data are available

Cover photograph ©2005 Corbis Photos

Manufactured in the United States of America

*McFarland & Company, Inc., Publishers
Box 611, Jefferson, North Carolina 28640
www.mcfarlandpub.com*

Contents

Preface	1
Abbreviations and Acronyms	3
Part I. An Overview of Volunteerism for Seniors	7
1. Volunteerism	9
2. The American Volunteer Tradition	26
3. Redefining Aging and Retirement	40
Part II. The Scope of Senior Volunteerism	61
4. How Many Seniors Volunteer?	63
5. Where Do Seniors Volunteer?	69
6. Why Do Seniors Volunteer?	73
Part III. Volunteer Opportunities	83
7. Government Programs	85
8. National Programs	116
9. International Programs	139
10. Clearinghouses	150
11. Virtual Volunteering	156
Part IV. Appendices	171
1. A Profile of Older Americans: 2003	173
2. Volunteering in the United States: 2003	180
3. Internet Tutorials	188
Internet Glossary	191
Sources	195
Index	203

Preface

"Past the beggar and the suffering walks he who asks, 'Why, oh God, do you not do something for these people?' To which God replies, 'I did do something. I made you.'"

—SUFI SAYING

One of the best advantages of being a retiree or a senior is that you are likely to have more time to do the things you may have always wanted to do. Time and isolation can be the enemy of the idle elderly. Don't let the winter of your life become a winter of discontent. Don't give up; give back. Volunteer!

Volunteers of all ages have traditionally been the backbone of community services in America. Retirees and seniors provide, perhaps, the most reliable service, given their wisdom, life experience and maturity. They are "senior capital," the largely untapped wealth of our nation.

If one of your ambitions has always been to help others, you'll find a wealth of opportunities to do so as a volunteer, and you'll derive immeasurable personal satisfaction and feelings of self-fulfillment from the experience.

Each one of us has a duty to our fellow humans (those now living and those yet to be born) and to the environment to give back a small part of the many benefits we have received. That kind of giving is important if a community, a nation—indeed, the world—is to be a better place for everyone. Many nonprofit organizations in our communities are struggling with shortages of volunteers, supplies, and funding, while the demand for their services and the numbers in desperate need of them continue to increase. More help is needed. Volunteers are a vital resource. There are numerous opportunities to volunteer and many roles you can play. Don't wait to be asked.

The purpose of this book is to help seniors find ideal volunteer opportunities. Preparation of this book involved an extensive review of the current literature on volunteering. Numerous citations and quotations from authoritative sources on the topic are included, most derived from the Internet. Also drawn largely from the Internet is the information on most of the volunteer opportunities listed in the book. In most cases, further information is available on the Worldwide Web. For the "newbie" to the Web, a number of tutorials are listed in Appendix 3. These may prove helpful if one's grandchildren or great-grandchildren are not readily available—or willing—to consult.

The eminent German-born Harvard psychologist Erik Erikson (1902–1994) once said that the final challenge in life is coming to terms with the notion, "I am what survives of me." If he is correct, then volunteerism—especially that form of service which has an impact on the lives of the young members of our society—is essential to the long and fruitful lives of the old members of our society.

No single individual can solve the world's problems, but what little you might do can make your small corner of the world, or the many other corners, a happier, healthier, safer place to live for those who need your help. Together we can make a difference by finding ways to help that will make our efforts worth the time and trouble we invest in them. Volunteering is one of these ways!

Abbreviations
and Acronyms

AARP	Prior to 1999, the American Association of Retired Persons; now the full name of that organization.
ACE	Army Corps of Engineers
ACS	American Cancer Society
AHA	American Heart Association
AIUSA	Amnesty International USA
AoA	Administration on Aging
ARC	American Red Cross
BBBS	Big Brothers Big Sisters
BLM	Bureau of Land Management
BLS	Bureau of Labor Statistics
BOP	Bureau of Prisons
CCC	Civilian Conservation Corps
CFR	Code of Federal Regulations
CIRCLE	Center for Information and Research on Civic Learning and Engagement
CNS	Corporation for National and Community Service
CNVS	Catholic Network of Volunteer Service
CPS	*Current Population Survey*
DVUSA	Dominican Volunteers USA
EASI	Environmental Alliance for Senior Involvement
EPA	Environmental Protection Agency

FBCI	Faith-Based and Community Initiatives
FEMA	Federal Emergency Management Agency
FGP	Foster Grandparent Program
FWS	Fish and Wildlife Service
GVN	Global Volunteer Network
IESC	International Executive Service Corps
JVC	Jewish Volunteer Corps
LCE	Legal Counsel for the Elderly
LTC	Long Term Care Ombudsman
MOWAA	Meals on Wheels Association of America
MRC	Medical Reserve Corps
NCIC	National Crime Information Center
NCOA	National Council on the Aging
NIA	National Institute on Aging
NIH	National Institutes of Health
NMSS	National Multiple Sclerosis Society
NOAA	National Oceanic and Atmospheric Administration
NRCS	Natural Resources Conservation Service
NRVC	National Retiree Volunteer Coalition
NSC	National Service Corps, National Safety Council
OAA	Older Americans Act
OPM	Office of Personnel Management
PASEC	Pennsylvania Senior Environmental Corps
PBS	Public Broadcasting Service
RSVP	The Retired and Senior Volunteer Program
SAVE	Senior Attorney Volunteers for the Elderly
SBA	Small Business Administration
SCORE	The Service Corps of Retired Executives
SCP	The Senior Companion Program
SYVP	Senior, Youth, and Volunteer Programs
UMVIM	United Methodist Volunteers In Mission
UNICEF	United Nations Children's Fund
UNV	United Nations Volunteers
UNDP	United Nations Development Program
URL	Uniform Resource Locator
USACE	U.S. Army Corps of Engineers

VFW	Veterans of Foreign Wars
VIMI	Volunteers in Medicine Institute
VISTA	Volunteers in Service to America
VMB	Volunteer Management Branch (BOP)
VOA	Volunteers of America
VSO	Voluntary Service Overseas
YMCA	Young Men's Christian Association
YWCA	Young Women's Christian Association

PART I

An Overview of Volunteerism for Seniors

1. Volunteerism

"Volunteerism is the voice of the people put into action. These actions shape
and mold the present into a future of which we can all be proud."
—HELEN DYER

What Is a Volunteer?

Although the concepts of "volunteer" and "volunteerism" are generally
familiar to most individuals, they are not consistently defined. A review of the
extant literature reveals a disparity of definitions; many do not appear to encompass the full scope and prevalence of the volunteerism we witness in our national
and global society today. Mary V. Merrill notes: "Although published literature
and definitions contained therein are 'timeless' in the academic world we would
suggest that 'volunteer' and 'volunteerism' are not. Should we ... confine our
professional focus to traditional concepts and definitions of 'volunteer' and 'volunteerism'? Should we strive for more inclusive definitions that incorporate
traditional human behaviors into contemporary programs and institutional
structures?" (Merrill, "In Search of a Contemporary Definition of Volunteerism,"
2000).

In 1983, Park suggested that "the heart of volunteerism is the countless individual acts of commitment encompassing an endless variety of ... tasks" (Park,
Meaning Well Is Not Enough: Perspectives on Volunteering, 1983, 118). A few years
later, Smith defined volunteers as individuals who reach out, beyond the confines
of their paid employment and of their normal responsibilities, to contribute time
and service to a not-for-profit cause in the belief that their activity is beneficial
to others as well as satisfying to themselves. Although functional definitions of
volunteerism are as varied and contrasting as the volunteers themselves, a uni-

fying concept is the idea that volunteers are not paid for their services (Smith, "Taking Volunteerism into the 21st Century," 1989)

Our government, in its inimitable wisdom, has propounded official definitions of "volunteer." As rendered by the United States Department of Labor in the Fair Labor Standards Act (29 CFR §553.101), a volunteer is:

> An individual who performs hours of service for a public agency for civic, charitable, or humanitarian reasons, without promise, expectation or receipt of compensation for services rendered…. Individuals shall be considered volunteers only where their services are offered freely and without pressure or coercion, direct or implied, from an employer…. An individual shall not be considered a volunteer if the individual is otherwise employed by the same public agency to perform the same type of services as those for which the individual proposes to volunteer [U.S. Department of Labor].

The Department of Agriculture defines a volunteer as any person, adult or teen, in a leadership capacity who contributes time to the promotion, organization, assistance, or leadership of an organization, and is not paid for services rendered.

> Beyond these legal definitions of volunteers, it should be acknowledged that there are, in fact, many variations of the meaning of the term "volunteer." For example, *Webster's Dictionary* simply defines a volunteer as one who enters into or offers oneself for a service of his/her free will. In this sense the volunteer is basically distinguished as one who is not coerced to perform services. Further, while normally voluntary services are performed for which the individual neither expects nor receives compensation, it does not, in many cases, preclude the payment of expenses—such as per diem, travel allowances, stipends or living allowances, child care, or educational expenses [Young, "Volunteerism"].

Mary Merrill proposes four tenets that should comprise a contemporary definition of volunteerism. She believes that these "encompass traditional, contemporary and emerging perspectives of this human behavior."

• Volunteerism implies active involvement—active participation or contributions of time, energies, or talents—not merely the giving of financial or material resources as a donor or sponsor.

• Volunteerism is (relatively) uncoerced. Those who give of their time, energies, and talents do so of their own free will, primarily from intrinsic motivations, individual altruism.

• Volunteerism is not primarily motivated by economic gain. Traditionally, organizations have reimbursed volunteers for certain personal expenses incurred during their service. Some senior citizens, who may have a strong desire to volunteer, but who may have limited financial resources, may not be able to afford such expenses. For them, some monetary aspect of volunteerism in the form of financial remuneration may be necessary and appropriate.

• Volunteerism focuses on the common good. Although motivation to volunteer can be intensely personal and individual—perhaps even self-serving—the focus must remain on the common good. Altruism should serve as an ultimate goal as well as a means toward that goal. Research has shown that volunteers recognize that personal gain is possible from volunteering—satisfaction, self-confidence, and recognition. However, such personal benefits *per se* are strongly perceived to be the wrong reasons for volunteering. (Source: Merrill, "In Search of a Contemporary Definition of Volunteerism," 2000.)

In short, volunteerism is any activity that is relatively uncoerced, intended to help others in some way, conducted without any thought of monetary gain, and is a form of labor and not merely recreation or diversion. A volunteer is any person, young or old, who makes available to others his or her time, energy, knowledge, experience, and talents, while expecting nothing in return. Such people are willing to learn, to share their own wisdom and embrace that of others; in so doing, they experience personal inner growth and satisfaction. They appreciate the importance of time and kindness and the immeasurable value of both to others in society who may be less fortunate.

What Are the Benefits of Volunteering?

A study by Independent Sector, a prestigious coalition of philanthropic and charitable organizations, found that volunteering—among its many benefits—adds value to services, promotes social harmony, and creates public trust (Independent Sector, "Giving and Volunteering in the United States 2001," 2001).

Specifically, what are some of the benefits of volunteerism? First, a review of the literature demonstrates that volunteers provide a real economic cost savings—the "value to services" identified by Independent Sector. Second, volunteerism is recognized as an effective way to include citizens' participation in non-profit or governmental operations and decision-making processes.

It is believed that volunteers "can see and understand firsthand," through their various voluntary experiences, that public interests and needs are indeed being seriously and competently pursued and, where possible, successfully met. The literature, in many cases, suggests that volunteers improve citizenship and serve as an effective conduit to educate individuals outside philanthropic and governmental circles as to the merits of public service.

In addition to the two main benefits of volunteerism noted above, in 1995

J. L. Brundy, writing in *Volunteer Management Handbook*, identified a number of other benefits commonly associated with the use of volunteers in the public sector. He said that volunteers

- Add to the quality and capacity of programmatic services;
- provide enthusiasm, extra resources and, many times, much needed skills;
- supplement the normal workforce during times of crisis and especially when workload demands peak;
- provide a ready pool of applicants for employment;
- and often provide services outside the normal purview of government employees, such as fund raising and advocacy (cited in Young, "Volunteerism").

There are many benefits any individual can derive from volunteerism. These include reward in the form of psychic income; the satisfaction of realizing the benefits to the receivers of one's efforts; improvement in one's personal repertoire of skills; relaxation and reduction of personal stress; community betterment; and socialization.

Volunteering can enable the individual to acquire or enhance the knowledge and skills needed in personal life. There are new talents to be discovered in a novel experience—talents that may be latent and unrealized. You can meet new friends who may bring new experiences and talents to the encounter. From them you can learn about yourself and the world around you. Discovering more about yourself is one of the greatest benefits to be derived from the volunteer experience. You will have the self-satisfaction which comes from taking time to give a little of that self to help others. You will not be diminished; you will grow! You will learn to appreciate new aspects of your community and critically assess your past views about that community and your role in it.

The simple act of volunteering at a homeless shelter or soup kitchen can enable the volunteer to better understand the factors that contribute to hunger and homelessness. Tutoring or mentoring a child can enhance one's understanding of the status of education in a particular community and the needs of the children in the system. Volunteering to clean up a local stream, river, or park can contribute to appreciation of environmental issues facing one's own community and the nation at large.

> Volunteers provide the human capital to alleviate community problems, advocate for social change, research new discoveries, protect neighborhoods, and worship together in community. While volunteers are doing this work, they are making new connections, building their own sense of community, learning new skills, fostering heightened self-esteem, and cultivating leadership capacities. Additionally, volunteering has been shown, when coupled with reflection, to develop the skills of citizenship and greater political

efficacy; it raises the volunteer's awareness of important societal issues and makes the volunteer a more informed citizen.

For volunteer service to reach its greatest potential, it must also provide common ground for people to meet and know one another across differences. Volunteerism can serve as a platform for meaningful exchanges that bridge chasms of class, race, and power. Service provides unique ground for diverse people to work together toward common goals and to create social cohesion.

In order to maximize the societal benefits, volunteer projects must allow both sides of the volunteer exchange—server and served—to learn from one another. A powerful volunteer exchange is one in which the reciprocal nature of the volunteer experience is evident (Nunn, "Building Social Capital").

Reasons People Volunteer

In making a final decision to volunteer, consider these reasons for volunteering that have been identified by those who have done so:

- After a lifetime of taking, retirement can be a time to give back.
- It promotes a feeling compassion for those in need.
- It provides a way to be useful, help others, and do good deeds.
- The work is enjoyable and makes one feel needed and appreciated.
- You can help somebody not as healthy or fortunate as you.
- You have a deep personal interest in the activity or work.
- You gain a new perspective on life.
- Your own personal development is enhanced.
- Volunteerism increases self-esteem and confidence.
- You experience feelings of personal empowerment.
- You discover personal fulfillment and satisfaction.
- Your ability to deal with your personal problems develops.
- Improved interpersonal skills enrich your life.
- You exercise leadership and problem-solving skills.
- Volunteer work helps you meet new people and break down barriers of misunderstanding, mistrust, and fear.
- It keeps you connected to the community.
- It provides a way to tap a wealth of experience, expertise, and wisdom, and channel it into new directions, and share it with others, especially those in greatest need.
- Volunteerism can lead to creativity, learning new skills, and a renewed vigor and enthusiasm for life. (Source: AARP, "Serve Your Community.")

Individuals volunteer for a variety of personal reasons. They may wish to give back—perhaps to an organization that has responded to their needs in the past. They act out of appreciation—just to say "thank you." Perhaps they wish to support a specific cause or the organization espousing it. They desire to meet new people and gain new experiences. Volunteering may be their mechanism for coping with the stress of life's problems. Perhaps they simply enjoy it; they have the time and they intend to use it to the best advantage. They do it just because they want to. It makes them feel good!

Deciding to Volunteer

Helen Dennis, author of "Ten Trends That Will Change Retirement," advises would-be retirees and volunteers that before they take the step, they should think long and hard about whatever it is that makes their life meaningful. "Take a clue from your past 30 years.... You are who you are, but what you have is an opportunity to express it differently." And whether you plan to work at a paying job or volunteer, lay the groundwork before you retire. Being busy is not enough. It's what you're busy doing that counts" (cited in: Streisand, "Today's Retirement Journey," 2004).

There are several considerations in making such a decision; ask yourself:

1. Why, in addition to making a difference and helping others, am I interested in volunteering?
2. Do I want to learn something new, or try something different?
3. Would I prefer to use my current experience, knowledge, skills and special strengths?
4. Would I like to meet new people with similar interests and broaden my own personal community, or would I prefer a more individual experience?
5. What benefits do I hope to experience from volunteering?" (Source: AARP, "Serve Your Community.")

AARP advises: "Remember—there is no single 'best' motivation for volunteering; it's a very personal choice that should be based on your situation and preferences. The clearer you are on what you hope to get out of volunteering, the more likely you are to make that happen as you select a volunteer role" (AARP, "Serve Your Community").

When a value is placed on the service that a volunteer gives, the value to that individual's personal life is endless. When that value is diminished in any way, self-esteem, confidence, and all of the noble qualities are diminished. Among the best reasons to volunteer are those you may not have considered—those that make it worth your while to give back a little effort and time. Individuals who have volunteered have confirmed that they have received in satisfaction and joy far more than they ever expend in inconvenience or effort—what they receive in return is immeasurable.

The Changing Face of Volunteerism

The faces of today's volunteers are showing more wrinkles than those in the past. The United States is experiencing an increasing trend in volunteerism by persons age 65 or older. Their numbers have increased 400 percent since the early 1960s. This is an encouraging development in a society that has historically failed to exploit the resources represented by the experience, knowledge, and talents of its increasing elderly population. As Marc Freedman states in his book, *Prime Time: How Baby Boomers Will Revolutionize Retirement and Transform America*, "America's burgeoning older population is poised to become the new trustees of civic life in this country" (Freedman, 2002, 19).

"Baby boomers" (some call them "younger seniors") are defined as those persons born between 1946 and 1964; millions of them will turn 65 in 2011. Eighty percent of baby boomers say they expect to perform volunteer work in their later years—but will there be enough volunteer opportunities to go around? Research suggests no, according to The National Council on the Aging (The National Council on the Aging, "Boomers Want to Revitalize Communities but Need New Volunteer Opportunities," 2004.)

Studies by the NCOA and other organizations have shown that the anticipated retirement of an estimated 77 to 80 million baby boomers in the coming decades is already directing the redefinition of growing older in America this country as well as that of retirement. The question is raised: How will our society persuade the largest age group in the nation to participate in the building of stronger, more vital communities, and convince them that this is an integral part of vital, productive aging?"

Wisdom Works

On November 7, 2003, the National Council on the Aging, with a $400,000 grant from the MetLife Foundation, announced the initiation of the program "Wisdom Works: Building Better Communities." It was described as "an initiative to foster increased civic engagement among people aged 60+ … a multidimensional program that includes consumer research, public education, and small grants to support innovative projects in which local groups of adults aged 60 and over come together to address community problems within a specific time frame. It is an opportunity to become part of a national redefining of aging by providing new ways to use the knowledge and skills of older adults to become actively involved in community service" (National Council on the Aging, "Wisdom Works"). "Civic engagement" was defined as individual and collective actions by older people as volunteers designed to address critical community needs. At that time, NCOA President James P. Firman said: "The time, talent and compassion of retirees are America's greatest underutilized resource to address community needs. We need to develop compelling new opportunities that enable both the older Americans of today and the retirees of tomorrow to mobilize and make genuine contributions" (National Council on the Aging, "Wisdom Works," 2003).

The goal of the NCOA project is to identify and foster innovations in civic engagement that use the knowledge, skills, and wisdom of older adults to address critical community needs, and that have the potential to be replicated in hundreds of communities throughout the United States. The program will provide demonstration grants to the best of community involvement programs to either launch new or expand existing programs to address these needs.

The programs must include adults age 60 and over who work in self-directed teams that most effectively use their skills, abilities, and life experiences.

> Through a multi-dimensional approach, the initiative will embrace strategies to increase awareness of the public and to enable self-directed "teams" of older people—with minimal support and guidance from organizational or agency staff—to reach beyond their individual personal lives to address specific community problems that they, along with a number of their peers, have a passion to solve.... Our hope is that these programs will not only build the capacity of community organizations to mobilize older volunteers, but also will be replicated across the country, enabling thousands of older Americans to make genuine contributions [National Council on the Aging, "Wisdom Works," 2003].

Programs that effectively use senior volunteers and that seek to develop volunteer leadership among seniors are most likely to receive one of the demonstration grants. Agencies and programs interested in applying for a grant can find complete details on the NCOA web page: www.ncoa.org/content.cfm?sectionID=65&detail=461.

Cheryl M. Keyser, in her essay "The Importance of Civic Engagement to Older Americans," said:

> But volunteering among older adults is changing. It is no longer ... "lick-'em and stick'em" jobs.... (T)oday's and especially tomorrow's volunteers are no longer looking for opportunities to lick stamps and stuff envelopes; they are looking for new ways to be useful, to learn, to use their skills, to engage in meaningful work, and to follow their passion. There is a movement occurring right now. It is in its formative stages and is very quiet. It

is being driven by demographics. Baby boomers are entering this pre-retirement age; many have been successful and now they want to give back.... Studies indicate that there is an untapped well of people who want to make a contribution. For every two older volunteers, there is another person willing if the opportunity is put in front of them [Keyser, "The Importance of Civic Engagement to Older Americans," 2003, 9–13].

Mark Keyser in his report "Reimagining Work: The Next Chapter," suggests that to attract these persons, these potential resources, the volunteer experience should be redefined. "We should serve it up in a different way, as a form of self-enrichment and staying vital, of feeling you have adventures ahead of you" (Keyser, "Reimagining Work," 2003).

Retirees and Seniors as Volunteers

As discussed under the topic in this book "How Many Seniors Volunteer?," an estimated 57 million Americans participate in volunteer activities. Of these 15 million, about one-third are older persons. Despite the large number of people who share their time and talents, however, the needs of our communities and those of the nation far surpass the number of people who volunteer. A significant disparity exists between the boundless capacities and opportunities of older Americans and their efforts to make significant contributions as volunteers. Older Americans, especially retirees, are in an excellent position to do so. They not only have the time, but also the experience and expertise to help in a variety of activities. They are in an ideal position to mobilize their time and talents and become an enormous resource for their communities and for society at large.

In Madrid, on April 8, 2002, at the Second World Assembly on Ageing, the Honorable Josefina G. Carbonell, then-Assistant Secretary for Aging, U.S. Department of Health and Human Services said:

> Like all of you, the United States values the contributions that older persons have made and continue to make to society. Today, we reaffirm our commitment to them and to identify steps we can take to further improve their lives and the lives of their families and caregivers.... We are also urging seniors to stay socially active, especially through volunteering in their communities.... In March [2002], President Bush announced the USA Freedom Corps, a new program that offers service opportunities to Americans of all ages who are looking for ways to serve their community, our country, and the world [United Nations, "Statement by USA at the Second World Assembly on Ageing," 2002].

On November 4, 2003, during the Independent Sector annual conference in San Francisco, a report—"Experience at Work: Volunteering and Giving Among

Americans 50 and Over"—was released. The report was the result of a collaboration by Independent Sector and AARP. It is the fifth in Independent Sector's "Giving and Volunteering Signature Series," which is supported by the MetLife Foundation. The study analyzes the giving and volunteering patterns of the American baby boom generation and finds enormous potential for Americans over the age of 50 to contribute time and money to the nonprofit sector. This generation "represents the largest untapped pool of potential volunteers for the nonprofit community in recent history…. As baby boomers begin to approach retirement age, nonprofit organizations will be faced with unprecedented opportunities and challenges to engage this population" (Independent Sector, "Experience at Work," 2003).

The study presents an analysis of the over-50 population in the United States by examining the current giving and volunteering patterns of this age group and comparing the philanthropic habits of Americans still in their working years, age 50 to 64, with those who are retired, age 60 and over. The study shows that members of the younger population are more likely to have graduated from college, volunteered in their youth, and watched their parents volunteer—all indicators of high civic involvement.

In the coming decade, the report states that the population of persons over the age of 50 in the U.S. is expected to increase by 18.3 million people, including some 13.9 million people between the ages of 50 and 64. Because most of these individuals will still be working, they are expected to become the most generous givers and have more time for volunteer activities as they approach retirement age. "Nonprofits would be well served to customize their approach to recruit these volunteers and demonstrate the value of their service to the individual volunteer and the organization he or she serves. If [the study] gives us one recommendation, it is that nonprofits ought to seize this opportunity to engage older Americans" (Independent Sector, "Experience at Work," 2003).

What Types of Volunteer Opportunities Should You Consider?

In its "Multicultural Study 2003" AARP states: "Volunteering independently—on one's own—is often more prevalent than volunteering through an organization. For example, about half of our sample reports that all of their efforts on behalf of the elderly are informal, while only 9% say they volunteer for organizations concerned with the elderly. Similarly, 25% report supporting the environment on their own, whereas only 9% volunteer for environmental organizations" (AARP, "Multicultural Study 2003," 5).

Your service can be formal or informal—on a regular basis or periodically as you have time. It's important to think about what kind of role you would like to play—active or behind the scenes—and in what type of organization. When selecting volunteer activities, AARP suggests that you ask yourself:

- What really interests me?
- What are my natural strengths and gifts?
- What comes easily to me?
- What do I enjoy doing?
- What do I dislike doing?
- Do I enjoy working with others, or being on my own?
- Would I rather work with people, things, or ideas?
- Would I prefer a small local organization, or a larger one—national, international?
- Would I prefer to do something in my own neighborhood only?
- What issues do I care about most?
- If I choose to volunteer on a regular basis, do I want to do the same type of activity consistently, or would I prefer a variety of experiences?
- How will my desire to serve fit in with my current time commitments?
- Do I want to volunteer periodically or on an ongoing basis?
- How much time do I want to give (monthly or weekly)?
- Are weekends or weekdays best for me?
- What time of the day—morning, afternoon, or evening—do I prefer?
- Am I able to travel within my community or to sites outside my area?
- How far can I travel?
- What will be the economic effects; can I afford it? (Source: AARP, "Volunteer.")

Types of Volunteer Activities

The Bureau of Labor Statistics identifies several activities which volunteers engage in consistently. The list below presents these in predominant order.

- Teaching or coaching   24.4%
- Canvassing, campaigning, or fundraising   22.9%
- Collecting, making, serving, or delivering goods   22.2%
- Serving on a board, committee, or with an association   16.3%
- Consulting or administrative work   14.0%
- Providing care or transportation   12.3%

(Source: U.S. Bureau of Labor Statistics, *Volunteering in the United States, 2003*, 2003.)

There are numerous opportunities to volunteer. There are many roles you can play. The following are some examples:

ACTIVITIES

- Accounting, tax filing
- AIDS ministry
- Arts and crafts
- Building and construction
- Child care
- Communications
- Community organizing
- Computer training, database management
- Counseling
- Education/tutoring
    - Adult
    - General
    - Literacy
    - Primary
    - Secondary
    - Special
- Elderly outreach
- Environmental awareness
- Food service
- Fundraising
- Health care
- Homeless ministry
- Hospice team
- Hotline counselor
- Immigration and refugee services
- Maternal care
- Medical and dental care
- Minority ministry
- Nursing care
- Peace and justice advocacy
- Prison ministry
- Recreation
- Religious education and ministry
- Social services
- Therapy—occupational, physical, speech, etc.
- Translating
- Transportation—volunteer, coordinating
- Visitor for the homebound
- Youth mentor
- Youth ministry

SITES

There are many settings in which citizens of all ages can volunteer, working alongside agency staff as a team member, in appropriate and effective ways. Consider the following places where volunteers can routinely be found:

- Animal shelters
- Businesses
- Churches
- Community centers
- Community choirs, bands, orchestras, playhouses
- Day-care centers—adult or child
- Family and child counseling and protection services.
- Foundations
- Fraternal organizations
- Fund-raising groups
- Halfway houses
- Historical restorations—monuments, battlefields, national parks
- Homeless shelters
- Hospices

- Hospitals—community, military and veterans
- Legal system—courts, jails, prisons; probation and parole departments
- Libraries
- Local park and recreation programs
- Mosques
- Museums and art galleries
- Nature centers
- "Neighborhood Watch"
- Nursing homes
- Parks—national, state, community
- Political campaigns
- Retirement communities
- Schools
- Senior advocacy groups
- Shelters—family, homeless
- Soup kitchens or food pantries
- Special interest groups
- Substance abuse rehabilitation centers
- Synagogues
- Youth—organizations, sports teams, after school programs
- Zoos

Behind the Scenes Roles

You can help organizations achieve their missions by providing support to employees and other volunteers behind the scenes. Some examples:

- Administration
- Advertising/publicity
- Community outreach coordinator
- Event coordinator
- Fundraiser—door-to-door, telephone, direct mail
- Office support/clerical
- Volunteer recruiter
- Writer/editor

Where Do You Begin the Volunteer Adventure?

Volunteerism is an ideal way for older adults to remain active, creative, and productive in their later years. As we will discuss in a following section, a number of medical studies have confirmed the health benefits of volunteering. Seniors are urged to contact their local agency on aging, senior center, or volunteer resource center for ideas as to where to go to volunteer. At times, newspapers will publish articles or announcements about where volunteers are needed. Usually it does not matter how much time or energy you have to contribute. There is so much need in so many areas that every little bit helps and will be appreciated.

Many paths to the adventures will be discussed in detail in Part III "Volunteer Opportunities." At this time the reader should consider the fact that there is a desperate call on the part of local, national and international organizations for volunteers. The desperation is exacerbated by deficits in funding, materiel, and interest—at times bordering on apathy—in the face of an ever-increasing demand for volunteer services. "Like our nation, volunteering is more diverse than ever. In today's America, people across the spectrum volunteer—representing a wide variety of nationalities, income levels, ages and backgrounds. People working full-time volunteer, as do teens and 20-somethings, children and older adults. There are numerous places to volunteer—and many roles you can play" (AARP, "Serve Your Community").

Rights and Responsibilities of the Volunteer

As a prospective volunteer you should be aware that you have certain rights and responsibilities in that capacity that will help ensure the success of your volunteer experience. Before making a commitment, assure yourself that you have had sufficient time to research the organization with which you intend to volunteer. Do you fully understand and concur with its philosophy, goals, and methods of operation? Will it meet your needs? Can you fulfill the needs of the organization's members? Will it be a good fit for both sides? These efforts will not only help you to feel comfortable with your decision, but will also enable you to critically evaluate the experience throughout its course and determine whether or not both you and the organization are satisfied with the encounter.

YOUR RIGHTS AS A VOLUNTEER

You have the right to:

• Select an assignment that allows you to effectively utilize your experience and skills;
• Select appropriate alternative assignments as necessary;
• Receive adequate training and orientation;
• Expect an organized and mutually convenient schedule so that your time will be utilized most effectively;
• Receive timely evaluation of your performance;
• Be appreciated and respected as a contributing member of the organization; and
• Receive appropriate encouragement and recommendation for your efforts.

YOUR RESPONSIBILITIES AS A VOLUNTEER

You have the responsibility to:

• Accept only those assignments that you believe you are capable of carrying out efficiently and effectively;
• Respect the organization's policies and procedures and competently effect them;

• Concur in, and fully support, the organization's mission;

• Act as a responsible individual and promptly notify the organization of any anticipated absences or delays so that a substitute can be found;

• Volunteer as long as you are able to, and honor your commitments;

• Use time wisely—yours, theirs, the clients';

• Notify the organization of any limitations or special needs that you may have that may affect your performance; and

• Provide suggestions so that the organization can continue to grow in its volunteer opportunities and its service to the community. (Source: Fourinfo.com, "Volunteerism, The Volunteer's Rights and Responsibilities.")

Ten Tips on Wise Volunteering

The source of the following tips—the website of Independent Sector—encourages everyone to "please feel free to reprint this information." In appreciation for its courtesy and with its urging, we do so for the benefit of the reader.

1. *Research the causes or issues important to you.*
   Look for a group which deals with issues about which you feel strongly. You might already be giving money to one of these organizations, and that might be a good place to begin your volunteer experience. If you can't find such an organization, here's a challenging and intriguing thought: why not start one yourself? You can rally your neighbors to clean up that vacant lot on the corner, patrol the neighborhood, paint an elderly neighbor's house, take turns keeping an eye on the ailing person down the street, or form a group to advocate for a remedy to that dangerous intersection in your neighborhood. There is no end to the creative avenues for volunteering, just as there is no end to the need for volunteers.

2. *Consider the skills you have to offer.*
   If you enjoy outdoor work, have a knack for teaching, or just enjoy interacting with people, you may want to look for volunteer work which would incorporate these aspects of your personality. Many positions require a volunteer who has previous experience with certain equipment, such as computers, or who possesses certain skills, such as ability in athletics or communications. For one of these positions you might decide to do something comparable to what you do, or had done, on the job during your work day, or something which you already enjoy as a hobby. This sort of position may allow you to jump right into the work without having to undergo extensive training to prepare for the assignment.

3. *Consider volunteering as a family.*
   Think about looking for a volunteer opportunity which would be suitable for parents and children—grandparents and grandchildren—to do together, or for husband and wife to take on as a team. When a family volunteers to work together at a nonprofit organization, the experience can

bring them closer together. Teach young children the value of giving their time and effort. Introduce everyone in the family to skills and experiences never before encountered, and give the entire family a shared experience as a wonderful family memory.

4. *Would you like to learn a new skill or gain exposure to a new situation?*

Consider seeking a volunteer opportunity where you'll learn something you never knew before or which will provide you with novelty or change. Many nonprofits seek out people who are willing to learn, especially if the needs they serve are specialized or unique. Many of them have a demonstrated need, but few volunteers skilled in what it takes to fill that need. Realize beforehand, however, that such work might require much more of an effort or a time commitment for training before the actual volunteer assignment begins. Assure yourself that you are willing and able to commit to the necessary responsibilities.

5. *Don't over-commit your schedule.*

Make sure the volunteer hours you want to give fit into your hectic life, so that you don't frustrate your family, exhaust yourself, shortchange the organization you're trying to help or neglect your day job. Do you want a long-term assignment or something temporary? If you are unsure about your availability, or want to see how the work suits you before making an extensive commitment, see if the organization will start you out on a limited number of hours until you get the feel of things. Better to start out slowly than to commit yourself to a schedule you can't—or don't want to—fulfill.

6. *Nonprofits may have questions, too.*

While most nonprofits are eager to find volunteer help, they have to be careful when accepting the services you offer. If you contact an organization with an offer to donate your time, you may be asked to come in for an interview, fill out a volunteer application, describe your qualifications and your background—just as you would at an interview for a paying job. It is in the organization's interest to make certain you have the skills they need, that you are truly committed to doing the work, and that your interests match those of the nonprofit. Furthermore, in volunteer work involving children or other at-risk populations, there are legal ramifications for the organization to consider.

7. *I never thought of that!*

Many community groups that are looking for volunteers may not have occurred to you. Most of us know that hospitals, libraries, and churches use volunteers for a great deal of their work, but there are some volunteer opportunities which may not have crossed your mind.

Combine your goals. Look for volunteer opportunities that will also help you achieve your other goals for your life. For example, if you want to lose a few extra pounds, pick an active volunteer opportunity such as cleaning a park or working with kids. [The reader is referred to the section "Where Retirees and Seniors Volunteer" for a detailed listing and discussion.]

8. *Give voice to your heart through your giving and volunteering!*

Bring your heart and your sense of humor to your volunteer service, along with the enthusiastic spirit which is, in itself, a priceless gift. What you'll get back will be immeasurable!

9. *Virtual volunteering?*

Yes, there is such a thing! [We will discuss the concept in Part III of this book.] If you have computer access and the necessary skills, some organizations now offer the opportunity to do volunteer work over the Web. It may be typing letters or other documents for a person with a disability, or simply keeping in contact with a shut-in who has e-mail. This sort of volunteering might be well-suited to you if you have limited time, no transportation, or a physical disability which precludes you from getting about freely. Virtual volunteering can also be a way for you to give time if you simply enjoy computers and want to employ your computer skills in your volunteer work.

10. *Be a year-round volunteer!*

We all tend to think more of those in need during the holidays; but volunteering is welcome and necessary all year. The need for compassion doesn't stop with the new year, and warm spring weather doesn't fill empty stomachs or decrease the litter in public parks. We all need to be aware that making our communities, our nation and our world better is a 365-day-a-year responsibility—and there is always something we could be doing to help! [Source: Independent Sector, "Ten Tips on Volunteering Wisely," no date.]

2. The American Volunteer Tradition

"Voluntary initiative has helped give America her national character."
—MERLE CURTI, PULITZER-PRIZE WINNING HISTORIAN

A Brief History of Volunteerism in America

A number of scientific studies have confirmed that the United States is the most advanced nation in philanthropy in two important respects—the percentage of its citizens' income donated to charities, and the average number of hours devoted to volunteerism. Various reasons have been identified as accounting for this phenomenon. Much of the literature notes that America traditionally possesses a strong belief in community relations and charity. Helping those in need within their communities, and across the nation, is ingrained in the American way of life—our ethos. Religion and diversity have also been identified as contributing to a heightened, enduring sense of, and dedication to, the principles and practice of volunteerism.

Social activist and onetime government official John Gardner has said, "Almost every major social breakthrough in America has originated in this voluntary sector. If volunteers and voluntary organizations were to disappear from our national life, we would be less distinctly American. The sector enhances our creativity, enlivens our communities, nurtures individual responsibility, stirs life at the grass roots, and reminds us that we were born free. Its vitality is rooted in good soil—civic pride, compassion, a philanthropic tradition, a strong problem-solving impulse, a sense of individual responsibility and an irrepressible commitment to the great shared task of improving our life together" (Cited in O'Connell, "America's Voluntary Spirit," 1998, 12).

In their now out-of-print book, *By the People: A History of Americans as Volunteers*, authors Susan J. Ellis and Katherine H. Noyes state:

> The journey from barn raising to computer user groups spans three and a half centuries of American volunteering. These pages have catalogued the remarkable achievements of citizens, individually or in groups, whose voluntary decisions to participate made social progress possible. What is important is not the number of volunteers engaged in each activity noted, but the cumulative effect of all their accomplishments large and small. Volunteerism is both reactive and proactive. It is a response to current events, social problems, and community needs that volunteers are often the first to identify. Volunteers can take action before institutions and government are willing to offer services. As such, volunteers are pioneers and experimenters, unlimited by the restrictions of tradition, public statutes, need to make a profit, or availability of initial funds.
>
> By creating or urging others to create programs, volunteering challenges the status quo. This is the inherent political side of volunteer work. The irony is that pressure in one direction elicits pressure in the other; whenever one group of volunteers works toward change, another group often reacts to preserve tradition or advocate yet another alternative. This is why volunteers will continue to be found on both sides of an issue—and at all points along the political spectrum [Ellis and Noyes, *By the People: A History of Americans as Volunteers*, 1978, 5].

Volunteerism for the common good has always been an American tradition. It is neither a new concept nor an uncommon activity. Historically, America has long recognized the importance of a societal responsibility to join in, to give freely of one's time to assist or aid others. It is an ideal of this country embedded in the national ethos. This ideal is frequently iterated in the literature. In 1831, Charles Henri Maurice Clérel Alexis de Tocqueville, (1805–1859), French lawyer, historian, and political scientist, then only 25 years old, came to the America to report on the prison system.

He spent nine months traveling throughout the United States observing and recording. De Tocqueville recognized that America is great because Americans are good—all over this country—and they demonstrate their fundamental goodness and decency to their fellow citizens and to the world when they volunteer and serve. He recorded his thoughts and observations on America's social and political institutions and reported precisely on the structure of government and the judicial system. On his return to France, in 1835 he published his monumental work, the penetrating political study *De la Démocratie en Amerique* (*Democracy in America*), which brought him great fame in Europe and in America. This book, derived from the voluminous diaries of his journey, set the stage for discussions about democracy that are still being carried on today. It is required reading in many political science courses.

In Chapter V de Tocqueville propounds:

Among democratic nations, on the contrary, all the citizens are independent and feeble; they can do hardly anything by themselves, and none of them can oblige his fellow men to lend him their assistance. They all, therefore, become powerless if they do not learn voluntarily to help one another. If men living in democratic countries had no right and no inclination to associate for political purposes, their independence would be in great jeopardy, but they might long preserve their wealth and their cultivation: whereas if they never acquired the habit of forming associations in ordinary life, civilization itself would be endangered. A people among whom individuals lost the power of achieving great things single-handed, without acquiring the means of producing them by united exertions, would soon relapse into barbarism [de Tocqueville, *Democracy in America*, 1839].

De Tocqueville observed that Americans did not wait for the government to act to solve a problem affecting the community. He noted that America is a "nation of joiners" that regularly form groups to meet or accomplish common goals. If a school or church was needed, the citizens of the community built it. He marveled at how Americans constantly came together to meet common goals; and to this day, no nation in the world has such a vast network of clubs, church and civic groups, and neighborhood organizations. In his observations of American society, de Tocqueville saw this country's system of voluntary organizations not so much as simply service providers but as "the moral associations" where such values as charity and responsibility to others in society are created and perpetuated. However, as significant as moral and religious influences may have been, we cannot attribute our tradition of voluntary action solely to their lessons of charity and altruism. The concepts of mutual dependence and assistance are essential.

In a *Business Week* article "Volunteerism: What Makes America Great," Michelle Nunn said: "Service can be a powerful platform for building community and social capital. Volunteering has long been a strong American tradition with support coming from diverse groups—including our businesses, religious institutions, and volunteer organizations" (Nunn, "Building Social Capital," 2003). Contributing to that same article, John Bridgeland said: "Our Nation is the greatest force for good in history, and we sustain that force through our service to others. Americans can boast a long tradition of service to others at home and abroad, and by continuing to serve, we connect to generations of Americans long gone, many of whom died to protect the freedoms we enjoy now, and also to the generations of Americans to come, who will inherit the world strengthened by our legacy of service" (Bridgeland "Why Serve?," 2003).

Brian O'Connell has said: "Through our voluntary initiative and independent institutions, ever more Americans worship freely, study quietly, are cared for compassionately, experiment creatively, serve effectively, advocate aggressively and contribute generously. These national traits are constantly beautiful and must remain beautifully constant" (O'Connell, "America's Voluntary Spirit," 1998, 12).

American Presidents Reflect on Volunteerism

Throughout our history, many of our presidents have spoken of the importance of serving our communities and nation.

• Thomas Jefferson, third president: "A nation, as a society, forms a moral person, and every member of it is personally responsible for his society."

• Abraham Lincoln, sixteenth president: "Let us have the faith that right makes might, and in this faith let us to the end dare to do our duty as we understand it."

• Woodrow Wilson, twenty-eighth president: "We are expected to put the utmost energy, of every power that we have, into the service of our fellow men, never sparing ourselves, not condescending to think of what is going to happen to ourselves, but ready, if need be, to go to the utter length of self-sacrifice."

• Harry S. Truman, thirty-third president: "We know that helping others is the best way—probably the only way to achieve a better future for ourselves."

• John F. Kennedy, thirty-fifth president: "The energy, the faith, the devotion which we bring to this endeavor will light our country and all who serve it, and the glow from that fire can truly light the world."

• Lyndon B. Johnson, thirty-sixth president: "If there is one word that describes our form of society in America, it may be the word—'voluntary.'"

• William J. Clinton, forty-second president: "Service to one's community is an integral part of what it means to be an American.... Volunteers enrich our lives every day with their generosity and compassion. This spirit of citizen service has deep and strong roots in America's past. By nurturing this spirit we can help ensure a better future for our nation."

The Calls to Action

BY RECENT PRESIDENTS

The origins of senior citizens' service began largely in the summer of 1963 when President John F. Kennedy delivered a landmark speech on aging in which he decried the loneliness and isolation so pervasive in this population of Americans. He characterized the situation as "heightened by the wall of inertia" that formed a barrier between a large number of seniors and the communities in which they lived.

At that time, the president enthusiastically proposed the establishment of a National Service Corps (NSC). He had alluded to the Corps in a speech at American University on June 10, 1963: "We must show it in the dedication of our own lives—as many of you who are graduating today will have a unique opportunity to do, by serving without pay in the Peace Corps abroad or in the proposed National Service Corps here at home" (Henchman, President Kennedy's speech at American University, 1963).

As conceived, the NSC would have provided "opportunities for service for those aged persons who can assume active roles in community volunteer efforts." Kennedy's plan constituted a significant departure from accepted practice and attitudes in America. At the time, only an estimated 11 percent of the older population were involved in volunteer activity—formal or informal. National service had historically meant youth service. President Kennedy recognized and encouraged the potential contributions of both older and younger Americans. Each would be given equal value in the new National Service as he envisioned it.

According to attorney general Robert Kennedy, who was chairman of the task force charged with developing the new program, the NSC was a call to service to "college students and retired persons," a challenge to youth but also to "millions of older and retired people whose reservoir of skill and experience remains untapped." In his testimony before the Senate special committee convened to review the feasibility of the NSC, the attorney general delivered an impassioned plea for a prominent role for older Americans in the area of domestic service: "Millions of Americans who have years of productivity and service to offer are dormant. Retired teachers, craftsmen, tradesmen really don't want to go to the seashore to fade away. They want to help. So many of these people have come forward that I am convinced they can accomplish something unique in this country, something un-done by all the federal, state, county and private agencies, something still to be done." A week later, Sergeant Shriver, the founding director of the Peace Corps, assured the same committee that "a substantial number of retired people ... would apply for the National Service Corps and that they could be effectively used" (Shapiro, "A History of National Service in America," 1994).

Despite the backing of President Kennedy and his administration, the National Service Corps was defeated in congress where, as one writer alleges, "reactionary lawmakers portrayed it as a back door to racial integration in the South" (Shapiro, "A History of National Service in America, 1994).

President George W. Bush supported so-called "faith-based initiatives," or religious charities, (the reader is referred to the discussion on that topic) and proposed the USA Freedom Corps to coordinate federal volunteer projects. His predecessor, William Clinton, launched the AmeriCorps national domestic service program.

On February 10, 2003, President Bush released a 2004 budget for the Corporation for National and Community Service (CNS) that would have provided opportunities for 2.5 million Americans to serve their communities and country through Senior Corps, AmeriCorps, and Learn and Serve America. The Corporation's programs were a vital part of President Bush's USA Freedom Corps initiative to build a culture of service, responsibility, and citizenship that strengthens communities and helps those in need. The 2004 request would support 75,000 AmeriCorps members, nearly 600,000 senior volunteers, and 1.65 million students in service-learning programs (FirstGov for Seniors, "President Calls for Senior Volunteers," 2003).

On January 31, 2002, President George Bush, in remarks to Senior Corps Volunteers at Daytona Beach, Florida, said:

> America can change, one heart, one soul at a time. We understand that a compassionate tomorrow and a safe tomorrow requires presidents and governors and mayors and county officials to rally the true strength of the country, which is our people.
>
> We basically ... have said there are numerous seniors who have got a lot to offer—people who might be retired, but their brains haven't retired, and their experience hasn't been retired. So let's figure out how to get them involved in the community [*Senior Journal*, "President Bush's Speech on Senior Corps," January 31, 2002].

BY RECENT PRESIDENTIAL HOPEFULS

Patriotic calls for public service seem to be *de rigueur* for politicians aspiring to the White House (exceeded in occurrence only by their fervent, ubiquitous, and largely hollow promises for programs that would benefit seniors—Medicare is the piñata of political candidates).

On October 14, 2003, Wesley Clark, one of the several Democratic presidential contenders at that time, proposed the establishment of a civilian volunteer corps for service at home and abroad. In a speech at Hunter College in Manhattan, he presented a plan to create a "Civilian Reserve Corps" that could be called up for service, much like the National Guard, in national emergencies, such as terrorist attacks, and natural disasters, such as earthquakes, forest fires, and floods. Saying that more than 59 million Americans had performed volunteer service in 2002, Clark affirmed that there could be a greater effort. "In this new world with the challenges we are facing at home and abroad, we need more. We know we have the generosity for a new wave to help others, a new wave of service" (McCool, 2003). Clark quoted the powerful appeal of President John Kennedy, who, in his 1961 inaugural speech said: "Ask not what your country can do for you. Ask what you can do for your country."

The top Democratic presidential contender in 2004, Massachusetts Senator John Kerry, also presented a proposal for national service. In a speech in Manchester, New Hampshire, on May 19, 2003, he propounded "A New Era of National Service" and stated:

> I believe service can define the life of the nation.... I have come to New Hampshire today to call for a new era of national service open to everyone in the nation.... To protect our nation and meet our potential, we will have to harness the faith, the energy, and the commitment of people of all ages in communities across the country.
>
> Yet, too often today, citizenship and duty are dismissed as peripheral or as fond memories of a forgotten past. But day after day, they are a way of life for millions. And they have sustained and strengthened our democracy for more than two centuries.
>
> All over this country, Americans are demonstrating their fundamental goodness and decency to their fellow citizens and the world when they volunteer and serve.... [A]ll of us have something to give and each of us has a responsibility to serve. Today, I propose not only to build on that tradition, but to go beyond it—because today, our challenges are different and our commitment must be even greater. We need a new era of service—not an effort for one time, one purpose, or one group—but a permanent and national endeavor. For America now, service is not just an option, but an obligation of citizenship. So I am proposing that we fulfill that obligation by creating a seamless web of service where every American—young and old, rich and poor, of every race, religion, and background—can enlist in a new army of patriots who will serve on all the frontlines of our future— guarding our nation from danger abroad, strengthening our homeland security, reducing illiteracy, preserving our environment, providing after-school care, helping our seniors live in dignity, building new homes for those who need them—and in all of this, building a nation that is more truly one America.
>
> .... I propose service not just for the young in years, but for those who still have so much to contribute after finishing their careers. As Robert Kennedy once said, "Youth is not a time of life, but a state of mind." I believe in calling on older Americans to contribute to a nation that continues to need all that they have to offer. My proposal for Older Americans in Service will enlist those who have now retired—because beyond the jobs they did, they have so much more to give.
>
> There are those in the Greatest Generation who are doing that today. And now the generation of the 1960s is entering their 60s. Today's Americans are living longer and staying healthier into their retirement; we need their experience and their energy.... They have already done so much for their country.... Our older Americans are retired, not tired—and America cannot afford to waste their wisdom and vitality [Kerry, "A New Era of National Service," 2003].

During his campaign, Senator Kerry unveiled his "Compact with the Greatest Generation" touted as "a guarantee that will give seniors the protection they have earned from Social Security and Medicare, help seniors afford their medicine, and ensure long-term care…. [N]ow that the Greatest Generation is getting older, I think it is the responsibility of all Americans to make sure we do our part for America's Seniors" (Kerry, "Compact with the Greatest Generation").

The Compact espouses four priorities:

1. Protect Medicare and Social Security
2. Ensure affordable prescription drugs
3. Provide quality options for seniors with long-term care needs
4. Ask America's Greatest Generation to help the next

"The Greatest Generation has another battle yet to fight—to help strengthen American [sic] for generations to come.

• 100,000 Older Americans in Service

For 10 hours of service a week, members will earn up to $2,000 a year, tax free, that they can apply to an education grant for a grandchild or other family member, another young person.

• Older Americans in Our Schools

When seniors spend time tutoring, they free up over-strained teachers to teach, and children to get extra help learning.

• Seniors Helping Each Other

Members will be able to offer seniors support to live independently by helping them pick up their prescriptions or checking in on them to make sure they are doing alright" (Kerry, "Compact with the Greatest Generation").

Volunteerism in America Today

Brian O'Connell, founding president of Independent Sector, professor of public service at Tufts University, and author of *Voices from the Heart: In Celebration of America's Volunteers* and *Civil Society: The Underpinnings of American Democracy* has said:

> The question is asked, is there still a civic spirit in the United States? There is a pervasive view that in earlier times, Americans were far more willing than we are today to help one another and to become involved in causes and public issues. It almost seems a given to some that we are now a less caring society and that we should worry about what's happened to all that neighborliness, public spiritedness and charity.
>
> Actually, the past was not nearly as good as remembered and the present is far better than perceived. A far larger proportion and many more parts of our population are involved in community activity today than at any time in our history.

Most often the participation is attributed to our Protestant ethic and English ancestry; but as important as they are, they are only two of many sources. What we identify as Judeo-Christian impulses were also brought to our shores by each wave of immigrants—from Sweden, Russia, China, India or elsewhere—who followed Jesus, Moses, Mohammed, Buddha or other sages and prophets.

...As important as religious influences have been, we can't ascribe our tradition of voluntary action solely to their lessons of goodness. The matter of mutual dependence and assistance cannot be overlooked. ...One of the most striking points about the origins is that we shouldn't assume that these characteristics and traditions were imported.... [H]istorian Robert Bremner makes clear that the Native Americans treated us with far more "Christian" goodness than we practiced on them [O'Connell, "America's Voluntary Spirit," 1998, 9–10].

Volunteerism today is not the same as it was a century ago. At the beginning of the twentieth century, as a consequence of the Industrial Revolution, there was a prevailing and growing need for social welfare. Charitable efforts, including volunteering, were, to a large extent, unorganized. They involved individual, informal, rather than organizational, methodical, efforts. The current interest in volunteering in America occurs in a society that has changed substantially in just the past 100 years. The new environment in which volunteerism is taking place has shifted the focus of the efforts, both for volunteers and for those who are served.

In discussing the implications of this new focus of volunteering for the senior members of our society, M.L. Hadley of the Centre on Aging and Centre for Studies in Religion and Society, University of Victoria, Canada, has affirmed:

Volunteerism, many have observed, has little to do with being a "do-gooder." It is about valuing the person, and increasing the value of social and human resources; it is about self-esteem, freely sharing one's talent and wisdom; it is about being valued, not paid; it is about empowerment, growth and creativity; it is about enhancing the community's quality of life. It is also about having fun in the process—the third stage or "Troisieme Age" of human development—is a time when we can give back to society the lessons, the wisdom and resources that we have derived throughout our long and productive lives. This "Troisieme Age" is a special period when we can deepen our wisdom and personal sense of spiritual identity. Whatever emphasis each of us might place on this stage of life, our full engagement implies an enhancement of the common good [Hadley, "Themes and challenges for future service and research," 1998, 42–43].

Minorities and Volunteerism

According to estimates released by the Census Bureau on June 14, 2004, a marked growth among Hispanics and Asians fueled a surge in the U.S. population between 2000 and 2003. The Hispanic and Asian populations continued to grow at much faster rates than the U.S. population as a whole. They far outpaced an approximately 3 percent increase in the population to an estimated 290.8 million at that time.

The number of Hispanics, the nation's largest minority group, rose 13 percent between April 2000 and July 2003 to 39.9 million, according to the Census Bureau data. This group accounted for about one-half of the 9.4 million residents added to the nation's population since the census of 2000. Their growth rate over the 39-month period was almost four times that of the total population (3.3 percent).

Hispanics may be of any race—the federal government treats Hispanic origin and race as separate and distinct concepts. "Non-Hispanic white" is what would generally be considered the majority group in the U.S. population, though it is not officially designated as such. The population of Hispanics and, to a lesser extent, Asians, rose in nearly every state during the 1990s, due in large part to immigration.

Asians were the next-fastest-growing among the large minority groups, up 12.6 percent to 11.9 million, while the black population rose nearly 4 percent to 37 million. During the same time period, the number of people who reported being Asian grew 12.5 percent to 13.5 million. Following Asians were native Hawaiians and other Pacific Islanders (5.8 percent, to 960,000), American Indians and Alaska natives (3.3 percent, to 4.4 million) and whites (2.8 percent, to 237.9 million).

Whites remain the single largest group at 197 million, up just 1 percent between 2000 and 2003. That number refers to those U.S. residents who are not of Hispanic ethnicity and who selected only white as their race. Over two-thirds of U.S. residents are white. Bureau projections released earlier in 2004 predicted that whites and minority groups overall would be roughly equal in size by 2050. (Source: U.S. Census Bureau. "Hispanic and Asian Americans Increasing Faster Than Overall Population," June 14, 2004,) Members of minority groups are projected to represent 26.4 percent of the older population in 2030, up from 16.4 percent in 2000, and 17.2 percent in 2002. Between 2000 and 2030, the white population is projected to increase by 77 percent compared with 223 percent for minorities, including Hispanics (342 percent), African-Americans (164 percent), American Indians, Eskimos, and Aleuts (207 percent), and Asians and Pacific Islanders (302 percent).

Approximately 34 percent of the nation's Hispanics are younger than 18, compared with only 22 percent of non–Hispanic whites. Fifteen percent of whites are 65 or over, a rate three times as high as that of Hispanics. The youthfulness of minorities and the aging of the white population overall provide further evidence suggesting the nation's demographic future. The expected continued influx of younger Hispanic and Asian immigrants could also replenish the U.S. labor force as the massive baby boom generation approaches retirement age, says William Frey, a demographer at the Brookings Institution in Washington. (Cited in Armas, 2004.)

In the same time period, there were 35.9 million people age 65 and over. Fifteen percent of non–Hispanic whites reporting only one race belonged to this age group. That proportion surpassed that of all other race and ethnic groups. Nationally, 12 percent of the total population was 65 years and over. A total of 4.7 million people were in the "oldest old" category (age 85 and over). About 2 percent of non–Hispanic whites reporting only one race were in this age group, higher than any other race or ethnic group. (Sources: Administration on Aging. *A Profile of Older Americans: 2003*; Armas, "An Explosive Growth Among Hispanics," 2004; U.S. Census Bureau. "Hispanic and Asian Americans Increasing Faster Than Overall Population," 2004.)

The 2003 Bureau of Labor Statistics study—included as Appendix 2—had previously revealed several changes in volunteer rates among these demographic groups. The rate for whites rose from 29.2 percent for the year ended in September 2002 to 30.6 percent for the year ended in September 2003, while the rates for blacks and Hispanics were little changed. About 18.7 percent of Asians performed some sort of volunteer work through or for an organization over the year ended in September 2003. (Data for Asians were not tabulated in 2002.) The data on volunteering among these demographic groups in 2003 are shown in the table below.

Volunteer Rates for Demographic Groups
(Numbers in thousands, September 2003)

	Number	Percent of Population
White	55,572	30.6
Black	5,145	20.0
Asian	1,735	18.7
Hispanic	4,364	15.7

(Source: U.S. Department of Labor, Bureau of Labor Statistics. "Volunteering in the United States, 2003," 2003)

> Volunteerism is deeply rooted in U.S. ethnic and racial components. The public and researchers have not fully acknowledged the value of volunteer activities—especially within ethnic groups. There is wide diversity within

and across cultural groups. The following characteristics only begin to demonstrate a few specific differences:
• African Americans, through families, neighborhoods, friendships, fraternal and social groups and churches, have long served their communities
• Chinese family associations or benevolent societies have provided information, guidance, support and sustenance to the needy
• Native American pueblos demonstrate their shared communal experiences in an agrarian lifestyle
• The Latino communities' high regard for family and expectation of service and support has been recognized
[University of Missouri, Kansas City, "Volunteerism."]

The AARP Study of Volunteering Among Minorities

In a landmark study among African-Americans, Hispanic-Americans, and Asian-Americans over the age of 45, conducted between July 2 and July 30, 2003, AARP attempted to assess actual behavior among more than 2,000 respondents that may be considered to have an impact on their community—behaviors that AARP believed might be missed by traditional survey questions. Several multicultural organizations advised AARP in designing the study.

The AARP study defined differences in the distinct community service activities among members of racial and ethnic groups in the sample group; however, their assumption that African-Americans, Hispanic-Americans, and Asian-Americans are more likely to be involved in informal volunteering was not borne out by the survey. The survey questions, designed to discern informal and individual volunteering, revealed that members of all races and ethnicities are extensively involved in informal service to their communities—but none are more likely to do so than white Americans (AARP, "Multicultural Study 2003," November 2003).

In discussing the role of race and ethnicity in volunteering the AARP report states:

> "The results of the survey indicate that African-Americans, Asian-Americans, Hispanic-Americans and white Americans are more similar than dissimilar in their actions and motivations to give of their time and money.
> • African-Americans are among the most active volunteers, and are especially likely to report volunteering on their own, apart from organizations. Their efforts focus on homeless and hungry people, the rights of minorities, religious institutions, neighborhoods, and people who need tutoring.
> • Asian-Americans are more likely to volunteer on occasion rather than regularly, and are most likely to support museums, theaters, libraries, or other cultural and arts organizations. On average they donate larger amounts of money to help others than do the other groups we queried.

• Hispanic-Americans volunteer the most hours per month. They are the most likely to provide help to other immigrants in this country and send money to help people in other countries.
• Whites tend to donate more financially and are likely to volunteer to help animals, the environment and public servants.
[AARP, "Multicultural Study 2003," November 2003.]

PBS has said: "It should be noted that Hispanics do not volunteer in the traditional American pattern. Hispanic volunteerism usually takes place in the home and, secondarily, in the neighborhood and church. As a result, elderly Hispanics, who may be inclined to follow this pattern, remain a valuable, untapped resource for mainstream, community-based organizations" (PBS, "Aging in the Hispanic Community").

Independent Sector reports that: "Seniors of every age, ethnic and racial group volunteer to some level. Over 46 percent of persons ages 55 to 74 reported performing some type of volunteer work in the past year [1999]. Almost 34 percent of those 75 years and older reported volunteering. Significant numbers of seniors in minority groups reported volunteering, including 37.4 percent of blacks and 38.9 percent of Hispanics. These groups constitute a growing portion of American society and a valuable resource of volunteer time" (Independent Sector, "Senior Volunteers in America," June 2000).

"In many minority communities volunteerism is a close-knit and personal obligation.... [U]ndocumented volunteerism is alive and well in most minority communities. Most people refer to this as 'helping out.' This tradition of community involvement indicates that minority communities possess a rich and as yet untapped volunteer pool" (National CASA Association, "Recruiting Minority Volunteers," 1999).

In an effort to identify reasons why this pool is not being tapped, The United Way of Santa Clara, California, conducted a research poll. These were some of the reasons given by respondents:

• Minorities were not asked
• Fear of being used as a token
• Do not feel connected to the mainstream community
• Lack of personal time
• Emphasis of minority culture on family involvement over community involvement
• Lack of identification with agencies that are serving minority clients
• Lack of knowledge about volunteer opportunities
• Belief that minority input is not taken seriously
• Uncertainty about benefits of involvement
• Economic hardship

These were not all the reasons given by respondents, but are those that present serious challenges to recruiting minorities. (Source: National CASA Association, "Recruiting Minority Volunteers," May 1999.)

Celebrating Volunteerism in America

In May of each year, the United States celebrates "Older Americans Month"—a time when all are reminded of the contributions and sacrifices of the elder population of our citizenry. In 2002 the theme was "America: A Community for All Ages"; the theme for 2003 was: "What We Do Makes a Difference." "Aging Well, Living Well" was the theme selected for 2004 to celebrate and recognize older Americans who are living longer, healthier, and more productive lives. The 2005 theme was "Celebrate Long-Term Living."

Older persons are not only adding years to their lives, they are also improving the quality of their lives. "In addition to achieving a healthier lifestyle, older persons must also take steps to prepare for later life. These steps include seeking opportunities for community participation and social engagement, including access to volunteer activities" (Administration on Aging, "Older Americans Month, 2004").

Each year National Volunteer Week is also celebrated. On April 17, 2004, President George W. Bush signed a proclamation which designated the week of April 18 through April 24, 2004. The announced theme was "Volunteers Inspire by Example." In 2003, the theme was "Celebrate Volunteers—The Spirit of America!" In his proclamation, the president stated:

> "The strength of America lies in the hearts and souls of our citizens. Across our country, citizens are donating their time and talents to improving lives and strengthening communities. During National Volunteer Week, we recognize and celebrate those who serve a cause greater than self.
>
> Through the dedicated efforts of America's volunteers, we are building a culture of service, responsibility, and compassion, particularly among our young people. Volunteers can make a difference in many ways…. Their acts of kindness have a profound effect on people's lives and on the future of our country…. America's volunteers set a fine example for our nation, and I encourage all Americans to look for a challenge in their communities and step forward to lend a hand.
>
> I call on all Americans to recognize and celebrate the important work that volunteers do every day across our country. I also encourage those who have not yet answered the call to explore ways to get involved" [The Whitehouse, "National Volunteer Week, 2004"].

3. Redefining Aging and Retirement

"Here is a test to find whether your mission on earth is finished: if you are alive, it isn't."

—RICHARD BACH

The aging boom is upon us. Life expectancy nearly doubled in the twentieth century. "Americans have received a tremendous gift in the past 100 years—the doubling of life expectancy. Currently, a person age 50 can expect to live another 30 years. Because of advances in medical care, this 'third age' of life is as productive as any other time. This longevity bonus means that Americans may work longer, and also remain productive to the nation in other ways" (AARP, "Multicultural Study," 2003).

In 2001, persons reaching age 65 had an average life expectancy of an additional 18.1 years (19.4 years for females and 16.4 years for males). A child born in 2001 could expect to live 77.2 years, about 30 years longer than a child born in 1900. Much of this increase has occurred because of reduced death rates for children and young adults. However, the past two decades have also seen reduced death rates for the population aged 65–84, especially for men—by 29.0 percent for men aged 65–74 and by 22.5 percent for men aged 75–84. Life expectancy at age 65 increased by only 2.5 years between 1900 and 1960, but has increased by 3.8 years from 1960 to 2001. (Source: Administration on Aging, "A Profile of Older Americans, 2003," 2003.)

The older population itself is getting older. In 2002, the 65–74 age group (18.3 million) was eight times larger than in 1900, but the 75–84 group was more than 16 times larger, and the 85+ group was almost 38 times larger. These oldest-old constitute the fastest growing segment of the U.S. population. By 2050, this population—currently about 4.6 million persons—could exceed 19 million. Living to be 100 years old will become more commonplace. In 1950, only about 3,000 Americans were centenarians; by 2050, there could be nearly 1 million. This is the future of aging. (Source: Administration on Aging, "A Profile of Older Americans, 2003," 2003.)

> Aging is a complex natural process potentially involving every molecule, cell, and organ in the body. In its broadest sense, aging merely refers to changes that occur during the lifespan. However, this definition includes some changes that aren't necessarily problematic, and usually don't affect an individual's viability.... To differentiate these superficial changes from those that increase the risk of disease, disability, or death, gerontologists prefer to use a more precise term—"senescence"—to describe aging. Senescence is the progressive deterioration of many bodily functions over time [National Institute on Aging, *Aging Under the Microscope: A Biological Quest*, 2002, 3].

The reader who may be interested in recent scientific findings on the biology and the physiology of aging is referred to the 2002 National Institute on Aging (NIA) publication cited above. This is a free 50-page booklet that explains, in somewhat technical language, what scientists are learning about aging. In addition to describing the progress scientists have made in unlocking the secrets of aging, the booklet details how these insights may help move us closer to the ultimate goal of promoting health and independence throughout our lifespan.

Among the questions the booklet addresses are: What is aging? What is senescence? What is the difference between life expectancy and lifespan? Why do we age? What role do genes play in aging? How do hormones affect aging, and what influence, if any, does hormone replacement therapy have on this process? Can cutting caloric intake increase lifespan and improve health? The NIA publication is intended to be a resource for journalists, educators, students, policymakers, and the general public.

Copies of the booklet are available from the NIA, which is part of the National Institutes of Health (NIH) at the U.S. Department of Health and Human Services. A copy can be downloaded or ordered online at the URL shown in "Sources" at the back of this book. For additional information about aging contact:

NIA Information Center
P.O. Box 8057, Silver Spring, MD 20898-8057
Phone: 1-800-222-2225
E-mail: niaic@jbs1.com
Website: www.nia.nih.gov

Redefining Aging

In order to redefine retirement, we must first redefine aging. Successful aging is the key to successful retirement. John W. Rowe and Robert L. Kahn, in their book, *Successful Aging*, derived from their collaboration in a MacArthur Foundation study (described below), compiled research results over a decade, focusing on 1,000 individuals who aged well. "More and more people will follow the model of successful aging that this [MacArthur Foundation] study proposes. Elders who age 'successfully' avoid disease and disability by avoiding risk factors such as smoking, obesity and inactivity. They also use their cognitive and physical abilities and capacities. Furthermore, they remain productively engaged with life by entering into reciprocal, not dependent, relationships and by participating in productive or meaningful behaviors" (Cited in Dennis, "Ten Trends That Will Change Retirement," 2002).

An important impetus to the redefinition of aging began in 1984, when the John D. and Catherine T. MacArthur Foundation brought together a group of scientists from widely diverse fields to undertake an intensive, 10-year study of aging. This group, known as the "MacArthur Network on Successful Aging," took a simple but radical approach to its research. Rather than focus on the array of problems of disease and disability associated with aging—which was the prevailing approach of research in gerontology at the time—the Network focused its research on persons who age well—not just physically, but also psychologically. "The goal was to move beyond the limited view of chronological age and to clarify all the factors responsible for retaining and even enhancing people's ability to function in later life" (MacArthur Foundation, "A New Perspective on Growing Old," 2003).

The Network's research redefined what it means to grow old, setting a new standard for scientific, clinical, and policy experts in the field of aging. The study concluded that genetics plays a much smaller role than had been thought and that successful aging is largely determined by lifestyle choices. Results showed that only 30 percent of how we age can be attributed to our genetic inheritance; the remaining 70 percent is determined by our choices of lifestyle. "Twenty years ago, most scientists associated old age with decline and disability. If you aged well, they believed, it was because you were lucky—you held a winning ticket in the genetic lottery of heredity. Today, the concept of aging has been transformed. We take it for granted that with proper diet, exercise, rich human relationships, and intellectual stimulation, people can live healthy, productive, satisfying lives well into their 70s and 80s" (MacArthur Foundation, "A New Perspective on Growing Old," 2003).

When does old age begin? It's not the candles on the cake. According to older Americans, the importance of chronological age alone is a less important indicator of old age than a number of other factors. In a study by the National Council on the Aging (NCOA), when asked "what best defines the beginning of old age?" 41 percent of the respondents said a "decline in physical ability"; 32 percent said a decline in mental functioning is the key determinant of old age. Only 14 percent said reaching a specific chronological age is a definitive indicator of old age.

Forty-four percent of those age 65 and older described the present as "the best years of my life." Among those respondents age 65 to 69, 49 percent echoed that opinion. (Among Americans of all ages, 66 percent described the present as their best years.) Many persons in their 70s (44 percent) and 80s (33 percent) concurred. And regardless of the persistent misperceptions about aging, 84 percent of all respondents affirmed that they would be happy if they lived to be 90 years old. (Source: The National Council on the Aging, "Myths and Realities of Aging," 2000.)

Demographic trends in the United States indicate a substantial expansion of the population of the healthiest and best-educated generation of older Americans in the nation's history. Individuals over the age of 65 represent a growing resource of experience, time, energy, and talent with the potential to effectively address the needs of communities and their fellow citizens nationwide. "Wisdom Works: Building Better Communities," the National Council on the Aging/MetLife Foundation initiative discussed previously, has as its goal increasing civic engagement, which is defined as, "collective actions by older people in volunteer teams engaged in addressing critical community needs" (The National Council on the Aging, "Wisdom Works: Building Better Communities," 2003).

"Science is reshaping the way we think about the older body, memory and sex drive. More and more, how we grow old is a personal choice…. This is a good thing, according to researchers who have found that negative stereotypes about aging can actually shorten your life. A Yale University study last year [2003], in the *Journal of Personality and Social Psychology*, found that people who have a positive perception of aging tend to live seven and a half years longer than those who don't. The difference may be the result of a better response to stress or even just the will to live, according to the study" (Lawson, "Aging's Changing Face").

The Negative Stereotypes About Aging

There are many frequently held misconceptions about aging. Doctor Roger Landry has studied the myths and stereotypes of aging and has identified five generally held fallacies:

1. Aging means Alzheimer's or some inevitable decline in cognitive functioning.

Fact: Research has shown that of those persons over age 65, only 10 percent have Alzheimer's disease. Most forms of decreased mental function and dementia are caused by disuse, not disease—letting the mind get lazy. Depression has also been identified as a causative factor. The elderly can help prevent the decline of mental function and some forms of dementia by involving themselves in activities that stimulate the brain.

2. Aging means a decline in physical activity—slowing down.

Fact: Seniors are not only capable of physical exercise, but require it to maintain independence, good mental function, and to reduce the risk of disease and injury.

3. Aging means reducing or discontinuing one's contributions to society.

Fact: Current retirees are more interested in an active life, including continuing to work in an "active retirement," and also in volunteering, than their parents' generation. As we will see in the section of this book "How Many Seniors Volunteer," about 3.7 million older Americans (12 percent of the population) were in the labor force in 1998—approximately 2.8 percent of the U.S. labor force. And 15 million older persons—nearly half the population in the U.S over the age of 65 volunteer.

4. Aging means the end of learning.

Fact: Learning is a lifelong process. Seniors with no training have embraced computer technology and are the most rapidly growing computer-literate demographic group. Likewise, seniors have mastered other technologies that were unknown when they were young. More and more, educational institutions are realizing the expanding demand for continuing education opportunities in this population of our citizens.

5. Aging means isolation, loneliness, and depression.

Fact: Unfortunately, this was the sad fate of many previous generations of older Americans. It came about primarily because society had no role for them; there were perceived as no longer useful and unable to make a contribution. Today's seniors increasingly are finding alternatives to being alone, such as home-sharing or moving to senior living communities, where they can maintain social connections, continue to learn, and contribute to the larger community through employment or volunteerism. (Source: Landry, "Facts on Aging Are Brighter," 2003.)

Doctor Roger Landry has commented:

> Ironically, while examples of seniors enjoying productive lives abound, most Americans continue to view aging as a totally negative process. Out

of ignorance or perhaps fear, Americans view aging as a process of decline and steady erosion of the joys of living.

The good news for seniors, as well as those who will one day become seniors, is that a good deal of the negative associations with aging are, in fact, wrong or exaggerated…. Recent research has smashed the stereotypes of aging. Growing older can be rewarding and fun. Seniors who take charge of their health, stay engaged in life, and use, rather than lose, their physical and mental capabilities, can enjoy later years filled with vitality and joy. As former Washington Post publisher Katharine Graham once put it: "No one can avoid aging, but aging productively is something else" [Landry, "Facts on Aging Are Brighter," 2003].

Lillian Hawthorne has been the author of the "Finishing Touches" column in SeniorWorld Online. Prior to retirement, she enjoyed two separate careers of approximately 20 years each, both relating to working with people—first as a school teacher, and second as a clinical practitioner and university professor in the field of social work. In her article "The Rest of Our Years, the Best of Our Years" Hawthorne said:

> The society in which we live now defines not only when we grow old, by its policies toward aging; it also influences how we grow old, by its attitudes toward aging. The problem is that society sends us confusing, and sometimes contradictory, messages about being older…. Although aging is a process that eventually affects all of us, if we live long enough, many of us really do not know much about it; nor do we always want to know, or even think much about it. Perhaps this is because growing older reminds us of, and brings us closer to, our own mortality. As a result, many myths and stereotypes have arisen about age, virtually all of them negative. Older people are pictured as frail and failing, anxious and unhappy, insular and incompetent. They are thought to be bored, or boring, or both; too rigid to change or learn, and too self-centered to care about other people or other problems [Hawthorne, "The Rest of Our Years, the Best of Our Years," 1999].

Robert Knechtel has said:

> "What changes is not older peoples' capacity to be vigorous, productive and creative. Rather, society is unwilling to see seniors as vital and active contributors far beyond traditional retirement age. It's assumed that people of a certain age suddenly turn senile and accept being seen as useless and dispatched to decades on the golf course, playing bingo, or just plain idleness as a way of life. You're expected to embrace inconsequence and oblivion.
>
> Why should we suppose that older people, whose way of life has been vital, interesting and productive, would not want to sustain that life as long as possible?
>
> Much of human dignity is experienced and expressed through work. As social creatures we need to feel valued and empowered, feelings which

come from knowing we are contributing to our fellow humans" [Knech-tel, "Productive Aging in the 21st Century"].

The Aged in the Origins of Civilization

The elderly may have been crucial to the evolutionary success of the human race—they may hold the key to our civilization as it is today. This is the conclusion of researchers who published their findings in the journal *Proceedings of the National Academy of Sciences* on July 13, 2004. The scientists, Rachel Caspari of the University of Michigan and Sang-Hee Lee of the University of California at Riverside, believe there had to be a distinct evolutionary advantage to large numbers of people growing older. Their study of the human fossil record has shown that elders played an important role in the dramatic spread of human civilization some 30,000 years ago.

They believe that groups in which old people survived better were more successful, in turn allowing more people to live into old age. On the one hand, it would have led to more disease and disability. On the other, it would not only have encouraged social relationships and kinship bonds, but also the passing of information from old and experienced individuals to younger generations. They found evidence that, around 30,000 years ago, many more people started living into old age, fueling a population explosion. Human lifespan took a sudden leap about 32,000 years ago, allowing people to grow older and wiser. A five-fold jump in longevity may have been the key factor that shaped modern civilization.

Perhaps around this time, people started to value and take care of the weak and the old, and benefited from their wisdom and experience. The researchers credit grandmothers with helping to raise their extended families, contributing to a group's success. The findings support the so-called "grandmother hypothesis," Caspari said. Anthropologists have long suspected that older people may have played an important role in the development of early human societies by providing extra care for children, helping to accumulate useful information and strengthen kinship bonds. Experts have argued that grandmothers are useful because of the knowledge they pass on to their reproductive-age daughters, and eventually to their grandchildren.

"There has been a lot of speculation about what gave modern humans their evolutionary advantage. This research provides a simple explanation for which there is now concrete evidence—modern humans were older and wiser.... We live in a society that is so geared towards younger people. It is nice to realize that it might be older people that make us human after all" (Caspari and Lee, "Older Age Becomes Common Late in Human Evolution," 2004).

The Socioeconomic Implications of an Aging Society in the Present

Between 2011 and 2030, an estimated 77 to 80 million baby boomers will be approaching age 65—an age once associated with early bird dinner specials and slow driving in the fast lane. There are many who believe that America, today, is wholly unprepared to accept obligatory changes in ways of thinking and feeling about seniors in society. They interpret the numbers as ominous; for them, the increasing population of elderly portend dire consequences for our economy, and for social services and the health care delivery systems that will be overburdened by such numbers.

"If you heed the doomsayers, the graying of the U.S. population is a catastrophe. Look a little harder, and those fears are overblown…. The graying of America is enough to send most public-policy analysts running for the medicine chest, seeking relief from visions of impending disaster: Spendthrift Americans aren't saving enough for their retirement. Social Security is hurtling toward insolvency. The health-care system is out of control. The aging of society is a demographic tidal wave that will swamp the economy" (Farrell, "The Not-So-High Cost of Aging").

Listen to Laurence J. Kotlikoff, economist at Boston University and co-author of *The Coming Generational Storm: What You Need to Know*:

> I think we're heading for sizable tax hikes, benefit cuts, hyperinflation, and high interest rates…. The phrase "we can't afford growing old" reverberates from gloomy Congressional testimony to somber economic conferences…. In 2030, as 77 million baby boomers hobble into old age, walkers will outnumber strollers; there will be twice as many retirees as there are today but only 18 percent more workers. How will America handle this demographic overload? How will Social Security and Medicare function with fewer working taxpayers to support these programs?… [I]f our government continues on the course it has set, we'll see skyrocketing tax rates, drastically lower retirement and health benefits, high inflation, a rapidly depreciating dollar, unemployment, and political instability. The government has lost its compass… and the current administration is heading straight into the coming generational storm [Kotlikoff and Burns, *The Coming Generational Storm*, 2004].

Christopher Farrell is a bit more positive: "Look, none of this is to say that getting old is fun—believe me—or that an aging society doesn't confront all of us with public-policy challenges. But there are many positive fundamental forces at work that deserve emphasis. Business is more productive than at any time since the 1960s. The elderly are more vital than before. Yes, we can afford to grow old" (Farrell, "The Not-So-High Cost of Aging").

James Scheibel, a former vice president of the Corporation for National Service addressed some misconceptions:

> The aging of the United States population could present a great challenge if senior citizens were drains on society taking resources away from younger Americans. That is how seniors have been portrayed on occasion. In fact, however, the aging of the nation is providing a remarkable opportunity for engaging the best-educated and most vigorous group of retirees in U.S. history to help wrestle with the challenges contemporary U.S. society poses.
>
> As more and more seniors and retirees seek to become involved in community service, the challenge to policymakers is to provide more opportunities for older citizens to serve—both part-time and full-time. Harnessing the potential of the United States seniors could go far in building a better U.S. society for all Americans [Scheibel, "Seniors: A Vital Resource"].

Defining Retirement

The term retirement is still perceived as negative by many to whom retirement still means going from "Who's Who," to "Who's that?" The English word derives from the French "*retirer*" meaning to withdraw, disengage, or take back. The root word "*tirer*" means to draw out. As used in English, the term has largely lost its traditional connotations. For example, in 1999 the American Association of Retired Persons expunged that name and adopted the acronym AARP as its official appellation, in part because the organization found that 40 percent of its members are actively working and not retired, as officially defined. In the summer of 2004, AARP was considering another name change. The phrase "senior citizen(s)" would likely *not* be included; the editor of the AARP publication *AARP The Magazine* had specifically forbidden its use in any AARP publications!

Yes, our government has also defined the term "retired." The U.S. Department of Labor offers two criteria, both of which must be fulfilled before an individual can be considered "retired." First, a person may not be working full time. For the Department, full time is considered to be 40 hours per week or more. The second criterion is that the person must be receiving some portion of regular income from a pension or pension-like source. This can be a private saving IRS-type plan, a company pension, an annuity, or Social Security. This means that a person could still be working up to 39+ hours weekly, and be receiving as little as 5 percent of their total income from a pension and be considered retired for legal purposes. The point is that people can be working quite actively, and still be considered retired—an "active retirement."

A Brief History of Retirement in America

Many are inclined to believe that the concept of retirement has been part of American culture for a long time. It has not. In reality, the concept only emerged at the beginning of the twentieth century. It arose from the socioeconomic climate of the Industrial Revolution, which created a predominantly male workforce that literally needed to rest after the age of 65. It has continued to evolve continually since that time and has been radically transformed several times. And it continues to change today. Today's retirees are finding that after leaving the job market, they now have the time, the energy, and the will to devote themselves to volunteer activities that they had insufficient time for while working. We are now experiencing a "retirement revolution" which carries with it new challenges and opportunities. Understanding how retirement has evolved over the last century will help us understand why retirement is the way it is at present, and why it will most likely be far different in the future.

In its 2002 study, "Re-Visioning Retirement," AIG SunAmerica defined four phases of retirement as it has developed in America.

- Phase One: No Retirement

Until the beginning of the 20th century, workers did not retire. They continued to work until they were no longer able or until they died. Whichever event occurred first dictated their "retirement." Working was simply a matter of survival—their own and that of their families. The assumption was that everyone would work until overtaken by illness or old age and no longer able to contribute. For many, however, their retirement period was measured in a few years, not decades.

- Phase Two: A Very Short Retirement

This picture began to change as the labor force slowly migrated from rural farms to urban factories, where age was viewed as a liability. The speed, strength, and agility of a young man were to his advantage in an industrial setting—and in surviving there. Older workers were considered unable to physically or mentally compete. This problem was exacerbated during the Great Depression of 1929. To address the problem, the government began developing a program that would simultaneously remove the problematic older workers from the workforce and employ younger, quicker hands. The result was the creation of Social Security in 1935. Retirement of older workers was officially institutionalized.

- Phase Three: The Golden Years

In the years following, retirement evolved into the "Golden Years," a decades-long vacation at the end of life. Americans began retiring earlier and earlier. The average age of retirement dropped from 70 in the 1930s to 62 today. Moreover, retirees were becoming wealthier due to increasingly generous company pensions and government programs. Poverty among the elderly abated to some degree. Health care and longevity improved markedly. Retirement was reborn as a time to enjoy life, health, and wealth. The elderly were no longer burdened with the perceived need to be productive, to work.

• Phase Four: Today's Retirement Revolution

The "Golden Years" has remained the archetype for retirement for almost four decades. But this perception is changing. Increasingly, retirees are not content with this traditional model of retirement. They desire to stay active and socially engaged. Many still want to work, continue to learn and make themselves useful and productive in society. Today's emerging retirees have greater energy, drive, and expectations for fulfillment in their later years. "In short, there is a new kind of retiree: energetic, vigorous, productive, driven; and not about to settle into a retirement of inactivity and endless leisure" (Source: AIG SunAmerica, "Re-Visioning Retirement," 2002).

Redefining Retirement

Considering the retirement revolution, perhaps we simply should "retire" the concept of retirement. "Retirement, as we know it, is dead," says Ken Dychtwald, Ph.D., president of the consulting firm, Age Wave, one of the nation's foremost experts on aging and retirement, and author of many books on baby boomers and aging. "It's no longer an end. It's a turning point. A chance to take a break and then reinvent yourself" (Cited in Streisand, "Today's Retirement Journey," 2004).

Not winding down but continuity, work, learning, travel, and new experiences are what most people want. These are the sentiments derived from a nationwide survey of more than 1,000 randomly selected adults age 55 and older who were contacted by telephone between October 29 and November 17, 2001. The survey was conducted by Harris Interactive for AIG SunAmerica. The researchers, under of the direction of Dr. Dychtwald, were commissioned to develop an understanding of the emerging new era of retirement and a portrait of the different experiences of retirement living. From their research, a new face of American retirement emerged that challenges conventional norms. The majority of respondents did not regard retirement as a time of rest and relaxation. Rather, they saw it as a new, active stage of their lives characterized by continued personal growth, personal reinvention, and new beginnings in work and leisure. The study revealed that retirement is not "one size fits all" (Source: AIG SunAmerica, "Re-visioning Retirement Survey," 2002).

> Over the 67 years since President Franklin D. Roosevelt introduced the Social Security System in 1935, it seems that most people saw successful

retirement as a peaceful time of old age and winding down after the stresses of a long working life. If one were lucky enough to still enjoy reasonable health and financial security, it was a time to stop working, relax and enjoy the grandchildren and, perhaps, to do a little gardening. Many retirees— like old soldiers—just faded away. That is not what most people want now. As life expectancy, health status and standards of living have all increased, retirees' hopes and expectations have changed dramatically [AIG SunAmerica, "Re-visioning Retirement Survey," 2002].

Doctor Dychtwald has said: "An entirely new paradigm for retirement is emerging in the twenty-first century, yet we have found that no research had been done to define how the retirement experience had actually changed, or to segment retirees by their commonly shared experiences, good or bad. Considering how extended longevity has multiplied the number of healthy, productive years in maturity before this study, there simply wasn't any effective blueprint for this complex and expanding state of life" (AIG SunAmerica, "Re-visioning Retirement Survey," 2002).

For the first time, research indicated four distinct segments that now define the contemporary retirement experience in America. Those over the age of 55 were divided into these four groups depending on "their commonly shared experiences"—their expressed hopes and expectations.

1. "Ageless Explorers"
These personify the new ideal for retirement. They are not satisfied with traditional norms of retirement. They want to live life to the fullest by being active and independent in retirement. They want to avoid boredom by participating in numerous recreational, leisure, and personal growth activities—including volunteering. They desire to make the most out of this stage of their life.

2. "Comfortably Contents"
This group embraces the more traditional view of retirement and its members are quite content to relax and enjoy the fruits of their lifetime of labor. They are satisfied with their life as it is now. They do not wish to see any stress in their retirement. Working in retirement holds no attraction for them; they have "been there, done that." This is the group that is least likely to feel a need to contribute to society. They are content to live their golden years in relaxation and play.

3. "Live for Todays"
This group is trying to be active and adventurous in retirement. It's followers share many of the same retirement ideals and aspirations of the Ageless Explorers and, in fact, may be even more interested in personal growth and reinvention of self and lifestyle. They dream of having the time to do all of the things they never had time for before retirement—including hobbies, travel, and participation in community affairs.

4. "Sick and Tireds"

For this group, gray hair brings gray clouds. They have low expectations for retirement and are pessimistic about all aspects of their future. For them, retirement is the worst possible scenario. They are less educated, and may lack the financial resources of other retirees. A significant number of this group are likely to be widowed and in poor health—frequently the principal cause of their retirement. In retirement, they expect to accomplish little in taking advantage of what life and social interaction has to offer. They are less likely to travel, engage in any leisure activities, visit family and friends, participate in community events, or utilize their own talents and experience. They are just trying to hang on. Perceiving their years of good health and productive employment to be behind them, they are convinced that there is little that they can do now to improve their situation. They are likely to view their retirement years as an inexorable winding down of their lives—truly the winter of their discontent (Source: AIG SunAmerica, "Re-visioning Retirement Survey," 2002).

The key findings of the AIG study were:

• The concepts of retirement as a "winding down" or an "extended vacation" are obsolete.
• Retirement no longer means the end or work, and relegation to inactivity.
• Satisfaction in retirement is positively related to the number of years one saves for that retirement. "One of the most compelling findings was the connection between feeling financially prepared for retirement and satisfaction with the retirement experience." (This aspect was, understandably, a major focus in the study. SunAmerica, the retirement savings division of American International Group, specializes in this area and the marketing of related investment products and services.)

A recent survey conducted for NCOA and MetLife Foundation by Harris Interactive revealed that "having something meaningful to do" in retirement would have the most favorable impact on future quality of life; and the socialization, friendship, and sense of accomplishment developed through volunteer service helps to promote improved health, a feeling of optimism, and a higher quality of life.

Very few of their survey participants wanted to "take it easy and relax most days" in their retirement years. Despite the proven value of becoming involved in one's community, and the stated desires of this segment of the population to perform community volunteer work, less than half of them actually do so. In fact, service falls off sharply after retirement, and civic engagement among older

Americans is lower than any other age group (Source: National Council on the Aging, "Wisdom Works: Building Better Communities," 2003).

These findings are corroborated by a 2002 study by the Center for Information and Research on Civic Learning and Engagement (CIRCLE), of the University of Maryland. The Center assessed civic engagement among four groups ("Matures," born before 1946; "Baby Boomers," born between 1946 and 1964; "Generation X," born between 1964 and 1976; and the "DotNets," the almost 40 million young adults now between 15 and 30 years of age, born after 1976. They found that while the "Matures" are the most politically active age group, they lag behind younger people in their involvement with community service. (Center for Information and Research on Civic Learning and Engagement, "The Civic and Political Health of the Nation," 2002, 12, 19–20). (The full text—49 pages in PDF format—of the CIRCLE study cited is available online at the URL shown in "Sources.")

Marc Freedman, in his book, *Prime Time: How Baby Boomers Will Revolutionize Retirement and Transform America*, shows how retirement as "a time to take it easy, enjoy leisure activities and a much-deserved rest from work" is a social construct created in the 1950s and 1960s by Del Webb and Sun City, Arizona. It is losing its hold on the American imagination. Freedman contends that baby boomers—at the forefront of societal change since their coming of age in the 1960s—are seeking a new, more engaged vision of retirement—a vision more attune with "our deep hunger to live lives that matter, to use our experience and knowledge in ways that will have lasting benefit, and—in the process—to continue learning and growing" (Freedman, *Prime Time: How Baby Boomers Will Revolutionize Retirement and Transform America*, 2002, 6). "Retirement is a fluke of the 20th century," says David Ekerdt, a sociologist at the University of Kansas's Gerontology Center. "For people who are active and healthy, it's destructive. You can only play so much golf" (Cited in Streisand, "Today's Retirement Journey," 2004).

Retirement is not as easy to define as it once was. The trend toward increasing longevity that has been identified in numerous research reports has caused society and academia to redefine, reshape, and transform the traditional concept of retirement as most Americans have historically known it. "Across the nation, millions of older active Americans are retiring old notions of what it means to be retired. They are 'America's New Retirees,' a growing army of people who are using their later years to rethink and revitalize their lives. They are reinventing retirement—trying new careers, launching new businesses, volunteering eagerly, returning to school, and pursuing other paths that build on the interests, skills and wisdom they've acquired through the years" (Duka and Nicholson, "Retirees Rocking Old Roles," 2002).

The coming retirement of 77 to 80 million baby boomers will almost certainly require a redefinition of the meaning and implications of growing older in America. According to a 2002 study by the National Council on the Aging, 80 percent of today's baby boomers (age 35–53) report that they expect to do volunteer work in their later years. More than 50 percent of this group says "using their skills" will be important. "Will more retirees turn to community service as a means to sustain their vitality and build their communities? To achieve this outcome, America will need to develop the organizations that invite, facilitate and channel the time and talent of retired people. It will need to develop compelling new opportunities that enable older Americans to make genuine contributions, educate the public about this connection, and develop volunteer opportunities that are meaningful to the participants, both in terms of outcome and nature of their involvement" (The National Council on the Aging, "American Perceptions of Aging in the 21st Century," 2002).

Writing in the foreword to the book, *Productive Aging: Concepts and Challenges,* edited by Nancy Morrow-Howell and her colleagues, Robert N. Butler asks rhetorically:

> Will 69 million baby boomers suddenly drop out of the work force when they turn 65? It is difficult to imagine this generation, with its talent, education, and experience, idling away the last thirty years of their life. Old age has been historically thought of as a period of frailty and dependence, yet studies show that with the help of advances in health and medicine, current populations will live longer and remain healthier than previous generations. As average life expectancies rise traditional concepts of retirement need to be reconsidered on all levels—from government policy to business practice to individual life planning. In this volume, leaders in the field of gerontology explore these changing conditions through the concept of "productive aging," which has been developed by leaders in the field to promote older adults' contributions to society in social and economic capacities [Morrow-Howell et al., *Productive Aging: Concepts and Challenges,* 2000].

The concept of retirement has taken on an entirely new aspect—an entirely new definition. For so long society thought of retirement as a definitive point in life—the "beginning of the end." It started at age 65, and you pretty much stopped working, contributing, and living actively. Today we think of retirement as a pause before a new beginning, a hiatus rather than a halt—a transitional period between stages. The transition we call retirement is perceived as the beginning of a new phase of life called renewal. Increasingly, individuals are "retiring" for an interlude of reappraisal before making the transition to this new phase that manifests a redefinition of achievement and a distinctive combination of continuing education, personal growth, and active contribution to society.

Retirement no longer means "I'm finished!" It means "I'm just beginning!" Contrary to the popular media view of retirement, the most important thing that those individuals preparing for and anticipating it are looking forward to is personal fulfillment and enrichment—a sense of purpose, usefulness, and meaning rather than idle leisure. It can be a time to take advantage of opportunities we could not take advantage of before. It is a time to learn new skills, try a new career, or give back to the community. There is great hope inherent in retirement—hope for new life, directions, and endeavors. Retirement is a commencement, not an end!

Today's retirees are rocking stereotypes instead of chairs. Older Americans "harbor a profound anger at being labeled anything—they hate being labeled as retired," says Ruth Wooden, author of a study released in March 2002 titled "Recasting Retirement: New Perspectives on Aging and Civic Engagement." Wooden described her findings at the opening general session of the 2002 Joint Conference of the National Council on the Aging and the American Society on Aging, held in Denver in April 2002.

Wooden's focus-group participants revealed "a sense of denial about what's going on in their retirement. They resisted being labeled with chronological or stage-related terms. Sometimes they mythologize retirement, and they talk about how great it is to play golf, go to the movies whenever they want, or be able to read stacks of books." Often respondents refused to say anything negative about retirement, she says. They reveled in their new freedom, the research group found, but further investigation showed that it is "a lonely freedom." Wooden continues: "They had an unsettling sense of loneliness, and it came from a sense of purposelessness. Deeper exploration showed that many in the focus groups missed the collegiality of the workplace. What they were missing was a purpose where they worked together with people to solve problems ... joined together in that common purpose." A principal coping strategy among retirees was to become extremely busy. "They fill their calendars with activities" she says. (Wooden, "Recasting Retirement: New Perspectives on Aging and Civic Engagement," 2002).

In an article originally appearing in the *Los Angeles Times*, and later reprinted in *The Detroit News* on May 17, 2000, Jocelyn Y. Stewart describes how the golden years are now filled with part-time work, hobbies, and volunteering. "Retirement has always been the ultimate goal for the American worker, the payoff for hectic years of work. People have seen it as a time when their lives become their own; when they can rest, travel and play at their own pace. But ... more people are finding that traditional notions of old age and retirement are about as useful as an eight-track tape player. As people live longer and enter old age in better health, the generally accepted goals for this stage of life do not apply quite as universally—if they ever did" (Stewart, "Retired No Longer Means No Work," 2000).

A national survey by the *Los Angeles Times* portrays a generation of older

Americans who are poised not only to defy long-standing views of aging but to redefine this stage of life. Also, the expectations of those entering this generation are different from their predecessors, a trend that will only intensify, experts say, as baby boomers age. "They're not ready to withdraw, sit on the periphery and watch the parade go by from their rocking chairs" (Cited in Stewart, "Retired No Longer Means No Work," 2000).

James Firman, president of the National Council on the Aging has said: "Sixty-five may be meaningful as a speed limit, but it means less and less as a retirement age. The stereotypical notion of working until age 65, moving to a warm and sunny climate and rocking on the porch has gone the way of the gold retirement watch.... We are in the midst of a fundamental reformulation of retirement" (The National Council on the Aging, "National Study Says Retirement Not Determined by Work Status," 2000).

In 2002, 4.5 million (13.2 percent) Americans age 65 and over were in the labor force (working or actively seeking work), including 2.5 million men (17.9 percent) and 1.9 million women (9.8 percent). They constituted 3.1 percent of the U.S. labor force. About 3.6 percent were unemployed. Labor force participation of men 65+ decreased steadily from 2 out of 3 in 1900 to 15.8 percent in 1985, and has stayed at 16–18 percent since then. The participation rate for women 65+ rose slightly from 1 of 12 in 1900 to 10.8 percent in 1956; fell to 7.3 percent in 1985, and has been around 8–10 percent since 1988 (Source: U.S. Department of Labor).

Their mounting numbers form the vanguard of what Helen Dennis, a lecturer at the Andrus Gerontology Center, University of Southern California, Los Angeles, as well as a respected consulting expert on aging, employment and retirement, calls "a retirement revolution." "Retirement beyond the year 2000 will be influenced by increased longevity, the size and influence of the boomer generation, and higher expectations for retirement life" (Dennis, "Ten Trends That Will Change Retirement," 2002).

Richard Johnson in his 1999 book *Creating a Successful Retirement: Finding Peace and Purpose* has a far more optimistic view. He writes:

> Two separate trends are converging to create the greatest demographic experiment we have ever seen. First, people are retiring earlier than they ever have before.... Second, people are living longer.... This is not a tragedy for our culture, on the contrary, it's a bonanza if we can truly squeeze from our retirement years all the potential for personal and individual achievement that is there. If the "armies" of retirees can be inspired to address some of the cultural problems that plague our society today, if we can find the motivation to begin addressing these problems, there is no doubt that radical changes can be accomplished in our world that we have never been able to successfully tackle before.... Age is not a criterion for a successful retirement. Age alone offers no guarantee that we'll gather the necessary

wisdom to exploit the opportunities of retirement and find the happiness lying as undiscovered treasure there. Age does not miraculously give us the requisite tools, competencies, knowledge, and attitudinal shifts that will ensure that your retirement will proceed maximally [Johnson, *Creating a Successful Retirement*, 1999, 8–9].

The organization ReFirement proposes:

What if we replaced the retirement concept with a new and positive vision of basing your life and work choices on your core values, your passions, a commitment to lifelong learning, an intentional connection to all generations, and a willingness to use your legacy as a starting point for deciding how you want to live today? Instead of waiting for retirement, or a major life crisis to change directions, the new paradigm would promote-multiple career portfolios, translating passions into life and work opportunities, and finding meaning and authenticity in our life journey. Why defer our dreams? [ReFirement, "What Is Refirement?"].

Preparing for Retirement

As previously noted, retirement, by definition, means to withdraw and retreat. But today's retirees are not retreating. They are vigorously attacking and filling their retirement years with activity and purpose. Rather than focus primarily on financial planning, they are devoting their energies to deciding how they will spend a meaningful retirement, and restructuring their priorities rather than their portfolios to fulfill lifelong dreams. They intend to thrive—not merely survive. "You already know you are likely to live longer than your parents. You will probably also be healthier and better able to enjoy your later years. Yet, living longer means making decisions about what to do with that retirement chunk of life, as well as how to do it. Our current generation of retirees and potential retirees are thrusting themselves happily into that chore. As millions of Americans start to think about and plan for their retirement, it becomes obvious we have completely reinvented the concept of retirement. It's not your father's retirement anymore" (Berger, "Reinvent Retirement Completely," 2002).

TOP TEN WAYS TO REINVENT RETIREMENT

Begin by asking yourself some important questions: What do you like to do? Were there things you longed to do but didn't have time for when you were working? These are the activities you should begin building into your retirement days.

The website Too Young to Retire suggests ten ways to reinvent retirement. Summarized, they are:

1. Retire the word "retirement" from your vocabulary. Remember it means to "withdraw" or "retreat." Let "renaissance" describe your post-retirement life.

2. Realize that retirement is a relatively new concept in our society. Only a few generations ago, before Social Security and full-time leisure became the norm for our culture, the elderly were esteemed members of society; valued for their contributions, and respected for their wisdom and skills.

3. Restructure your priorities around those things that are most important and of greatest value to you.

4. Realize that learning is a life-long process. Renew your pursuit.

5. Revitalize your energy by associating with those who share your hopes and ideals.

6. Be willing to take risks. Do not be afraid to make mistakes. If not you, then who? If not now, when?

7. Actively seek out and respond to new opportunities. Remain open to the endless possibilities that life has to offer. Strive to realize your full potential.

8. Revitalize yourself through regular physical and mental activity. Find those that are stimulating and enjoyable and make them a part of your daily wellness program.

9. Revisit the dreams of your youth. It's never too late to be who you wanted to be—might have been—can yet be.

10. Remember that the wisdom to discover and act on your deepest passion is within you (Source: www.2young2retire.com, "Top Ten Ways to Retire Retirement").

Volunteering in Retirement

Volunteering allows you to use your life experiences, skills and talents to help others in your community. There are numerous organizations that need help. If you decide to volunteer, choose something you enjoy and are familiar with; that way, you'll be volunteering some time while dealing with people who have interests similar to yours.

Studies have confirmed a national trend toward service by retirees. In the summer of 2002—July 22 to July 31—the organization, Civic Ventures, undertook its second national survey focusing on the attitudes of the next generation of retirees toward continuing to contribute to society. The effort was conducted by Peter D. Hart Research Associates of Washington, D.C. and was funded by the David and Lucile Packard Foundation.

The poll surveyed 600 older Americans age 50 to 75, including 300 volunteers and 300 non-volunteers. The results were released on August 19, 2002. These showed that older Americans are in the midst of redefining retirement. In place of the old "golden years" notion of a leisured later life—or recent predictions that today's retirees will simply work "til they drop"—the men and women surveyed made it clear that they are poised to assume a leadership role in rejuvenating the nation's civic life.

Data from the study which defines attitudes about retirement and civic engagement shows that:

• More than half of those surveyed said volunteering and community service will be an important part of their retirement.

• 59 percent of respondents saw retirement as a time to be active and involved, to start new activities, and to set new goals.

• 56 percent say civic engagement will be at least a fairly important part of retirement.

• 57 percent report having volunteered in the past three years, with one-quarter of those devoting at least five hours a week.

• An additional 21 percent of older Americans would commit at least five hours a week to volunteering if they received a small monetary incentive for their service—effectively doubling the current older adult volunteer workforce, from 25 percent to 46 percent. Nearly one in three older adults say they would serve 15 hours a week for such an incentive.

• Working with children was found to be the most appealing volunteer activity among older adults, with 35 percent seeing that as most enjoyable, followed by service to religious organizations, other seniors, and hospitals.

• More than half (52 percent) believe that the government should do more to fund programs that provide volunteer and community involvement opportunities for older adults. (Sources: Civic Ventures, "The New Face of Retirement," 2002, 1–18; OASIS, "Volunteers Find Fulfilling Ways to Serve Their Communities," 2003.)

SENIORS AS SOCIAL CAPITAL

There are many who have planned well for a comfortable and financially secure retirement and have no great desire or need to acquire more wealth. However, they believe that they can make a contribution to society and, therefore, seek out volunteer opportunities. Volunteering often gives retirees or seniors a chance to use the skills they spent so many years cultivating. They may not need financial capital—they *are* capital!—social capital.

"Despite the decline in political and civic engagement, as evidenced by lower voter participation and fewer people actively involved in the political parties, volunteer activity in the United States is on the rise. More than ever before, individuals, communities and scholars are examining how changing patterns of volunteerism affect the creation of social capital" (Nunn, "Building Social Capital," 2002).

Robert Putnam, a public-policy professor at Harvard University, has defined social capital as the collective value of all social networks and the inclinations — the associated norms of reciprocity and trust — that arise from these networks to do things for each other. Social networks matter to the individual and the community. Volunteering is not only one of the most powerful mechanisms through which individuals build social networks, it is also an important indicator of social capital and a tool for building it (Source: Dennis: "Ten Trends That Will Change Retirement").

In his book *Bowling Alone*, Putnam focuses on what he perceived to be the decline in this nation's investment in its nonmonetary social capital and civic engagement in American society. His research demonstrated that "the United States has failed to invest in the social glue, the cohesiveness that a society needs to build on." Putnam's message is that we have become increasingly disconnected from family, friends and the social structure. He asserts that the shrinking access to social capital is a serious threat to civic and personal health. "Older people are a tremendous source of social capital and could serve as a valuable resource to American society in rebuilding the civic engagement that is vital to all communities. As this decade unfolds, more trends will emerge to shape what it means to age in American society" (Cited in Dennis "Ten Trends That Will Change Retirement," 2002).

"Civic engagement can be considered a type of community service in that healthy communities depend on involved citizens. Among middle age and older persons, civic engagement is largely limited to voting, discussing issues, and community activities through their religious organizations. Less than a third of this population directly contact elected officials, attend neighborhood or local government meetings, write letters to media, or take part in demonstrations" (AARP, "Multicultural Study, 2003").

PART II

The Scope of
Senior Volunteerism

4. How Many Seniors Volunteer?

"To the world you may be one person. But to one person you may be the world."

—ANONYMOUS

The Number of Seniors

Between 2000 and 2003, the national population count pushed closer to an estimated total of 300 million. In July of 2003, there were approximately 35.9 million people age 65 and over—12 percent of the population. Census Bureau projections predict that the older population will continue to grow significantly in the future. The projected population of persons age 65 and over in the year 2050 is 86.7 million—an increase of 147 percent between 2000 and 2050. By comparison, the population as a whole is expected to increase by only 49 percent over the same period. (Source: U.S. Census Bureau, "Older Americans Month," 2004.)

According to the census of 2000, the 65–74 age group (18.4 million) was eight times larger than it was in 1900, but the 75–84 age group (12.4 million) was 16 times larger, and the 85+ group (4.2 million, 1.5 percent of the population) was 34 times larger! Those at age 85 and older—the "oldest old"—comprise the fastest growing segment; this group is projected to increase from 4.7 million in 2003 to 9.6 million in 2030. (Source: Administration on Aging, "A Profile of Older Americans, 2003," 2003.)

Volunteering in the United States

Independent Sector's "Giving and Volunteering in the United States 2001" was the seventh in a series of biennial national surveys that reported national trends in giving and volunteering in the United States. The data from the study shows the following:

Giving and Volunteering	Percentage of Adult Population
Give only	46%
Give and volunteer	42%
Volunteer only	2%
Neither	10%

• Forty-four percent of adults over the age of 21 volunteered with a formal organization in 2000. Of these formal volunteers, 63 percent reported they volunteered on a regular basis, monthly or more often.

• Volunteers in formal organizations averaged just over 24 hours per month of volunteer time.

• An estimated 83.9 million adults formally volunteered approximately 15.5 billion hours in 2000.

• The formal volunteer workforce represented the equivalent of more than 9 million full-time employees at a value of $239 billion. Volunteers were more likely than their non-volunteering counterparts to belong to a religious organization (75.6 percent vs. 58.0 percent).

• Women were more likely to have volunteered than were men (46 percent and 42 percent, respectively).

"No differences were found in the number of monthly hours volunteered based on youth experiences, religious attendance, household giving patterns, age category, gender, race, or ethnicity. The amount of time people volunteered is independent of many of the differentiators examined in the giving and volunteering surveys" (Independent Sector, "Giving and Volunteering in the United States 2001," 2001).

The data also showed:

Percentage of adults who volunteered	44%
Total number of adult volunteers	83.9 million
Average weekly hours per volunteer	3.6 hours
Annual hours volunteered	15.5 billion hours
Estimated hourly value of volunteer time (2003)	$17.19 per hour
Total dollar value of volunteer time	$239.2 billion
Percentage of adults asked to volunteer	50%
Percentage of adults who volunteered when asked	71%

(Sources: Independent Sector, "Giving and Volunteering in the United States 2001," 2001; "Experience at Work," 2003.)

The Number of Retirees and Seniors Who Volunteer

America's retirees and seniors are an increasing part of our nation's demographics and a growing resource of time and talent. This number is expected to rise dramatically in the coming decades as millions of baby boomers mature and live longer than previous generations. The number of persons who retire every day is increasing. It is estimated that there will be approximately 77 to 80 million new retirees over the next 20 years, as the baby boomers reach age 65. Those in this group are retiring earlier; the average retirement age is now 57.5 years old. They are living longer than previous generations—average life expectancy has risen to more than 80 years.

Many in this group enjoy early retirement. Older Americans today are active, involved, and interested in helping, whether through charitable contributions or volunteer time. At more than 35 million in number, America's seniors are not only an increasing part of our nation's population; they are also recognized as a growing and largely untapped resource of time and talent. (Sources: Administration on Aging, "A Profile of Older Americans, 2003," 2003; U.S. Census Bureau.)

A 2001 study—"Experience at Work: Volunteering and Giving Among Americans 50 and Over"—which involved a national survey of 4,000 adults by Independent Sector, a research and advocacy group in Washington, D.C., in collaboration with AARP, offered good news for the future of volunteering: "The American Baby Boom generation represents the largest untapped pool of potential volunteers ... in recent history.... [There will be] unprecedented opportunities and challenges to engage this population." To do so, the study suggests that nonprofit organizations "seize this opportunity to engage older Americans ... and demonstrate the value of their service." To effect this change, it is suggested that they tailor their volunteer programs to meet the needs of the over-50 population by offering more flexible hours and accommodating volunteers who have disabilities and health concerns. These organizations should increase their efforts to create "virtual-volunteer" programs, (discussed in a section of the book to follow) that would take advantage of boomers' computer skills and allow them to actively volunteer without leaving their homes (Independent Sector, "Experience at Work, Giving and Volunteering in the United States," 2001).

In its 1999 study, "Senior Volunteers in America," Independent Sector noted that seniors of every age, ethnic and racial group volunteer at some level. "Over 46 percent of persons ages 55 to 74 reported performing some type of volunteer work in the past year [1998]." Almost 34 percent of those 75 years old and older reported volunteering. Significant numbers of seniors in minority groups reported volunteering. "These groups constitute a growing portion of American society and a valuable resource of volunteer time" (Independent Sector, "America's Senior Volunteers," 2000). (The reader is referred to the previous discussion on "Minorities and Volunteerism" for more recent Census Bureau data.)

In 2002 Civic Ventures reported that almost 44 percent of all people 55 and over volunteer at least once a year; more than 36 percent reported that they had volunteered within the past month. More than half (57 percent of individuals 50 and older) have done some volunteer work over the previous three years. These older volunteers give on average 4.4 hours per week to the causes they support. These are some of the main conclusions drawn from the latest round of interviews conducted for "The New Faces of Retirement: An Ongoing Survey of American Attitudes on Aging" by respected poll-taker Peter D. Hart, president of Hart Research Associates, Washington, D.C. He presented the survey results in October 2002 at the 4th annual Coming of Age conference held by the study's sponsor, Civic Ventures, a San Francisco-based nonprofit organization. For a growing number of people age 50 or older, Hart said, "Civic engagement is not just about filling time, but it's also about filling a need, and they need to be involved" (Civic Ventures, "The New Face of Retirement," 2002).

Commenting on the Hart study, Kleyman said: "[O]lder Americans are volunteering their time and energy to community programs in rising numbers. Also, many more probably would pitch in if programs had the tools they need to recruit and involve older volunteers. Small inducements could double the older-volunteer force in the United States" (Kleyman, "Study Shows How Older-Volunteer Force in the U.S. Could Double," 2003).

In a recent Gallup Poll, 45 percent of older people age 65–74 stated that they volunteer. Another 50 percent said they would if they were asked. In fact, the poll showed that 85 percent of those asked to volunteer did so (The National Council on the Aging, "Volunteerism," 2002).

On December 17, 2003, the Bureau of Labor Statistics (BLS) of the U.S. Department of Labor released *Volunteering in the United States, 2003*. (Appendix 2.) These new data on volunteer service were collected as a supplement to the September 2003 *Current Population Survey* (CPS). The CPS is a monthly survey of about 60,000 households that obtains information on employment and unemployment among the nation's civilian non-institutional population age 16 and over, including the extent and type of volunteer service done through or for organizations. Volunteers are defined as persons who do unpaid work (except for expenses) through or for an organization.

The BLS found that both the number of volunteers and the volunteer rate rose over the year ended in September 2003. About 63.8 million people did volunteer work at some point, from September 2002 to September 2003, up from 59.8 million for the similar period ended in September 2002. The volunteer rate grew to 28.8 percent, up from 27.4 percent.

About 25.1 percent of men and 32.2 percent of women did volunteer work in the year ended in September 2003, increases of 1.5 and 1.2 percentage points from 2002, respectively. Volunteer rates were lowest among persons age 65 years and over (23.7 percent) and among those in their early twenties (19.7 percent). Within the 65 years and over group, volunteer rates decreased as age increased. For the third year in a row, the percentage of "older adults," those 65 and older, who did volunteer work was second-lowest among all age groups, according to the U.S. Department of Labor. Among the age groups, volunteers age 65 and over devoted the most time—a median of 88 hours—to volunteer activities (U.S. Department of Labor, Bureau of Labor Statistics, "Volunteering in the United States, 2003," 2003).

Paul Kleyman observes that the Hart survey and the BLS data "reveal two sides of the same coin…. On one side, the studies show that volunteering has grown steadily since the 1960s, and older people continue to express a deeply felt yearning to do much more. On the other side is a paucity of the kind of volunteer opportunities capable of capturing the imagination of a new generation of older Americans…. [O]lder Americans are a group that might be described as all dressed up with too few places to go—and the Department of Labor numbers reflect this gap" (Kleyman, "Study Shows How Older-Volunteer Force in U.S. Could Double," 2003).

In "Multicultural Study 2003: Time and Money: An In-Depth Look at 45+ Volunteers and Donors," AARP found that most people age 45 and over take on some role as a volunteer and contributor. This AARP survey attempted a comprehensive assessment of the extent of civic engagement—community service—of the population over the age of 45. The study analyzed those behaviors identified by respondents that may be considered to have a salutary impact on their communities, but may not be adequately identified by traditional survey methodology. The study examined how persons volunteer with non-profit organizations, and also the efforts they make on their own and in their communities. Telephone interviews with 2,069 Americans age 45 and over, were conducted between July 2 and July 30, 2003. The survey found that the target population takes on various roles as volunteers (AARP, "Multicultural Study 2003," 2003).

About half (51 percent) of the 45 and older population reported volunteering when asked the traditional question about community service—would they volunteer for a non-profit organization, charity, school, hospital, religious organization, neighborhood association, civic or other group. In its conclusion AARP states: "We believe this survey is a good start toward a more adequate understanding of the range of socially beneficial behaviors that create and sustain civil society. There is more work to do, and more refined definitions of community service and charitable giving may result from this work, as well as a greater understanding of the impact of organizational, informal, and individual volunteering and giving. AARP welcomes this challenge and considers community service and

charitable giving to be essential elements of The Power to Make It Better™"
(AARP, "Multicultural Study 2003," 2003).

In discussing its report, AARP asks rhetorically: "How many age 45+ people who volunteer their time or make charitable donations are not being counted,
and thus having their contributions overlooked by methods traditionally
employed for identifying such activities? We know from other surveys that substantial proportions of 45 and older Americans volunteer; however, the specific
incidence levels can vary depending on definition, question wording, data collection methodology, and sampling procedures" (AARP, "Multicultural Study
2003," 2003).

The Monetary Value of Volunteers' Contributions

In "Giving and Volunteering in the United States 2001," Independent Sector reported that 83.9 million American adults volunteered in 2001, representing the equivalent of more than 9 million full-time employees, at a value of $239
billion. The National Council on the Aging reports that "In a recent Gallup Poll,
[no date indicated] 110 million Americans said they volunteered their time annually, valued at $201 billion (The National Council on the Aging, "Volunteerism,"
2002). According to the BLS, volunteers contribute an average of 3.5 hours per
week—totaling 20 billion hours per year; valued at $200 to $225 billion.

The estimated dollar value of volunteer time—as determined by the Bureau
of Labor Statistics—was $17.19 per hour in 2003. This figure is based on the aver-
age hourly earnings of all production and non-supervisory workers on private non-
farm payrolls. (Source: Independent Sector, "Value of Volunteer Time," 2004.)

Rank in 2002* of the Top Ten States by Dollar Value of a Volunteer Hour

1.	District of Columbia:	$24.75
2.	Connecticut:	$21.70
3.	New York:	$21.53
4.	Massachusetts:	$20.75
5.	New Jersey:	$20.55
6.	California:	$18.67
7.	Illinois:	$18.20
8.	Delaware:	$18.08
9.	Michigan:	$17.48
10.	Colorado:	$17.41
	Washington:	$17.41

(*2002 is the latest year for which state-by-state numbers are available.)
(Source: Independent Sector, "Value of Volunteer Time," 2004.)

5. Where Do Seniors Volunteer?

"We make a living by what we do, but we make a life by what we give."
—WINSTON CHURCHILL

Type of Volunteer Work Performed

Volunteering can take many forms. Seniors have a wealth of knowledge and experience that can benefit society in all areas of life. They can volunteer through an a service club, homeless shelter, church, synagogue, or mosque to name only a few organizations. However, much volunteerism happens informally—such as a visit to a home-bound neighbor on a regular schedule. Like our nation itself, volunteerism has become increasingly diverse. In today's America, persons across a broad spectrum volunteer. They represent all ages and a wide variety of races, nationalities, and socioeconomic backgrounds. Individuals who work full-time volunteer, as do children, young adults, and older adults.

In their 2002 study, "The New Face of Retirement: An Ongoing Survey of American Attitudes on Aging," Civic Ventures reported that respondents ranked those volunteer activities that they found most appealing. In order of preference the activities were:

1. Working with children and youth.
2. Volunteering with a religious organization.
3. Helping other seniors.
4. Volunteering at a hospital or medical facility.
5. Working with the homeless or poor people.
6. Working to preserve the environment.
7. Working for a political campaign or cause.

8. Volunteering with an arts organization or a museum.

9. Working to preserve homeland security. (Source: Civic Ventures, "The New Face of Retirement," 2002, 3.)

AARP has confirmed: "Efforts to assist neighborhoods, disabled people, community and religious organizations, the environment, and animals are ... popular causes of volunteers age 45 and over" (AARP, "Multicultural Study 2003," 2003). Seniors can volunteer in many ways to help fellow seniors—in their community, the nation, the world.

In their communities, they are most likely to volunteer at hospitals, nursing homes, libraries, and schools. Their efforts include:

• Assistance at community events, particularly those involving other seniors.

• Helping with various care and social activities in a nursing home, such as serving food, teaching arts and crafts, or planning recreational activities such as parties and outings.

• Adult daycare/respite—assisting seniors who are cognitively or physically impaired and spending time at a senior center or adult day care center can be very rewarding. This is a unique opportunity to help others in a very meaningful, personal way.

• Escorting and transporting—seniors can drive other seniors to various appointments; wait, and then take them back home. This enables those who are no longer able to drive to meet their medical appointments, at no cost or limited cost. This is a vital service in those areas where public transportation is limited and taxi or paratransit services are prohibitively expensive.

• Shopping assistance—volunteers either take seniors shopping and help them, or take a list of their needs and the funds required and go in their place. Many shopping tasks that are routine for most people present major challenges for an elderly person, who may require a cane, walker, or wheelchair.

• Delivering prepared meals for such programs as "Meals on Wheels." Drivers are the "eyes and ears" in the community and often report to social service agencies or authorities if they see any changes or problems with seniors they contact. The appropriate agencies can then intervene, as needed.

• Visitation—volunteers can spend an hour or so each week visiting seniors who are homebound, just to brighten their day and ease their isolation and loneliness. They can telephone several times a week; they can encourage seniors to call others.

• For many families, grandparents and their grandchildren are separated geographically. So many seniors fill that void by spending time with children at daycare or in after-school programs—reading to them, tutoring, and helping with homework.

Findings from the study by the Department of Labor (Appendix 2.) show that most volunteers provided their services through or for one or two organizations—69.2 percent and 19.2 percent, respectively. The main organization—the organization for which the volunteer worked the most hours during the year—for the majority of volunteers was either religious/sectarian (34.6 percent) or educational/youth-service related (27.4 percent). Another 11.8 percent of volunteers performed activities mainly for social or community service organizations, and 8.2 percent volunteered the most hours for hospitals or other health organizations.

Older volunteers were more likely than their younger counterparts to volunteer mainly for religious/sectarian organizations. For example, 46.5 percent of volunteers age 65 and over performed volunteer activities mainly through or for a religious organization, compared with 29.1 percent of volunteers age 16 to 24 years. (Source: U.S. Department of Labor, "Volunteering in the United States, 2003," 2003.)

AARP noted: "By looking into not only how people contribute within charitable, non-profit organizations, but also what they do on their own and in their communities for relatives and others, we found that most people age 45 and over take on some role as a volunteer and contributor. Specifically: About half (51 percent) the 45 and older population report volunteering when asked the traditional question about community service—would they volunteer for a non-profit, charity, school, hospital, religious organization, neighborhood association, civic or other group" (AARP, "Multicultural Study 2003," 2003). These data are similar to those reported by the Independent Sector study "Giving and Volunteering in the United States 2001."

How Do Seniors Learn About Volunteer Opportunities?

Most senior volunteers learn about their volunteering options through religious institutions with which they are affiliated. Almost 50 percent of volunteers age 55 and over discover volunteer possibilities through their church, mosque, or synagogue—more often than through any other membership organizations or places of employment. Other voluntary organizations are also places where seniors find out about volunteering.

More than 80 percent of seniors surveyed claimed membership in a religious organization. Almost half of these members reported volunteering in the past year. Members of other organizations, such as social clubs, unions, or alumni organizations, were even more likely to volunteer. Of the 39 percent of seniors who stated that they were members of organizations, such as these, more than 65 percent reported volunteering. "Membership in organizations fosters the spirit of volunteerism among all adults. Regardless of the type of organization, these adults are more involved and have a greater link to other people in the community" (Independent Sector, "America's Senior Volunteers," 2000).

6. Why Do Seniors Volunteer?

"I shall pass through this world but once. Any good therefore that I can do or any kindness that I can show to any human being, let me do it now. Let me not defer or neglect it, for I shall not pass this way again."
—MAHATMA GANDHI

The Benefits and Rewards of Volunteering

Why would you, as a retiree or senior, want to volunteer your time and talents? The obvious answer is that you want to share the knowledge and experience that you have gained during your lifetime with those who can benefit from what you have to share. But volunteering is not just about giving; you will also receive an immeasurable return—new friends, new knowledge, new interests—all while realizing that you are making an immeasurable difference in the lives of others. These are some of the psychic dividends.

There are also physical benefits to be derived. Several scientific studies demonstrate that volunteering promotes good health—both physical and mental—among older persons. It also promotes longevity! The work of a number of researchers has documented that volunteers generally have higher levels of well-being and life satisfaction than non-volunteers, suggesting that engagement in volunteer work can play an important role in maintaining good health in later life, and perhaps in prolonging life. The research has proven the positive rewards of doing good for others and finding meaning in activities. Such meaningful activity greatly contributes to an older person's ability to age successfully.

Results of a survey conducted by the nonprofit organization, Independent Sector, reported that helping others significantly reduces stress and enhances personal health. However, they identified only a certain kind of help as most therapeutic—that which involves personal contact with those helped, repetition at

73

least every other week, and helping strangers rather than just family or friends. Such volunteers, the scientists say, who focus outside themselves, can derive the maximum benefits. (Source: Independent Sector, "Experience at Work: Volunteering and Giving Among Americans 50 and Over," 2003.)

Marcia Kerz of the OASIS Institute has affirmed: "Volunteering in our communities has an enormously positive impact on our lives and the lives of those we help.... It was not surprising to learn in a recent study that older adults who volunteer each week are living happier and healthier lives" (OASIS, "Volunteers Find Fulfilling Ways to Serve Their Communities," 2003). The comprehensive scientific study to which Ms. Kerz referred was done by Nancy Morrow-Howell and her colleagues, and published in the *Journals of Gerontology* (Morrow-Howell, et al., "Effects of Volunteering on the Well-Being of Older Adults," 2003).

The authors of that study researched the connection between volunteer service and improved mental and physical health. The participants were several thousand older adults, age 60 and over (67 percent were female). The researchers' objective was to test the effects of volunteering on the well-being of older adults— including the effects of level of engagement, the moderating effects of demographic and social factors, and the effects of the nature of the volunteer experience. Conducted over an eight-year period, the study found that the well-being of participants improved with the amount of time they volunteered, up to 100 hours a year, or two to three hours a week. They concluded that older adults who volunteer just two to three hours a week were living happier and healthier lives!

Compared to those who did not volunteer, the researchers found that volunteers had better assessments on three measures of well-being: functional status, self-rated health, and depression. Jim Hinterlong, one of the authors of the study, said: "Our findings support the perspective that volunteering is important in the larger context of successful aging.... [P]eople do not have to volunteer a lot of hours to reap the benefits of better mental and physical health."

Volunteer programs are enriching the lives of many more people. At the same time, those who volunteer find their own lives enriched through their service to others. Morrow-Howell and her co-authors also noted that "non-profit organizations have embraced the enormous potential of an aging population by providing opportunities for people to pursue successful aging on their own terms by challenging their bodies, minds and—most importantly—their civic spirits" (Morrow-Howell, et al., "Effects of Volunteering on the Well-Being of Older Adults," 2003).

The results demonstrated that older adults who volunteer and who engage in more hours of volunteering report higher levels of well-being. This positive effect was not moderated by social integration, race, or gender. There was no discernible effect as to the number or types of organizations for which the older adult volunteered.

Perhaps the most significant finding in this study was the discovery that even limited amounts of time spent volunteering can improve well-being—regardless of the nature of the volunteering—and that greater amounts tend to have an even greater effect, at least to some optimal level of volunteering. This work contributes to a knowledge base that points to the development of social programs and policies that maximize the engagement of older adults in volunteer roles. (Source: Morrow-Howell, et al., "Effects of Volunteering on the Well-Being of Older Adults," 2003.)

In a study which she had previously published in September 2000, "Productive Engagement of Older Adults: Effects on Well-being," Nancy Morrow-Howell said: "Activity has long been associated with improved well-being in later life. However, there are numerous types of activity. In fact, the 'busy ethic' that has shaped modern retirement seems to suggest that any activity will do. However, it is possible that all activity is not created equal—to the individual, the family, and society" (Morrow-Howell, "Productive Engagement of Older Adults," 2000). This study focused on a specific subset of activities—productive activity. Productive activity is any activity that produces goods or services, whether that activity is or is not paid. Activities included in this definition are volunteering, working, and caregiving. These are clearly a subset of activities in which older adults engage, and that have a common element—they have social benefits; benefits that extend beyond the individual. Doctor Morrow-Howell concluded:

> There is evidence that future generations will seek more engagement in these meaningful roles; and there may be increased demand for elders in these roles in future years. Thus, we need to know more about the effects of this type of engagement on well-being outcomes for the older adult. If older adults come forward in larger numbers to fill these roles in the extended late-life period [or if our society increases the demand on older adults to fill these roles], what will be the effect on the individual? To some extent, there is an assumption that productive engagement, in and of itself, is a good thing. Indeed, this assumption is supported by a great deal of literature about the benefits of social engagement. Yet a more refined research agenda is needed to understand the effects of the types, quantity, and conditions of activity on older adults.
>
> We are in the midst of a longevity revolution. How we will spend time in these extended years is not fully determined and the possibilities are numerous. Hopefully, we can be purposeful in the roles and expectations that we create for this new "third age" of human life. We need to define the possibilities and create the opportunities based on knowledge about what improves society and what improves the health, mental health, and life satisfaction of our large older population. Our 21st century society may seek the involvement of its older citizenry in work, volunteer, and caregiving roles, and the baby boomers and subsequent generations may seek increased involvement. How we shape and support these roles and how

we match opportunity to capacity and preference may influence the impact of these activities on older adults' well-being. Let us proceed with as much knowledge about the effects of productive engagement as possible [Morrow-Howell, "Productive Engagement of Older Adults," 2000].

Today's elderly have the lowest volunteer rate of any demographic group in the country—and the highest rate of depression (statistics show that white males in their 80s are the most suicide-prone age group.) The boomers apparently have every intention of changing that. Opinion surveys consistently find that the next generation of retirees expects that volunteering and community service will be a "very important" part of their lives (Streisand, "Today's Retirement Journey," 2004).

A national survey of 4,343 older adults, conducted by the Seniors Research Group in October 1999, reported that older adults who volunteer are more satisfied with their lives, and that seniors who engage in community service live healthier and longer lives. "Above all else, seniors who volunteer have more fun. When asked how worried they are about feeling bored, 75 percent of seniors who volunteer regularly acknowledge that they are not very worried or not at all worried about feeling bored, compared to 62 percent of seniors who do not volunteer in their community. Furthermore, those who do not volunteer are twice as likely to feel very worried or extremely worried about being bored than seniors who volunteer regularly" (Seniors Research Group, "Volunteerism Improves Seniors' Satisfaction with Life," 1999).

A study by The National Council on the Aging, conducted more than 40 years ago, revealed that nearly 40 percent of older Americans believed that being involved in the community contributes to having a meaningful life. Being connected to the community as a volunteer can be an integral part of a healthy lifestyle for older adults. It can enhance self-esteem by promoting the feeling of being needed as a valued, contributing member of society. Volunteerism is an ideal way for older adults to remain active and productive (The National Council on the Aging, "The Importance of Civic Engagement to Older Americans" 2003).

The formal study conducted in July 2002, under the auspices of Civic Ventures by Peter D. Hart Research Associates, Inc., included a series of questions to identify what is important in the lives of older persons—"not about volunteering, just about their lives," Hart noted. The findings of the study confirmed that "they want to be productive, intellectually stimulated, to have something significant to do, and to stay physically active. It's not the idea of shuffle board; it is not the idea of sitting back in a rocker—these people want to be engaged." The answers of those surveyed who volunteer revealed that "they believe volunteering will produce a better, happier, fuller life." Fifty-nine percent of all respondents confirmed their belief that retirement is a "time to begin a new chapter."

For those respondents who identified themselves as volunteers, an overwhelming 72 percent said they feel retirement "begins a new chapter." The latter group reflected a more positive outlook in their answers to a series of questions. Hart stressed: "Without a doubt, people who are volunteers are more optimistic ... feel more productive ... feel more empowered to improve the lives of others in their communities ... and they're likelier to feel healthier and more involved" (Civic Ventures, "The New Face of Retirement," 2002).

Senior citizens who volunteer constitute the backbone of American volunteerism—working not for financial rewards but to help their fellow citizens. Citing an excerpt of an article in the *San Francisco Chronicle,* the website of the Greater San Francisco Bay Area Combined Federal Campaign said:

> Giving back to society, either financially or socially, is a major motivation for volunteerism among seniors. Over 50 percent of senior volunteers reported that they volunteered because they wanted to give back to society some of the benefits they received individually.
>
> The desire to help others less fortunate is another major motivation for seniors to volunteer. The ability to help individuals meet their needs and the belief that those who have more should help those who have less were major motivations for seniors to volunteer in their community. They were also motivated by wanting to make good use of their time and the desire to enhance the moral basis of society. The number of seniors in the United States is growing every day. Volunteering is a learning experience—at any age" [Greater San Francisco Bay Area Combined Federal Campaign, "Volunteerism at Any Age"].

A 2002 study by Cornell University Gerontology Research Institute sociologist Phyllis Moen indicated that community involvement provides a sense of well-being. "Retired seniors often have more time than money to give to worthy causes. Those who contribute their time get a wonderful reward: a heightened sense of psychological and physical well-being.... Volunteering works for retired older folks because it connects them socially and provides routines, rituals and new or expanded roles in lives now largely devoid of them.... Since paid work seems to give workers a sense of purpose and well-being in the prime adult years, our study suggests that volunteering in community organizations does the same for retirees" (Moen, "Retired Seniors Gain Lots from Volunteering," 2002).

Moen's findings in 2002 corroborate those of her previous study in 1999. At that time she had recommended that the middle-aged become active in their communities early on, since volunteering rates do not rise with retirement. "Community participation gives retirees ... a sense of purpose and a strong sense of being connected. And being socially connected is a powerful predictor for high levels of well-being in older life" (Moen, "Senior volunteering connected to well-being," 1999).

Volunteering and Longevity

A number of studies have shown that retirees and/or seniors who volunteer and are actively involved in their communities, tend to live longer, healthier lives. In their 1999 study, Musick and his colleagues at the University of Michigan documented a remarkable link between moderate volunteer activity and longevity. According to their findings, seniors who spend less than an hour a week volunteering are helping themselves as well as others. "Quite a few people assume that older volunteers should benefit in terms of better health and well-being," says Marc A. Musick. "This study is one of the first to document that's true in a nationally representative sample of older Americans."

Musick and his associates surveyed 1,211 adults over the age of 65 (mostly retirees) in 1986 and followed up on them eight years later. They examined the association between volunteering and mortality among older adults to estimate the effects of volunteering on the rate of mortality among the subject group. The authors found that volunteering has a protective effect regarding mortality and identified a link between moderate levels of volunteer activity and increased levels of survival. Seniors who volunteer may actually add years to their lives. The authors were among the first to establish that people live longer because they volunteer, rather than that people volunteer because they're healthier and hence more likely to live longer.

Musick and his collaborators found that seniors who volunteered for a total of less than forty hours over the previous year were less likely to die over the next seven-and-a-half years than those who didn't volunteer at all. One possibility is that volunteering provides meaning and purpose in people's lives. Such qualities may in turn have protective effects on mortality and other health outcomes. Interestingly, the volunteers' focus seemed to be crucial: Volunteers who spread their time and efforts among several organizations did not gain any discernible advantage in terms of their longevity. "Volunteering for a greater number of hours did not reduce the likelihood of death, and even tended to increase it…. [T]aking on too much volunteer activity may incur just enough detriments to offset the potential beneficial effects of volunteering" (Musick, et al., "Volunteering and Mortality Among Older Adults," 1999).

Discussing the beneficial effects of volunteering, Musick and his colleagues noted: "We further find that the protective effects of volunteering are strongest for respondents who report low levels of informal social interaction." One explanation for these findings may be that volunteering provides meaning and purpose in people's lives. Such qualities may in turn have protective effects on mortality and other health outcomes.

Discussing the perceived link between volunteering and longevity, Donald Kausler, emeritus professor of psychology at the University of Missouri-Columbia comments:

Of great interest in gerontology is the extent to which voluntary activities aid the physical and/or mental well-being of older adults. There are reasons for believing that they may have both positive and negative effects, but with the positive greatly outweighing the negative. Positive effects are to be expected because activity of virtually any kind is healthier than inactivity and because being a volunteer provides a substitute role for roles lost with retirement. Negative effects are to be expected when older adults get carried away and do excessive activities to the point of straining themselves. However, the evidence indicates that the positive effect on mortality is true only for moderate amounts of volunteering [40 hours or less, over half a year]. Greater amounts have been found to have neither a positive nor a negative effect on mortality.

Which would be more beneficial to a senior citizen's health—exercising physically or volunteering at a hospital, school, theater or other facility in need of help? Surprise! Researchers are finding that volunteering carries positive health benefits for older people in terms of increasing their longevity. In fact, the reduction of mortality associated with voluntary activity has been discovered to be greater than that associated with exercising. Who knew? [Kausler, "The Graying of America," 2003].

Helping Others, Helping Society

Many seniors desire to do something meaningful and purposeful. Volunteering is perceived as a way keep them active in society, give them a sense of purpose, facilitate social interaction, and maintain physical activity and mental acuity. It is viewed as a positive way to help others who may not be as fortunate, to increase self-esteem and competence, and reduce the stress, isolation and depression that so often comes with aging.

Benefits ranked most highly in the Hart study, by the percentage who considered volunteering as fulfilling these needs include:

1. Contributing to society and making a difference.
2. Having something significant to do.
3. Feeling valued and productive.
4. Being able to share the lessons you have learned.
5. Working as part of a group of people with a clear and important purpose.
6. Feeling vital and physically active.
7. Being intellectually stimulated.
8. Having a sense of discovery and adventure.
9. Having a place to go.
10. Being able to use your career-related skills. (Source: Civic Ventures, "The New Face of Retirement," 2002.)

Membership in organizations promotes the spirit of volunteerism among seniors. Regardless of the of type of organization, its members are more actively involved with, and have more effective links to, others in the community—not only their peers. "One of the top motivations among 45 and older volunteers and donors is a sense of personal responsibility to help others. In addition, 45 and older volunteers and donors want to be involved with organizations that have a good track record; they want to make a difference, and help the communities where they live. Affiliation with a religious organization is also a motivation for many volunteers and donors. Personal interests also play a role. Volunteering can make the lives of 45 and older volunteers more satisfying by keeping them active or employing their skills for community needs" (AARP, "Multicultural Study 2003," 2003).

"The desire to help others less fortunate is a major motivation for seniors to volunteer. Senior volunteers stated most often that the ability to help individuals meet their needs and the feeling that those that have more should help those with less were major motivations that drive them to be volunteers in their community. Giving back to society, either financially or socially, are also major motivations for volunteerism among seniors. Over one-third of senior volunteers reported that they volunteered because they wanted to give back to society some of the benefits they received individually; they wanted to enhance the moral basis of society" (Independent Sector, "America's Senior Volunteers," 2003).

Every day, across the United States, countless numbers of people from all walks of life—as individuals or in groups—spend hours in service to others. Why will one person spend time helping someone he or she does not know, close to home or far away? There are no easy answers. Volunteering is, for some, a way of returning to the community some benefit received. For others, it is an ineffable experience that makes the volunteer "feel good." And for still others, it can be a transforming experience—changing one's perspective on people, on community and on society, and defining one's purpose in life.

The desire to serve others in society is an important factor in making a decision to volunteer; however, it may not be the only reason. "The opportunity to support something you believe in, while getting to know others with similar interests, often is a motivation. You can use skills and talents you've gained through a lifetime of experience and share what you know with others. It also can be a way to learn and develop new skills, check out possibilities in a different career field, or explore a new area of interest" (AARP, "Volunteer").

In his 2003 essay "Reimagining Work: the Next Chapter," Marc Freedman remarks:

> However, despite much progress, it would be a mistake to assume that millions of aging boomers are about to rush headlong into new roles as "senior

volunteers." The growth in volunteer numbers isn't necessarily indicative of a civic renaissance among the older population; it equally reflects the more pervasive activity revolution that's taken place over the past half century as Americans in their 60s, 70s and 80s [and beyond] swapped their rocking chairs for an array of more vital pursuits, volunteering among them. At the same time, it can be argued that U.S. society has paid far more attention to the goal of "keeping the old folks busy" than to the nature of what these individuals have actually been doing in volunteer roles. As a result a yawning gulf exists between the vast capacities of older Americans today and real opportunities for them to make significant contributions to most civic organizations. If the United States is to have any hope of capturing the imagination and expansive talents of the aging boomers, we will have to do much better. One reason for this challenge is that the generation of 76 million people born from 1946–1964 lack many of the civic habits of their parents' generation" [American Society on Aging, "Reimagining Work," 2003].

Reasons Why Seniors Do Not Volunteer

In the various studies reported in the literature and cited here, those seniors who did not volunteer frequently identified personal health issues and physical problems as the reason; for others, their age was the determining factor. A number cited other time commitments as the major reason why they were not able to volunteer; although seniors were less likely than their younger counterparts to say that their personal schedule was too full to volunteer. Seniors have the time to volunteer if given an opportunity and, perhaps most importantly, if asked. "Today's senior citizens are active, involved, and interested in helping others, whether through charitable contributions or volunteer time. This reservoir of time and talent is a rich resource for volunteer organizations to tap into. Studies have found that even more seniors would volunteer if only organizations would ask them" (Sokolowski, "Volunteerism").

Summary

In placing a high value on the efforts that volunteers give to an organization, it is a win/win situation for both the agency receiving the help and the volunteer providing it. Retirees and seniors who volunteer their time do much more than help themselves. "Older adults make important social contributions through voluntary commitments. They represent a large reservoir of knowledge, skills, cultural continuity, wisdom and civic responsibility. Since human beings are social animals, it makes sense that helping others and being connected to our community is a mutual benefit—especially since people are living longer and healthier lives" (Woolston, "Seniors and Volunteering").

The research cited here shows that seniors who engage in community service live healthier and longer lives. Volunteering changes the lives of the person receiving, the person giving, their families, their communities, and the world!

PART III

Volunteer Opportunities

7. Government Programs

"If you want to build a ship, don't drum up the women and men to gather wood, divide the work, and give orders. Instead, teach them to yearn for the vast and endless sea."

—Antoine de Saint-Exupery

A common misconception is that volunteering involves activities solely for nonprofit organizations. Because of the term "voluntary sector," the general presumption is that volunteer work and private voluntary agencies invariably go hand in hand. This is too narrow a view. In fact, a very large percentage of American volunteers assist a vast array of government agencies at the federal, state, and local levels.

Federal Government

Most federal government volunteer programs are actually located within a community and recruit volunteers from the surrounding geographic area for such agencies as the U.S. Forest Service, the National Park Service, Federal Bureau of Prisons, and a number of others. One key to building a strong volunteer corps for these program is in establishing ongoing partnerships. Partnering with a local entity can provide a steady stream of potential volunteers. As paid staff change—move up and around in the department or division—there is "institutional memory" with the partners about the way projects or events are carried out. Partners are also effective supporters of federal programs at the local level.

An examination of the interrelationship of government and volunteering in the United States must take into account four distinct categories:

• Volunteering done on behalf of government by citizen volunteers, by choice and without remuneration.
• Volunteering done by government officials and employees as an extension of their commitment to the community, but without additional compensation.
• Citizen activities seeking to affect political or social life through lobbying, protesting, advocating or advising, on a wide range of issues.
• Government programs that bring about community service by special categories of citizens." [Ellis, "Volunteerism and the Government Sector," In "The United States A Nation of Volunteers," 15–19.]

During the past century, we have seen many memorable examples of volunteerism in America. Those associated with federally sponsored programs are particularly notable. There have been many instances of government-created community service—service that has had its impetus in government legislation. These include the Peace Corps in the 1960s; the Volunteers in Service to America (VISTA) program, initiated during the same decade; and more recently AmeriCorps, Learn and Serve America, Senior Corps, and USA Freedom Corps— national programs that enlist thousands of volunteers to address virtually every kind of pressing human problem or need.

"A slew of federal government programs provide volunteer opportunities for older Americans, especially retirees. Among them are the Administration on Aging in the U.S. Department of Health and Human Services, the National Service Corps under the Corporation for National and Community Service, the Senior Corps of Retired Executives under the Small Business Administration, and the National Park Service's Volunteers in Parks. These programs draw on the diverse talents, experience and expertise of older Americans who now have time to meet some needs in their home communities through volunteer work" (Asmus, "Volunteering When Retired," 2001).

State governments also actively recruit volunteers for programs that provide essential services to their citizens. For example, volunteers provide various essential emergency services in the wake of natural disasters. They also assist in state and county courts and the correctional system. These latter efforts include the provision of probation and parole mentors, counselors, teachers and trainers. Volunteers are found in the many state "Adopt-a-highway" programs, and innumerable other state government-sponsored volunteer programs that exist across the nation.

Volunteer Opportunities from the Federal Government

VOLUNTEER.GOV/GOV/

A suggested starting point in exploring volunteering opportunities with the federal government is Volunteer.Gov/Gov/—"Proud Partner of the USA Freedom Corps Network"—whose stated mission is "to connect people with public sector volunteer opportunities to help Build America's Communities of Service." Volunteer.Gov/Gov/ is a partnership among the Department of Agriculture, Department of Defense, Department of the Interior, Department of Veterans Affairs, the Corporation for National and Community Service, the Army Corps of Engineers, and USA Freedom Corps, aimed at providing a single, easy-to-use web portal with information about volunteer opportunities.

The site allows you to search for volunteer opportunities by keyword, state, activity, federal agency partner, and/or date range. The Volunteer.Gov/Gov/ website can be found at: www.volunteer.gov/gov/aboutvolgov.cfm. In this section, we will discuss several of the volunteer opportunity links on this website.

OLDER AMERICANS ACT (OAA) PROGRAMS

Each year about 7 to 9 million older persons benefit from Older Americans Act (OAA) services, whose delivery largely depends upon the efforts of more than half a million volunteers. These volunteers work through state and territorial units on aging, area agencies on aging, and more than 20,000 local organizations that offer opportunities and services to active older persons as well as those elderly who need help.

Volunteer activities include:

- Assisting at group meal sites;
- Delivering meals to the home-bound elderly;
- Escorting frail older persons to health care or other needed services;
- Accompanying them on errands;
- Visiting homebound older persons;
- Providing telephone communication to help ensure their well-being through regular social contacts;
- Repairing and weatherizing the homes of low-income and older persons to ensure their safety and improve their mobility;
- Counseling older persons in a variety of areas, including health promotion, nutrition, legal and financial concerns;
- Serving as a nursing home ombudsman (discussed below) to resolve resident facility disputes and to help ensure the safety and well-being of residents;
- Providing a homemaking assistant to frail older persons; and
- Assisting in senior center, daycare, and other group programs for seniors.

LONG-TERM CARE OMBUDSMAN (LTC)

Administered by the Administration on Aging, the LTC Program was established under the Older Americans Act. Local ombudsmen work in hundreds of communities throughout the country as advocates on behalf of residents of nursing homes, board and care homes, assisted living facilities, and similar adult care facilities. Since the program began in 1972, thousands of paid and volunteer ombudsmen working in every state and three other jurisdictions have made a dramatic difference in the lives of long-term care residents. LTC ombudsmen work on behalf of individuals and groups of residents, provide information to residents and their families about the long-term care system, and endeavor to effect systems changes at the local, state and national level. They provide an ongoing presence in long-term care facilities, monitoring care and conditions and providing a voice for those who may be unable to speak for themselves.

About 1,000 paid and 14,000 volunteer staff (8,000 certified) investigate more than 260,000 complaints each year. They provide information to more than 280,000 people on a myriad of topics, including how to select and pay for a long-term care facility. For further information on the program, prospective volunteers can consult the LTC web page: www.aoa.gov/prof/aoaprog/elder_rights/LTCombudsman/ltc_ombudsman.asp.

Anyone interested in volunteering in Older Americans Act Programs should contact their local Area Agency on Aging. To locate an Area Agency on Aging near you, contact the Eldercare Locator: 800-677-1116, or visit their website: www.eldercare.gov.

USA Freedom Corps

In his 2002 State of the Union Address, President George W. Bush added more choices to the list of volunteer service corps sponsored by the government. Perhaps he raised the question, "Which government corps should you join?" and created some degree of confusion about where and how seniors can participate.

The President called upon every American to get involved in strengthening America's communities and sharing America's compassion around the world. He included all Americans, because everyone can do something. As part of that initiative, the president appealed to all Americans to devote the equivalent of two years—4,000 hours—over the course of our lives to the service of others in a major new citizen service initiative—the USA Freedom Corps, created to help all of us answer the call. The mission of the Freedom Corps is to coordinate citizen volunteer efforts, both domestically and abroad.

The president affirmed: "Americans of all ages are already serving others in countless ways, by mentoring a child, caring for an elderly neighbor, teaching someone to read, or donating food and clothing to those who need them.... While government cannot fulfill the need for kindness, for understanding, and for love in our communities, through the USA Freedom Corps, government can support the momentum of millions of acts of kindness and decency that are changing America one heart at a time" (USA Freedom Corps).

Coincident with the president's address and announcement, a news release from the White House stated that the USA Freedom Corps is "a comprehensive, integrated citizen service initiative" that includes three major programs. The proposed Corps, was to be an umbrella, overseeing several existing nationally sponsored volunteer programs such as the Peace Corps, AmeriCorps, and the National Senior Service Corps (Senior Corps). Senior Corps taps the skills, talents, and experience of older Americans to help solve pressing social problems. We will discuss Senior Corps in more detail in a section to follow.

The president had called particular attention to the last, a group of federally funded programs that allow retirees and seniors to utilize their time and talents in countless volunteer activities throughout their communities. These include:

• The Foster Grandparent Program, which started in 1965;
• The Senior Companion Program, which began in 1974; and
• The Retired & Senior Volunteer Program (RSVP), which was organized in 1971.

In his State of the Union Address on January 30, 2003, celebrating the one-year anniversary of USA Freedom Corps, President Bush said: "Last year, I called on my fellow citizens to participate in the USA Freedom Corps.... Tonight I ask Congress and the American people to focus the spirit of service and the resources of government on the needs of some of our most vulnerable citizens."

USA Freedom Corps Volunteer Network

The USA Freedom Corps Volunteer Network is one of the most comprehensive clearinghouses of volunteer opportunities ever available. It will be discussed further in the section, "Clearinghouses."

Citizen Corps

The Citizen Corps, launched in May 2002, supports local volunteer efforts that help communities prevent, prepare for, and respond to emergencies. Almost all fifty U.S. states and territories support state or territory-wide Citizen Corps Councils. In November 2003, more than 300 councils of first responder, local government officials, and volunteer service organizations were functioning. Volunteers are working with police departments through more than 320 Volunteers in Police Service programs. Doctors and nurses are joining Medical Reserve Corps units across the country.

Citizen Corps programs build on the successful efforts that are in place in many communities around the country to coordinate volunteer activities that will prevent crime, and better prepare us to respond to any emergency situation, including terrorism and disasters of all kinds. The Corps provides opportunities for citizens of all ages to participate in a range of measures to make their families, homes, and communities safer. Programs that started due to local innovation are the foundation for Citizen Corps and this national approach to citizen participation in community safety.

Citizen Corps is coordinated nationally by the Federal Emergency Management Agency (FEMA). In this capacity, FEMA works closely with other federal entities, state and local governments, first responders and emergency managers, the volunteer community, and the White House Office of the USA Freedom Corps.

To learn more about Citizen Corps, go to the website. You can volunteer online at: www.citizencorps.gov/citizenCorps/volunteer.do. In applying, you can select those programs that interest you. These include:

- Medical Reserve Corps (discussed below)
- Community Emergency Response Teams
- Neighborhood Watch Program
- Volunteers in Police Service
- Citizen Corps Councils

The Citizen Corps' Affiliate Programs and Organizations offer communities resources for public education, outreach, and training; represent volunteers interested in helping to make their community safer; or offer volunteer service opportunities to support first responders, disaster relief activities, and community safety efforts. These programs are discussed in the section of this book on national volunteer opportunities.

MEDICAL RESERVE CORPS (MRC)

The Medical Reserve Corps Program coordinates the skills of practicing and retired physicians, nurses and other health professionals, as well as other citizens interested in health issues, who are eager to volunteer to address their community's ongoing public health needs and to help their community during large-scale emergency situations. For more information, go to the MRC home page at: www.medicalreservecorps.gov/. A 26-page booklet, *Medical Reserve Corps—A Guide for Local Leaders*, a reference for local planners who wish to begin a Medical Reserve Corps unit in their community—can be downloaded from the site. The *Guide* may be of interest to potential volunteers as well.

Volunteers for Prosperity

Early in his first term, President George W. Bush had made combating global poverty and stimulating prosperity in developing countries a national priority. On May 21, 2003, at a commencement address at the United States Coast Guard Academy, he expanded his summons to volunteer service by issuing a call to Americans trained in professional specialties to serve as volunteers with nonprofit organizations helping to generate prosperity in countries around the world. A part of the president's USA Freedom Corps volunteer service initiative Volunteers for Prosperity would:

• Support new and existing U.S. government initiatives with highly skilled volunteers;
• Give Americans with appropriate technical expertise the opportunity to serve for flexible periods of time, such as weeks, months, or longer;
• Deliver skilled volunteers to developing countries and emerging economies to promote health and prosperity in a cost-efficient manner.

The President affirmed that Volunteers for Prosperity:

> [W]ill give America's highly skilled professionals new opportunities to serve abroad.... The program will enlist American doctors and nurses and teachers and engineers and economists and computer specialists, and others to work on specific development initiatives.... These volunteers will serve in the countries of their choice, for however long their project takes. Like generations before us, this generation of citizens will show the world the energy and idealism of the United States of America.
>
> These goals—advancing against disease, hunger and poverty—will bring greater security to our country. They are also the moral purpose of American influence. They set an agenda for our government, and they give idealistic citizens a great cause to serve. President Woodrow Wilson said, "America has a spiritual energy in her which no other nation can contribute to the liberation of mankind." In this new century, we must apply that energy to the good of people everywhere [Volunteers for Prosperity, President's Speech, 2003].

An executive order signed by President Bush on September 25, 2003, directed the Departments of State, Commerce, Health and Human Service, and USAID to create offices to manage components of the program (Volunteers for Prosperity, "Fact Sheet," 2003).

THE CORPORATION FOR NATIONAL AND COMMUNITY SERVICE (CNS)

Created in 1993, the Corporation for National and Community Service, part of USA Freedom Corps, and its programs are a White House initiative to foster a culture of citizenship, service, and responsibility, and to provide opportunities for Americans of all ages and backgrounds to serve their communities and country through three programs:

- AmeriCorps
- Learn and Serve America
- National Senior Services Corps/Senior Corps

Together these three programs engage more than two million Americans of all ages and backgrounds in community service each year, while helping to promote a lifelong ethic of service and good citizenship. For more information, visit the website. Or you can contact CNS for pamphlets, brochures, fact sheets, and program handbooks at:

Corporation for National Service
1201 New York Avenue, NW
Washington, DC 20525
Phone: 800-424-8867
Website: www.cns.gov

FAITH-BASED INITIATIVES

Included under the aegis of CNS are faith-based initiatives that are mentioned in this book. The Corporation for National and Community Service has been implementing President George W. Bush's directive to reach out more effectively to small faith-based and community organizations through a federal department and agency-wide initiative—Faith-Based and Community Initiatives (FBCI).

The president's Faith-Based and Community Initiatives is not a distinct program but an expansion of the way the Corporation and its three main programs—Senior Corps, AmeriCorps, and Learn and Serve America—typically operate. Those programs have a long history of working with grassroots organizations, both faith-based and secular. To date, FBCI activities have focused on strengthening the Corporation's existing partnerships, forging new state and community-level partnerships, creating improved performance measures, developing toolkits (and other technical assistance and training) geared to the needs of grassroots groups, and removing barriers in order to be even more welcoming to faith-based and small community organizations, particularly throughout the federal grants process.

One of President Bush's first official acts as president was to create the White House Office of Faith-Based and Community Initiatives, which was given the task of leading a "determined attack on need" by strengthening and expanding the role of faith-based and community organizations in addressing the nation's social problems. Called "Compassion in Action," the goal was to have faith-based and community groups assist people in need, transform lives with their compassion.

The intent was *not* to have the federal government fund religion—instead, the FBCI's purpose was to enable some of America's most effective social service providers to compete fairly for federal funding, to make a difference in the lives of our most vulnerable citizens without diluting the providers' religious identity. Through food banks, health centers, job training programs, drug treatment centers, and other efforts, these charities were to be supported in meeting immediate and long-term needs.

Initially President Bush created Centers for Faith-Based and Community Initiatives in seven cabinet departments—the United States Departments of Agriculture, Education, Health and Human Services, Housing and Urban Development, Justice, Labor, and the Agency for International Development—to promote the initiatives. The Departments of Commerce and Veterans Affairs and the Small Business Administration were included at a later date. Each department was charged with assisting grassroots organizations in navigating the federal funding process.

In his state of the union address on January 20, 2004, President Bush, speaking in support of FBCI, said:

> "It is also important to strengthen our communities by unleashing the compassion of America's religious institutions. Religious charities of every creed are doing some of the most vital work in our country: mentoring children; feeding the hungry; taking the hand of the lonely. Our country is blessed with a long tradition of and honorable commitment to assisting individuals, families, and communities who have not fully shared in America's prosperity. But despite efforts by the federal and state governments to battle social distress, too many of our neighbors still suffer from poverty and despair. In every corner of America, people of all ages and walks of life are calling out for help" [CNN, 2004, "Transcript of State of the Union Address"].

Faith-based initiatives have been referred to as "charitable choice" by religious conservatives and other proponents. Such initiatives are not altogether new. For generations, religious institutions in America have been at the forefront of providing care to the indigent and immigrants, and have long played a central role in the nation's communities. There have been opponents to FBCI. The questions come from conservative Republicans and liberal Democrats, from the politically connected and the not-so-connected. Their breadth runs the gamut. The primary concern has been the concept of separation of church and state, as dictated by the Constitution, and how FBCI might impinge on that proviso.

AMERICORPS

Created in 1993, AmeriCorps—part of the CNS—is viewed as the domestic Peace Corps. It is a network of national service programs that, every year, engage more than 50,000, predominantly young, Americans in intensive service, to meet critical needs in education, public safety, health, and the environment. Ameri-Corps members serve through more than 2,100 nonprofits, public agencies, and faith-based organizations. They tutor and mentor youth, build affordable housing, teach computer skills, clean parks and streams, run after-school programs, and help communities respond to disasters.

AmeriCorps, Learn and Serve America and Senior Corps, overseen by CNS, engage more than two million Americans of all ages and backgrounds in service each year. AmeriCorps is open to U.S. citizens or lawful permanent residents over the age of 17. Members serve full or part time over a 10- to 12-month period. Volunteers get a stipend for living and an education award after completing service. Complete information can be found on the AmeriCorps website: www.ameri-corps.org.

LEARN AND SERVE AMERICA

Learn and Serve America provides grants to schools, colleges, and nonprofit groups to support efforts to engage students in community service linked to academic achievement and the development of civic skills. In addition to providing grants, Learn and Serve America serves as a resource on service and service-learning to teachers, faculty members, schools, and community groups.

NATIONAL SENIOR SERVICE CORPS/SENIOR CORPS

Of the three programs of the CNS, the National Senior Services Corps is the one most relevant to the retiree or senior volunteer. The National Senior Service Corps has a thirty-seven-year history of leadership in volunteer service.

The Corps is a national network of federally supported programs that promote using the experience, skills, and talents of older Americans by enabling them to find volunteer opportunities to help local organizations meet community challenges and needs, and to become actively involved in community service. Tess Scannell, Director of Senior Corps, has affirmed: "People age 55 and over have much to offer through their work and personal life experiences. We want them to put those valuable skills and experiences to good use in tackling some of the serious social problems in their communities" (Senior Journal, "Senior Corps Seeks 100,000 Volunteers," 2003).

The Corps is "one-stop shopping" for senior volunteers—the service opportunities are endless. Senior Corps programs operate in local communities throughout the U.S. Depending upon your interests and availability, they can help you determine which program might be best for you.

Currently, more than half a million Senior Corps volunteers are engaged in activities such as tutoring and mentoring children with special needs, working with local police and fire departments to keep neighborhoods safe, helping homebound individuals remain independent in their own homes, and building houses for the homeless. They serve in all 50 states, the District of Columbia, Puerto Rico and the Virgin Islands.

To learn more about all of the Senior Corps programs or to find opportunities to volunteer, call 800-424-8867, or visit their website: www.seniorcorps .org/. There are actually three national programs under its umbrella. Through these programs more than half a million Americans, age 55 and over, assist local nonprofits, public agencies, and faith-based organizations in carrying our their missions. The programs are:

• Foster Grandparent Program, which links senior volunteers to children who need their help.
• Senior Companion Program, which places its volunteers with adults needing extra assistance to live in the community, such as frail older persons.
• Retired and Senior Volunteer Program.

FOSTER GRANDPARENT PROGRAM (FGP)

The Foster Grandparent Program, which started in 1965, is a network of national service programs that provide older Americans the opportunity to put their life experiences to work for local communities. Foster grandparents serve as one-on-one mentors, tutors, and caregivers for at-risk children and youth with special needs through a variety of community organizations, including schools, hospitals, drug treatment facilities, correctional institutions, and Head Start and daycare centers. In fiscal year 2001, more than 30,000 foster grandparents tended to the needs of 275,000 young children and teenagers. In 1999, 28,700 foster grandparents supported abused, neglected children, children with AIDS, developmental or physical disabilities, substance abuse problems, and delinquents, runaways and the terminally ill.

The program is open to people age 60 and over, with limited incomes, who are willing to serve at least 20 hours each week. All applicants undergo a background check and a telephone interview, as well as pre-service and in-service training. For their service, foster grandparents receive a modest stipend (tax free), reimbursement for transportation, meals during service, an annual physical examination, and accident and liability insurance while on duty.

Local nonprofit organizations and public agencies receive grants to sponsor and operate local Foster Grandparent programs. Organizations that address the needs of abused and neglected children, troubled teens, young mothers, premature infants, and children with physical disabilities work with the local FGP to place and coordinate the services of volunteers. These local partners are called "volunteer stations." Volunteer stations include children's services agencies, child and youth-oriented charities, and faith-based initiatives. For additional information on the program, those interested, who consider themselves qualified, can go to the FGP website: www.seniorcorps.org/joining/fgp/index.html.

SENIOR COMPANION PROGRAM (SCP)

The Senior Companion Program, which began in 1974, allows low-income seniors, 60 and older, to work one-on-one with other homebound seniors to help them stay independent. They too serve five days a week, four hours a day, and receive a small non-taxable stipend to help defray the cost of their service.

Senior Companions work with the at-risk or frail elderly and other homebound persons who have difficulty completing everyday tasks. They assist with grocery shopping, bill paying, and transportation to medical appointments, and they alert doctors and family members to potential problems. Senior Companions help elderly or homebound seniors and other adults maintain independence while living in their own homes. Because of the program, thousands of citizens are able to remain in their own homes longer, with an enhanced sense of dignity and independence. In fiscal year 2001, 15,500 senior companions tended to the needs of more than 61,000 adult clients.

The Senior Companion Program is open to healthy individuals, age 60 and over, with limited incomes. All applicants undergo a background check and a telephone interview, as well as pre-service and in-service training on such topics as Alzheimer's disease, diabetes, and issues related to mental health.

Local nonprofit organizations and public agencies receive grants to sponsor and operate senior companion projects. Community organizations that address the health needs of older persons work with the local SCP projects to place and coordinate the services of the SCP volunteers. These local partners — "volunteer stations" — include hospitals, Area Agencies on Aging, and home health groups. The stations' professional staff identify individuals who need assistance and work with SCP projects to place them with senior companions.

For their service, senior companions receive a small hourly payment (tax free), reimbursement for transportation, annual physical examinations, meals, and accident and liability insurance during their service. To learn more about the Senior Companion Program, go to the website: www.seniorcorps.org/joining/scp/index.html.

RETIRED & SENIOR VOLUNTEER PROGRAM (RSVP)

The Retired & Senior Volunteer Program was organized in 1971. The program matches seniors 55 years of age and older with meaningful volunteer opportunities that help to meet local community needs. RSVP is the third program of Senior Corps that provides older Americans the opportunity to apply their life experience to meeting community needs. RSVP volunteers serve in a diverse range of nonprofit organizations, public agencies, and faith-based groups.

Among other activities, seniors mentor at-risk youth, organize neighborhood watch programs, test drinking water for contaminants, teach English to immigrants, and lend their business skills to community groups that provide critical social services. In fiscal year 2001, approximately 480,000 volunteers served an average of four hours a week at an estimated 65,000 local organizations.

These organizations, both public and private, receive grants to sponsor and operate RSVP projects in their community. Although these projects recruit seniors to serve from a few hours a month to almost full time, the average commitment is four hours a week. Most volunteers are paired with local community and faith-based initiatives that are already helping to meet community needs.

There is no time commitment requirement for this program, nor is there any compensation to volunteers for the time served; but sponsoring organizations may reimburse them for some costs incurred during service. RSVP provides appropriate volunteer insurance coverage, and volunteers receive pre-service orientation and in-service training from the agency or organization with which they are placed.

Volunteers conduct safety patrols for local police departments, participate in environmental projects, provide intensive educational services to children and adults, and respond to natural disasters. RSVP volunteers provide these and a variety of other services that range from leading local museum tours to teaching adult education computer classes. To learn more about RSVP visit their website: www.seniorcorps.org/joining/rsvp/index.html.

The RSVP program is the fastest growing of the National Senior Service Corps programs. Retirees recognize the countless needs of their communities and rally to help with their time and talents. They volunteer to mentor, tutor, serve as resources for living history in the classroom, build habitat houses, monitor local waterways and streams, monitor air quality in school buildings, and teach other seniors how to use computers. The possibilities for volunteer opportunities are endless and limited only by your imagination.

ASK A FRIEND CAMPAIGN

The Ask a Friend campaign is a nationwide effort developed by Senior Corps in response to a challenge from President George W. Bush in his "Call to Service" message to all Americans. In June 2003, Senior Corps announced a nationwide search for 100,000 volunteers, age 55 and over, and launched "Ask a Friend, Share Your Volunteer Spirit," a campaign to recruit volunteers for activities that help support and strengthen their communities.

The campaign is supported by a website where individuals can find helpful resources and/or access volunteer opportunities. Among the features included are e-cards, fliers, and posters so that current volunteers are able to share information about volunteering with their friends. There is also a Fast-Match link so that individuals can match their personal interests with volunteer opportunities, by zip code, and there are inspiring stories about current volunteers and the contributions they're making in their communities.

Persons interested in the Ask a Friend campaign can log on to the website at: www.volunteerfriends.org. There is also a section that provides information to Spanish-speaking citizens. Individuals without web access can call a toll-free number (800-424-8867) to get information about the campaign or sign up to volunteer.

Ask a Friend was designed to address the primary reason people volunteer, which is simply because they are asked. The campaign uses the ask-a-friend method, because the likelihood of someone getting involved increases when a personal friend makes the request or suggestion. The goal of the campaign is two-fold: to encourage current Senior Corps volunteers to get a friend involved, and to encourage older non-volunteers to serve in projects that strengthen their communities.

As part of the campaign, on November 12, 2003, the Ask a Friend campaign announced a Thanksgiving volunteer drive that urged seniors to pledge their time and experience in an effort to encourage older adults to help strengthen their communities. The goal was to get 100,000 new volunteers to pledge service. (Source: Volunteer Friends, "Volunteer: Ask a Friend," 2003.) During that Thanksgiving week (November 24–30, 2003), adults age 55 and over were being urged to sign up to make a difference in their communities through the "Share Your Volunteer Spirit Pledge Drive." The campaign was hosted by Senior Corps, which was encouraged people to give thanks by finding local volunteer opportunities in their neighborhoods. "The holiday season is a time to reflect on the abundance in our lives.... We're providing an easy way to say 'thanks' for that abundance by volunteering for a cause or organization that benefits your community" (Corporation for National and Community Service, "Thanksgiving Volunteer Drive Urges Seniors to Pledge Their Time and Experience," 2003).

SERVICE CORPS OF RETIRED EXECUTIVES (SCORE)

The Service Corps of Retired Executives is a volunteer association sponsored by, and is a resource partner of, the U.S. Small Business Administration (SBA).

SCORE is made up of retired executives and small business owners. whose volunteers provide free and confidential counseling to small business owners as a public service. Teams of volunteer counselors assist clients in the areas of marketing, finance, sales, operations, planning, management, and offer seminars and workshops on major considerations in running a business. Volunteers work in or near their home communities to provide management counseling and training to first-time entrepreneurs and current small business owners. Working with nearly 400 local chapters, SCORE reaches clients across the country—from Maine to Hawaii. Volunteers meet with clients at a SCORE chapter office. To locate the office nearest you, call 800-634-0245 or visit the SCORE website: www.score.org.

THE PEACE CORPS

The Peace Corps traces its roots and mission to 1961, when then–Senator John F. Kennedy challenged students at the University of Michigan to serve their country in the cause of peace by living and working in developing countries. From that inspiration grew an agency of the federal government devoted to world peace and friendship.

Since that time, well over 200,000 Peace Corps volunteers have been invited by more than 136 host countries to work in the following areas: education, youth outreach, community development; health and HIV/AIDS; agriculture and environment; business development; and information technology. Within these areas, the specific duties and responsibilities of each Volunteer can vary widely. In 2003, approximately 7,000 Peace Corps volunteers were serving in more than 70 developing nations around the world.

The Peace Corps actively promotes a program for older volunteers. It is described in detail on the Corps web page: www.peacecorps.gov/diversity/older/index.cfm. Prospective applicants can read an overview of the issues facing older volunteers, find answers for a number of questions that may be of concern, and learn about the benefits and rewards of service for older volunteers. You can also call 800-424-8580 for answers to any specific questions you may have. Addressing older volunteers specifically, the Peace Corps affirms:

> Older Americans contribute tremendously to Peace Corps programs all over the globe. No single group has more to offer in terms of experience, maturity, and demonstrated ability. Many older Volunteers find their age to be an asset while serving overseas. You will have the opportunity to share a lifetime of work and wisdom with people of developing nations who respect and appreciate age. And because there's no upper age limit to serve, it's never too late. Volunteers who are well into their eighties have served and continue to serve.
>
> As an older Volunteer, you know you'll bring a wealth of knowledge and

experience to your Peace Corps service. What will you get in return? Well, first and foremost, there's the satisfaction of being able to make a difference in the lives of others who need your help [Peace Corps, "Older Volunteers"].

VOLUNTEERS IN SERVICE TO AMERICA (VISTA)

For more than 35 years, VISTA has been helping communities and individuals to move out of poverty. Today, more than 6,000 VISTA members serve in hundreds of nonprofit organizations and public agencies throughout the country—working to fight illiteracy, improve health services, create businesses, increase housing opportunities, or bridge the digital divide. They leave behind lasting solutions to some of our country's toughest problems.

"Strengthen low-income communities with AmeriCorps: VISTA! You know you can make a difference. You'd like to leave your mark on the world. Maybe you're looking to help people who haven't had the same opportunities as you by giving them the tools to help themselves. Maybe you've climbed that ladder yourself and want to help the next person up. Helping others help themselves is at the heart of AmeriCorps: VISTA" (VISTA).

As a VISTA member, you'll be assigned for one year, full-time, to a nonprofit organization—a shelter for abused or battered women, a health clinic for low-income families, or a disadvantaged school. Or you may be assigned to an organization that is helping people move from welfare to work, or introducing technology to an underserved neighborhood.

You'll recruit and train volunteers, raise funds and write grants, gather corporate sponsorship and donations, plan community meetings, and handle public relations—whatever it takes to make your project come together.

"Why do people join AmeriCorps: VISTA? First, there's the incredible work experience, tremendous responsibility, and great challenges. You'll develop new skills or further challenge abilities you've already developed. You'll also enjoy the satisfaction of making a real difference, helping a community help itself" (VISTA).

Applicants must be at least 18 years old; *there is no upper age limit*. Many VISTA members bring significant work and life experiences to their assignment. Most programs seek members with college degrees or at least three years of work experience. Self-initiative, flexibility, and organizational skills are a must. Fluency in one or more foreign languages (particularly Spanish) can also be helpful in certain assignments. You could find a project close to home, or you may choose to move to a new locale. You receive training, a living allowance, and health insurance; and your relocation expenses are reimbursed.

To obtain information on applying, or to read about members' experiences or examples of projects in any state, go to the VISTA website: www.americorps.org/vista.

ADMINISTRATION ON AGING (AoA)

The Administration on Aging programs enlist more than 500,000 volunteers nationwide, many of them retirees or senior citizens, to help older people in need. (Studies have found that senior volunteers are especially effective at aiding the elderly.) Volunteer activities include delivering meals to the homebound; escorting seniors to needed services; repairing homes of low-income people and seniors; assisting at senior centers; and counseling older people on health, nutrition, and finances.

SENIOR MEDICARE PATROL

The AoA Senior Medicare Patrol project teaches volunteer retired professionals, such as doctors, nurses, accountants, investigators, law enforcement personnel, attorneys and teachers, to help Medicare and Medicaid beneficiaries to be better health care consumers, and to help identify and prevent billing errors and potential fraud. Since 1997, these projects have trained more than 48,000 volunteers and conducted more than 60,000 community education events that have reached nearly 10 million people. To learn more about Senior Medicare Patrol, volunteers go to their website: www.aoa.gov/smp/.

AMERICA READS

The America Reads Challenge is a grassroots national campaign that calls upon every American to help all our children learn to read, including English language learners and students with disabilities. America Reads promotes collaborations between seniors, parents, educators, librarians, business people, college students, and community and religious groups. More than two million children have been taught, tutored, or mentored through national service programs such as America Reads, Foster Grandparents, AmeriCorps, and VISTA. The America Reads website includes a directory of hyperlinks by state. Those interested in volunteering can easily locate opportunities in their area.

The America Reads website announces:

> Children across America salute you for participating in the America Reads Challenge to every American to help all our children learn to read. From college students and citizens of all ages tutoring children, to seniors starting lending libraries, to businesses donating time, money and books and from policy makers and elected officials focusing on literacy, to parents reading to their children every night, to children themselves promising to read thirty minutes per day in the summer—everyone has an important role in meeting the Challenge. Keep up the good work! [America Reads].

BUREAU OF PRISONS (BOP)

Because of the national media, the public has experienced an increased interest in, and awareness of, the justice system at all levels. The Volunteer Management Branch (VMB), a branch of the Industries, Education and Vocational Training Division of the Federal Bureau of Prisons, fosters volunteerism throughout the BOP. This provides a unique opportunity to both the public and private sectors to expand the relationship between the community and the BOP.

Using volunteers, VMB is charged with developing an inmate reintegration program that will assist offenders in making the transition from the institution to the community and family. By role-modeling community values and helping inmates with their own self-development, volunteers have the opportunity to directly affect their lives. The BOP uses volunteers in all disciplines within the institution and community corrections facilities. By expanding partnerships with the local community, citizens grow to understand the unique role of correctional facilities.

VMB maintains and develops partnerships with schools and professionally based organizations to encourage staff volunteerism. In addition, VMB coordinates the development of training materials, newsletters, and videos and disseminates information about agency and civilian incentive programs to assist and encourage staff who work with and as volunteers.

Prospective volunteers must submit a BOP questionnaire, federal application forms (OF-612 and OF-330), a letter of reference from a member of the community (e.g., civic, employment or religious/organization leader) and an authorization for a National Crime Information Center (NCIC) check. Prospective volunteers are asked to indicate the location at which they would prefer to serve. They are also asked to indicate the category of service in which they would be most interested in volunteering. These include:

• Administrative
• Emotional: life skills training, counseling, victims assistance programs, marriage encounters
• Intellectual: education, literacy, languages, GED, higher education
• Occupational: career counseling
• Physical: recreation, disease prevention, drug abuse prevention, and health care
• Social: inmate organizations, hobbies and crafts, service projects
• Spiritual: religious services and ministry
• Other: (Applicant can specify.)

Volunteers are sought with experience or educational background in:

- Accounting/Finance
- Administration
- Computer Services
- Education
- Health Services
- Journalism/Writing
- Legal/Paralegal
- Office Support
- Security/Correctional Work
- Sports/Recreation
- Volunteer Work

For more information about volunteer opportunities in the BOP, call 202-307-3998. You can also visit the BOP website: www.bop.gov.

ENVIRONMENTAL PROTECTION AGENCY (EPA)

On its web page, "Help Us to Shape the Future: A National Agenda for the Environment and the Aging," the EPA provides a wealth of information about the Agency's efforts to protect the environmental health of older persons and how that population can become involved in those efforts. The Agency states:

> Due to the normal aging process, even older persons in good health may experience increased health risks from exposures to environmental pollutants. As we age, our bodies are more susceptible to hazards from the environment which may worsen chronic or life threatening conditions. Older persons also have accumulated a lifetime of environmental and occupational contaminants which are capable of remaining in their bodies.
>
> A major goal of the Aging Initiative is the development of a National Agenda for the Environment and the Aging. The National Agenda will prioritize environmental health hazards that affect older persons, examine the environmental impact of an aging population in a smart growth context, and encourage civic involvement among older persons in their communities to reduce hazards. The National Agenda for the Environment and the Aging, being developed through a public participatory process, will help guide the Agency's work to protect the health of older persons now and in the future. Information on this [EPA] website can help you learn more about our ongoing work and how you can contribute to—and benefit from—the National Agenda for the Environment and the Aging. We encourage you to join our efforts to shape an environmentally healthy future for our aging population [Environmental Protection Agency, Aging Initiative].

Information on the EPA Aging Initiative can be found at: www.epa.gov/aging/.

To encourage civic involvement among older persons, the EPA has also established the Volunteer Monitoring Program which "encourages all citizens to learn about their water resources and supports volunteer monitoring because of its many benefits. Volunteer monitors build awareness of pollution problems, become trained in pollution prevention, help clean up problem sites, provide data for waters that may otherwise be unassessed, and increase the amount of water quality information available to decision makers at all levels of government" (Environmental Protection Agency, "Volunteer Monitoring Program"). Many of EPA's ten regional offices are actively involved in volunteer monitoring. The EPA publishes a *National Directory of Volunteer Monitoring Programs* that lists volunteer organizations around the country engaged in monitoring rivers, lakes, estuaries, beaches, wetlands, and ground water, as well as surrounding lands. This electronic database contains updated information on volunteer monitoring programs nationwide. It is available online at: yosemite.epa.gov/water/volmon.nsf/Home?readform. EPA also publishes "Starting Out in Volunteer Water Monitoring," a brief fact sheet on how to become involved in volunteer monitoring. It is also available online at: www.epa.gov/owow/monitoring/volunteer/startmon.html. For general information on the EPA Volunteer Monitoring Program, go to the website: www.epa.gov/owow/monitoring/volunteer/epasvmp.html.

U.S. FISH AND WILDLIFE SERVICE (FWS)

Describing itself as a "Conservation Legacy," the FWS is the only agency of the U.S. government whose primary responsibility is fish, wildlife, and plant conservation. The FWS has served the nation for more than 125 years. Their stated mission is working with others to conserve, protect, and enhance fish, wildlife, plants and their habitats for the continuing benefit of the American people so that we may conserve and enjoy the outdoors and our living treasures. The service's major responsibilities are for migratory birds, endangered species, certain marine mammals, and fresh water and anadromous fish. (Source: U.S. Fish and Wildlife Service, "Conserving the Nature of America," 1999.)

Today, the service employs approximately 7,500 people at facilities across the country, including a headquarters office in Washington, D. C., seven regional offices, and nearly 700 field units. Among these are national wildlife refuges, national fish hatcheries, management assistance offices, and law enforcement and ecological services field stations.

In addition, the service conserves fish and wildlife worldwide under some 40 treaties, statutes, and agreements. The service cooperates with other nations on wildlife research and management programs, and responds to requests from foreign countries for technical assistance. The service's goal is to help cooperating countries develop their conservation capabilities in order to meet their own environmental goals and needs on a sustainable basis. Among the service's international programs are graduate education programs for fish and wildlife managers in Latin America; environmental education in the Near East, Asia, Africa, and Latin America; and special conservation efforts for tigers, rhinoceroses, and African elephants.

The volunteer program within the FWS was formally initiated in 1982, and began receiving congressionally appropriated funding in 1991. The program is as diverse as the individuals who comprise it. Whether volunteers are working at national wildlife refuges, fish hatcheries, wetland management districts, regional offices, or ecological service offices, each one helps the National Wildlife Refuge System and other FWS programs reach their full potential. The volunteer program provides people with hands-on opportunities to engage in wildlife conservation and be involved with lands that belong to them.

FWS volunteers are "individuals who want to give back to their communities, parents who want to be good stewards of the land and set examples for their children, retired people willing to share their wealth of knowledge, concerned citizens of all ages who want to learn more about conservation, and passionate people who enjoy the outdoors and want to spread the word about America's greatest natural treasures" (U. S. Fish and Wildlife Service, "Volunteers").

In promoting the volunteer opportunities, the FWS announces:

> Volunteers are welcome in the U.S. Fish and Wildlife Service! With more than 36,000 volunteers contributing in excess of 1.4 million hours of their time, skills and talents, the U.S. Fish and Wildlife Service's volunteer program is robust and continuing to grow. The tireless efforts of our volunteers complete more than 20 percent of the work conducted on national wildlife refuges alone. Volunteers play a vital role in helping the FWS fulfill its mission of conserving, protecting and enhancing America's fish, wildlife and plants and the habitats on which they depend. We hope you will consider spending time with us to help us help wildlife" [U. S. Fish and Wildlife Service, "Volunteers"].

Volunteers perform a wide variety of tasks. Some volunteers work full time; others, a few hours a week or month or during a particular season or special event. Some typical volunteer opportunities may involve:

• Conducting fish and wildlife population surveys;
• Leading tours and providing information and interpretation to the visiting public;
• Assisting with laboratory research;

• Taking part in special projects, such as bird banding;
• Assisting with habitat improvement projects, such as re-establishing native plants to a river bank;
    • Performing clerical and administrative duties;
    • Working with computers and other technical equipment; and
    • Photographing a variety of natural and cultural resources.

Generally, no special skills are required to be a volunteer. Any on-the-job training will be provided, if needed. Individual talents and skills are matched with volunteer interests and work opportunities.

Thousands of Americans volunteer with the U.S. Fish and Wildlife Service each year. Working side-by-side with service employees, volunteers serve as tour guides and educators and help with management activities such as bird banding, habitat restoration, wildlife population surveys, building trails, and staffing visitor centers. Many citizens also join "Friends" groups that support national wildlife refuges in their community.

To learn more about volunteer opportunities with the FWS, visit their website or contact a service office near you. The FWS recommends prospective volunteers go to the website, Volunteer.gov/gov (discussed in a previous note), an inter-agency website of national volunteer opportunities. At this site, you can also apply to participate in opportunities of interest by using the application link at the bottom of each volunteer position description. Should you be unable to find a volunteer opportunity of interest, or at a location where you would like to volunteer, contact the FWS directly by e-mail at: volunteers@fws.gov, to learn what other opportunities may be available.

Natural Resources Conservation Service (NRCS)

An arm of the U.S. Department of Agriculture, the NRCS is the primary federal agency that works with private landowners to help them conserve, maintain, and improve our natural resources and environment. The service's "Earth Team Volunteers" have been at work since 1981, when Congress passed legislation allowing NRCS to use volunteers in all programs. In 2002, more than 38,000 Earth Team Volunteers donated more than one million hours of their time to conservation practices. The total value of volunteer time in 2002 was estimated to be more than $17 million (Source: Natural Resources Conservation Service, "NRCS Earth Team Volunteers").

"We at the NRCS need people who are willing to commit their time and talent to conserving and protecting soil, water, and wildlife for their community and everyone in it. The Earth Team may be the perfect volunteering opportunity for you. Jump aboard by filling out this Volunteer Interest & Placement

Form! [online]. Upon submission, it will be e-mailed to the Earth Team's National Headquarters and a volunteer coordinator will contact you! Or look below [website link] for information about how to contact a state or regional Earth Team Volunteer Coordinator!" (Natural Resources Conservation Service). (Be advised that the online application form is a formidable 683 KB and is in .pdf format.)

U.S. ARMY CORPS OF ENGINEERS (USACE)

You can volunteer in the service of your country while enjoying the great outdoors in one of America's recreational parks or public service projects. Many thousands of retirees and seniors have discovered how to enjoy nature, contribute to improving the natural resources of the nation, and sometimes reduce their vacation costs. How? By volunteering to participate in the U.S. Army Corps of Engineers management of the hundreds of lakes, public lands, and outdoor projects nationwide.

The Corps of Engineers is the steward of almost 12 million acres of land and more than 300 lakes across the country. In these and many other projects, volunteers play an important role in protecting the natural resources and maintaining recreation facilities managed by the Corps. Volunteers serve as campground and park hosts, they staff visitor centers, conduct educational programs, restore fish and wildlife habitat, maintain park trails and facilities, and more. Lakes, parks, and visitor centers across the country need such volunteers. Nationwide during 1999, 70,000 volunteers contributed more than 1.2 million hours of work with an estimated value of $13.5 million. The Corps Volunteer Clearing House has confirmed that most of the people who volunteer their time to the USACE are retirees or senior citizens.

Volunteers are, by definition, not paid, but receive other valuable benefits. They gain skills, enjoy the pleasure of work outdoors in beautiful settings, meet new people, visit new areas of the country, and achieve a proud sense of helping the environment and their fellow citizens of all ages. Some Corps locations provide volunteers a free campsite with water, electricity, and sewer hookups. The dates available, tasks they will perform, responsibilities they will take on, and work hours are mutually agreed on by the supervising USACE ranger and the volunteer.

The U.S. Army Corps of Engineers Volunteer Clearinghouse is a nationwide, toll-free hotline number for individuals who are interested in volunteering their time with the Corps. To receive a "Point of Contact" list, telephone the hotline at 800-865-8337. A potential volunteer can express interest in any USACE project nationwide. While each project is listed by state, not every state has opportunities. The Clearinghouse will send the individual a packet of information containing a contact for the area requested, as well as written information about volunteer opportunities and maps. Callers should be ready to provide information about their interests, talents, and the location(s) at which they may want to volunteer. The hotline serves as a matchmaker, pairing up skilled, enthusiastic volunteers with USACE employees who can use their services, providing both with a memorable experience.

Interested persons can also sign up online. Current volunteer opportunity listings can be found on the Corps' volunteer website: www.orn.usace.army.mil/volunteer. You can also query by regular mail:

USACE Volunteers
P.O. Box 1070
Nashville, TN 37202-1070
Website: www.usace.army.mil

BUREAU OF LAND MANAGEMENT (BLM)

The U.S. Bureau of Land Management website states:

> "Did you know—this country's federally owned public lands are owned by every American, giving each of us a shared interest in their care and in their future? Nearly half of these lands—261 million acres—are managed by the U.S. Department of the Interior's Bureau of Land Management [BLM], making the BLM manager of the nation's largest land trust. That's a big responsibility! Fortunately, help is close at hand. Each year, over 20,000 Americans volunteer their time and talent. But there's always room for more. Young adults, single people, seniors, and families are invited to become BLM volunteers.
>
> You can make a difference! Working alone or with a group, BLM volunteers enjoy work that matches their interests and schedules. Some volunteers serve part-time and others enjoy a seasonal or full-time position. The important thing to remember is that even a few hours a month can make a big difference.
>
> The public lands administered by the BLM range from saguaro cactus desert to Douglas fir tundra. Overall, these lands, located primarily in the Western part of the United States, comprise nearly one-eighth of our nation's land area. The BLM's mission is to help sustain the health, diversity, and productivity of these public lands so they can be used and enjoyed by both present and future generations. BLM has an opportunity for you!"
> [U.S. Bureau of Land Management].

You can volunteer with BLM and:

• Help protect and restore streams, wildlife habitat, plant communities, and ecosystems.

• Serve as a river ranger, campground host, hiking leader, or interpretive guide.

• Share your talents as an educator or youth group leader by conducting field trips, visitor center programs and other educational activities inside and outside the classroom.

• Plant trees and shrubs in fire-damaged areas.

• Conduct fire prevention seminars.

• Update mineral survey maps and databases; assist with geological surveys and fossil excavations.

• Map and record ancient petroglyphs; discover, restore and protect historic areas; research the history and prehistory of the American West.

• Assist with soil and water conservation projects; plant vegetation; erect fencing to reduce erosion and pollution.

• Provide office clerical support; answer inquiries; supervise volunteers.

• Conduct orientation sessions for visitors.

• Write, edit or take photographs for publications; produce graphic artwork and videotapes.

• Monitor wilderness study areas and prepare management plans; maintain trails or teach low-impact camping.

• Assist with care and citizen adoption of wild horses; show trained animals at county fairs and horse shows.

• Construct and maintain facilities, signs, roads, and trailheads; work as a member of a cadastral survey crew.

• Operate the Land Information System—a computerized geographic-based system for processing natural and historic resources data.

• Computerize information for resource management plans; identify areas of critical environmental concern.

Many volunteer groups partner with the BLM to adopt a favorite stream or treasured wildlife habitat area. If your organization or group is interested in becoming a partner, you should contact a representative in your area. BLM provides general information regarding volunteer opportunities on BLM lands, including a list of state volunteer contacts. Volunteer applicants are selected without regard to gender, race, or age, and persons with disabilities are encouraged to apply. For more information on volunteer opportunities, go to the BLM website: www.blm.gov.

NATIONAL OCEANIC AND ATMOSPHERIC ADMINISTRATION (NOAA)

The National Oceanic and Atmospheric Administration conducts research and gathers global data about our oceans, atmosphere, space, and sun, and applies this knowledge to science and service that touch the lives of all Americans. NOAA's National Weather Service is the primary source of weather data, forecasts, and warnings for the United States. The NWS is the sole United States official voice for issuing warnings during life-threatening weather situations and operates the NOAA Weather Radio network, which broadcasts weather and other hazard warnings, watches, forecasts and post-event information 24 hours a day.

National Weather Service Cooperative Weather Observer Program is NOAA's nationwide network of private and academic volunteers. The network—considered the "backbone of the Nation's climate records" includes more than 11,000 weather observers across the United States who donate more than one million volunteer hours each year to collect the weather data that become our national climate records. Observers also add to the stream of information that the National Weather Service uses to forecast weather, water and climate conditions; issue severe weather and flood warnings; and record climates of the United States. (NOAA notes proudly that its efforts also include tracking the itinerary of Santa Claus each Christmas Eve!)

Thomas Jefferson envisioned such a nationwide network of weather observers as early as 1797, when he outlined a plan for providing weather instruments to a volunteer citizen in every county of Virginia, so that a regular statewide record might be maintained. A plan of this kind was not established until almost 100 years later when, in 1891, the Weather Bureau was charged with the task of "taking such meteorological observations as may be necessary to establish and record the climatic conditions of the United States." In compliance with these directions, the Weather Bureau relied heavily, as it does to this day, on voluntary "Cooperative Observers." Such observers come from all walks of life; some are farmers, ranchers, lawyers, storekeepers, ministers, teachers, construction workers, and retirees. You can learn more by visiting the NOAA website: www.noaa.gov.

VOLUNTEERING FOR THE COAST

Volunteering for the Coast is also a program of NOAA. It is for anyone interested in environmental stewardship through personal actions. "By volunteering for the coast, we can all help improve the condition of our threatened oceans, lakes, rivers, streams, and marshes." The information provided on their website is for individuals looking to volunteer, coordinate volunteer efforts, or seek ways to build successful volunteer programs. For further information check the link on the NOAA website: www.noaa.gov.

Volunteer Opportunities at National and State Parks and Forests

THE NATIONAL PARK SERVICE (NPS)

For retirees or seniors who like to travel—especially by RV—volunteering in our national or state parks and forests presents an ideal opportunity. You can take virtually free vacations! The National Park Service is entrusted with preserving more than 370 national parks in the United States. Each of the units of the National Park System, including the national trails and rivers, use volunteers to help accomplish the NPS's goals. Of the nearly 60 million Americans who participate in volunteer activities each year, the Park Service confirms: "Our volunteers are, without a doubt, Very Important People! In Fiscal Year 2002, 125,000 volunteers donated 4.5 million hours to national parks. Our volunteers come from all over to help preserve and protect America's natural and cultural heritage for the enjoyment of this and future generations. Young and old alike give of their time and expertise to assist in achieving the National Park Service mission" (U.S. Park Service, Volunteers-In-Parks Program).

Participants volunteer in almost every park in the National Park System— in big cities, in small towns, and in remote wilderness areas. Volunteers may work a few hours a week or month, seasonally, or fulltime. They work weekdays, weekends, during the day, or at night. As the expanding use of national and state park facilities in many cases exceeds the capability and budget of allocated personnel, park volunteers often help to provide services that might not otherwise be offered.

Volunteering at a national or state park offers the opportunity to meet new people, many of whom share a common interest in the outdoors, exploring nature, and a concern for protecting the environment. In the process, it affords individuals the opportunity to gain a sense of citizen ownership of a park and, in some cases, to receive valuable training and experience for their service.

Older persons with an interest in history and the great outdoors can volunteer their time with the National Park Service's Volunteers in Parks or VIP program. It is the centerpiece of the NPS's effort to enlist volunteer help. The VIP program was authorized by Public Law 91-357, enacted in 1970. The primary purpose of the program is to provide a medium through which the service can accept and utilize voluntary help from the public. The major objective of the program is to utilize this voluntary help in such a way that is mutually beneficial to the NPS and the volunteer.

Unlike regular employment opportunities, volunteer programs within the NPS are managed at the local level, so you will need to mail an application to your local national park office. As a volunteer, you will, of course, not be paid by the federal government, but some parks do reimburse volunteers for certain out-of-pocket expenses, such as local travel costs, meals, and uniforms (where required). A number of national (and state) parks provide volunteers with trailer pads with hookups, at no charge.

Volunteers are recruited and accepted from the public without regard to race, creed, religion, age, sex, color, national origin, or OPM classification laws, rules and regulations. But, they *must* be physically able to perform the work they volunteer to do. The superintendent of a park may request that the prospective volunteer complete a standard Form 256 (Self-identification of Medical Disability) or obtain a medical examination at government expense if there is a question regarding the volunteer's ability to perform any assigned duties.

Additional information is available at the National Park Service website: www.nps.gov. The VIP web pages on the website include general information on volunteering, a list of current volunteer opportunities, and a volunteer application form. Additional information on the VIP program is also available from local parks or from the National Park Service by calling 202-208-4747.

VOLUNTEERING IN THE NATIONAL FORESTS

The National Forest Service maintains Senior, Youth, and Volunteer Programs (SYVP): "Providing work, training, and education to the unemployed, underemployed, elderly, youth, and others with special needs in pursuit of our mission." The SYVP web page can be found at: www.fs.fed.us/people/programs/index.htm.

> In its volunteer recruiting literature, the National Forest Service states: "Volunteers are the heartbeat of the Forest Service. The types of work a volunteer can perform are many and varied; the only tasks a volunteer cannot carry out are those associated with law enforcement. Your talents and skills are matched with your work preference to obtain a role that satisfies you and best fulfills the mission of the Forest Service.
>
> You may work on a part-time or full-time basis. You can participate in a one-time project or serve over several months, seasons, or year-round. The commitment you make is up to you. Training may be provided to you if your job requires it. If you are retired or have summers free, you may wish to live on a national forest while you work as a volunteer.... A variety of jobs are available if you prefer the office environment. There are also numerous opportunities to perform vigorous but satisfying physical labor outdoors" [The National Forest Service, "Volunteering in the National Forests"].

Some typical volunteer activities in the National Forests include:

• Maintaining and hosting campgrounds;
• Answering phones, greeting visitors, and answering mail at visitor centers and ranger stations;
• Working with computers in Service administrative offices;
• Taking photographs;
• Planting trees and seeding damaged areas;
• Presenting environmental education programs;
• Building and repairing fences, nesting boxes, picnic tables, and other structures;

• Building barrier-free campsites, docks, and trails; and
• Restoring damaged stream banks and burnt-over areas.

Seniors interested in volunteering can apply by writing to, or calling, the volunteer coordinator of your nearest Forest Service office for information, and to request a volunteer application. A directory is available online at the FS web page: www.fs.fed.us/people/programs/index.htm, or you will likely find it in your phone book under "U.S. government, Department of Agriculture, Forest Service."

VOLUNTEER OPPORTUNITIES AT STATE PARKS AND FORESTS

In addition to volunteer opportunities in national parks and forests, there also are many available in parks, in individual states and U.S. territories. If you're interested in volunteering to work in an outdoor setting, there are a variety of options available in parks at state, county, or local levels—all across America, including Alaska, Hawaii, and the U.S. Virgin Islands. Volunteer opportunities also exist in Canadian—national and provincial—and other international parks. (See the note on the Canadian government at the end of this section).

Volunteer projects might include staffing information booths, conducting interpretive programs, monitoring wildlife, or maintaining computer databases. Group projects may involve park and trail cleanup or building restoration. If your time is limited, you might consider working on one-time projects. If time is not an issue, then consider volunteering for a seasonal or a year-round position. Some of the seasonal positions may include an application deadline. And remember, volunteers are usually provided with a free camp site, usually including a utilities hookup for an RV.

For an extensive list of links to information on seasonal and full-time job and volunteer opportunities at both national and state parks, the starting places are the websites: usparks.about.com/library/weekly/aa031699.htm, or, as previously noted, the U.S. Bureau of Land Management also provides general information on volunteer contacts for all state parks in the nation.

State Government

Each of the 50 states promotes volunteer opportunities for volunteers. Senior volunteers are a particular focus in the Commonwealth of Pennsylvania. The Pennsylvania Department of Aging actively promotes volunteering through the states' Area Agencies on Aging. "The Volunteer Services program provides a varied array of opportunities for seniors to serve other seniors and their community at large. It also provides meaningful opportunities for people of all ages to participate in providing services to older persons. The Volunteer Services program provides for the placement of persons in a variety of volunteer roles. It can provide short and long term projects that involve persons of all ages who can assist the Area Agency on Aging in the delivery of services to older persons. Where possible these volunteer efforts are coordinated with other volunteer initiatives. Some examples of volunteer efforts are friendly visiting and telephone reassurance" (Pennsylvania Department of Aging).

In 1997, the Pennsylvania Departments of Aging and Environmental Protection partnered with the Environmental Alliance for Senior Involvement (EASI) and established the Pennsylvania Senior Environmental Corps (PASEC). This program provides an opportunity for older Pennsylvanians to participate in volunteer projects that help the environment, such as monitoring water quality, stream restoration, debris removal from streams and banks, and education programs about protecting our natural resources. "EASI and the PASEC are making a difference through the volunteer efforts of thousands of seniors working with all generations to improve the environment, one community at a time" (Pennsylvania Senior Environmental Corps). The state also maintains the Conservation Volunteer Program, which utilizes volunteers in its 116 state parks and 2.1 million acres of forest land.

STATE GOVERNMENT WEBSITES

If you wish to explore volunteer opportunities in your particular state, there are several online resources. Searching for the keywords "volunteer," or "volunteering," should lead to the relevant web pages. These state website resources include:

• Global Computing
This site provides a complete list of the official websites for the 50 states. A simple click on the map will take you to your state's website. Go to www.globalcomputing.com/states.html.
• State and Local Government on the Net Directory
The directory provides convenient one-stop access to the websites of thousands of state agencies and city and county governments. Only those pages that are controlled and managed by state and local government agencies are included. The directory can be found at: www.statelocalgov.net/index.cfm.
• Volunteer Today
Another directory of state government websites can be found at: www.volunteertoday.com/GOVT/stategovt.html.

Local Government

Local governments, county and municipal, also rely on and utilize volunteers of all ages who provide invaluable services to libraries, schools, parks and recreational programs, senior centers, police, ambulance and fire-fighting units. (Statistically, for example, 80 percent of the manpower needs of local fire departments in the U.S. are provided by volunteers—including retirees and seniors.) Volunteers serve as foster parents, tax preparation assistants (a nationwide AARP program), as drivers for local "Meals on Wheels" programs, and in community hospitals, nursing homes, and other care-giving settings.

In cities and towns all over America, more and more volunteers are serving their communities. In their departments of parks, recreation, or public works, for example, they might:

- Document sidewalks in need of repair.
- Sand and paint hydrants.
- Wash emergency vehicles.
- Remove graffiti from public parks and buildings.
- Canvass neighborhoods and deliver information on upcoming events that affect residents.
- Inspect streams for pollutions sources.
- Set up and remove holiday decorations.
- Answer phones and document citizens' requests for services.

Canadian Government

The Canadian Ministry of Citizenship and Immigration maintains a comprehensive website for volunteers and volunteer agencies. This example of a government partnership with the nonprofit sector is a model that could be replicated in federal programs throughout the world. Information is available in English and French. For the English version go to: www.gov.on.ca/mczcr/english/ citdiv/voluntar.

8. National Programs

"You give but little when you give of your possessions. It is when you give of yourself that you truly give."

—KAHLIL GIBRAN

The following national resources may help you engage with other retirees and/or seniors in a variety of volunteering activities across the country, from working with youth to improving our environment. In addition to the national organizations listed in this section, there are many local nonprofit organizations—entities that have been created by a group of individuals who recognized a need in their community and organized their fellow citizens to help meet that need. These tend to be somewhat less structured and more hands-on; they may offer greater flexibility and more options to become involved. Examples of such local organizations include homeless shelters, food banks, and faith-based programs. To connect with a local organization in your area, you may wish to consult friends or other social contacts for suggestions. A volunteer center or agency, such as United Way, in your community can often facilitate a contact with prospective volunteers and those agencies that may need their help.

Many national organizations have affiliates in communities. Often identified as "chapters," they tend to take a more structured approach to volunteering—often in line with their national or international parent organization's policies and procedures. You can locate an affiliate in your area by checking the telephone book under the organization's name, search for and review the organization's website, or call the toll-free number's directory assistance (800-555-1212). Many national organizations have a toll-free number. All of this information is available on the Internet. A good starting place is: www.refdesk.com, which has hyperlinks to every conceivable WWW search engine and directory.

National Organizations

AARP

AARP is the nation's oldest and largest organization of older Americans, with a membership of more than 35 million. AARP has information centers, staffed by volunteers, to provide a place for other volunteers to locate and participate in projects, and a volunteer talent bank for members to share their knowledge and abilities with others. Two highly successful AARP volunteer programs are "Tax-Aide" and "Driver Safety Program." Their web pages, www.aarp.org/serve/ and www.aarp.org/volunteer/, and http://aarp.volunteermatch.org/aarp/index.html have a great deal of information on these and other AARP programs, and on finding local chapters.

At their volunteering section, you can learn about opportunities with AARP and those in your area; you can register your interests online, and discuss volunteering with like-minded individuals in their online community. Interested volunteers can find many organizations that need them. To find volunteer opportunities and all AARP activities in your state, visit: www.aarp.org/states/.

AARP Connections is the newsletter for and about AARP volunteers. Published nationally on a monthly basis, and on various schedules for state editions, *Connections* is mailed to AARP volunteers. Archives of the national edition only are online at: www.aarp.org/connections/archives.html. For additional information, you may contact AARP at:

The AARP Volunteer Center
601 E Street, NW
Washington, DC 20049
Telephone: 202-434-3200
E-mail: volunteer@aarp.org
Website: www.aarp.org

AMERICAN CANCER SOCIETY (ACS)

The American Cancer Society urges everyone to join the fight against cancer—especially breast cancer. The ACS website posts local events, activities and programs for volunteers to join the fight. These are ideal opportunities for seniors—particularly survivors of breast cancer or their families—to participate in a public service. "The success of Making Strides Against Breast Cancer [an ACS event] depends on our dedicated volunteers! We are looking for people of all ages who are interested in helping at the event. Volunteers are needed! You can make a difference!" Volunteers can also collect pledges for their efforts. You may be able to sign up online to volunteer at a Making Strides or any other ACS event near you. Volunteer activities in your community might include:

• Brochure distribution: Help spread the word by distributing brochures and promotional materials in your neighborhood.

• Office support: Help recruit new volunteers, coordinate walk materials and contact past participants by phone.

• Product sales: Help sell T-shirts and other promotional items at the event.

• Survivor tent: Assist in greeting cancer survivors who will participate.

• Registration: You must be good with numbers. This may involve pre-event training.

• Volunteer check-in: Sign-in and direct volunteers to their stations.

• Greeters and cheerers: Greet walkers and lead them to registration; cheer them on and give directions.

• Route marshals: Direct walkers to stay on the course. Duties include traffic control.

• Water stations: Distribute water to participants along the course of the walk.

• Refreshments: Set up and distribute food and refreshments to all participants.

• First aid: Provide medical attention, if needed. (Requires certification.)

• Set up/clean up: May involve heavy lifting, moving, and loading. (Source: American Cancer Society.)

To find volunteer opportunities in your area, go to: www.cancer.org/docroot/gi/gi_5.asp. You can also contact your local ACS chapter.

AMERICAN HEART ASSOCIATION (AHA)

"Volunteers are the backbone of the American Heart Association." They include heart disease and stroke survivors, people whose families or friends have been affected by these conditions in some way, and nurses, doctors, and scientists. AHA affiliates serve and raise money for important cardiovascular research. "Each year, the American Heart Association relies on people just like you to help us reduce disability and death due to heart disease and stroke." Volunteer opportunities include:

• Community programs: Educational programs seek to lower the risk of heart disease and stroke. AHA can use your help to reach the families and patients who can benefit from their services.

• Development or fund raising: AHA fundraising activities secure the funds necessary to support research and educational program activities. Examples of opportunities include organizing special events—e.g., auctions, dinners, galas, walks, fitness, or golf tournaments—soliciting major gifts, and recruiting other volunteers.

• Communications or public relations: The activities, events, and programs noted are promoted through these efforts. AHA can use your help in producing and distributing news releases, creating posters and flyers, and developing positive relationships with the media in your community.

• Public affairs: These activities help maintain AHA's reputation as a successful and credible voluntary health agency.

If you need information, including about volunteering, contact the American Heart Association at 800-AHA-USA1, or visit the AHA website: www.americanheart.org.

AMERICAN RED CROSS (ARC)

As a humanitarian organization of volunteers—with more than 950 chapters nationwide—acting under a Congressional charter and guided by the fundamental principles of the International Red Cross, for nearly 125 years the ARC's mission has been well defined. It provides relief to victims of disasters and helps all American citizens prevent, prepare for, and respond to emergencies by empowering them to take practical steps to make families, neighborhoods, schools, and workplaces safer, healthier, and more resilient in the face of adversity.

Through the "Together We Prepare" program, the ARC provides training for the public in community disaster preparedness, and response and lifesaving skills training (first aid and CPR). The program also encourages everyone who is able to donate blood and volunteer to help build community preparedness. The ARC website includes a directory of Red Cross local chapters and information about programs, events, and Red Cross initiatives. You can learn more by visiting the website: www.redcross.org.

AMNESTY INTERNATIONAL USA (AIUSA)

"In hundreds of communities across the country, local groups meet regularly to write letters and organize actions on behalf of victims of human rights violations.... Amnesty International is an international grassroots movement. Much of our work is done by our network of volunteer groups. We have groups in communities and churches and on high school and college campuses. There are professional networks of lawyers, health professionals, and educators. We very much hope that you will consider joining one of these groups" (Amnesty International).

For general information about AIUSA, go to: www.amnestyusa.org. To find a local group in one of the five regions near you, go to: www.amnestyusa.org/contact/volunteer.do. If you are interested in volunteering outside the U.S., contact your nearest national section.

ARTHRITIS FOUNDATION

"The Arthritis Foundation is the only national voluntary health organization helping the 70 million Americans with arthritis take greater control of their disease through a variety of actions. Volunteers at the Arthritis Foundation have always been the driving force behind the Foundation, contributing valuable resources (time, knowledge, skills and leadership) to serve in a variety of ways. The Arthritis Foundation values the commitment of our volunteers. We envision an organization in which volunteers can use their expertise and experience in business, leadership, marketing, health care, public relations, technology, fund raising, and government affairs to make a difference" (Arthritis Foundation).

Volunteers provide assistance in chapter offices, participate in programs and special events, and raise funds to support research in the prevention, control, and cure of arthritis and related diseases. To learn about volunteer opportunities in you area, go to the Foundation's web page at: www.arthritis.org/resources/Volunteer/position.asp.

BIG BROTHERS BIG SISTERS (BBBS)

Big Brothers Big Sisters has been the nation's preeminent youth-service organization for more than a century. "Our service is based on our volunteers. We have a proven success in creating and nurturing relationships between adults and children. Being a Big Brother or Big Sister is something that almost anyone can do. The only requirements are a willingness to make a new friend and a desire to share some fun with a young person" (Big Brothers Big Sisters).

The BBBS organization serves hundreds of thousands of children in 5,000 communities across America. Their expressed goal was to have provided "Bigs" to 400,000 children by 2004, the year of their 100th anniversary, and to one million children by 2010. You can volunteer with the BBBS program in your area by visiting their web page at: www.bbbsa.org/volunteer.asp.

BOY SCOUTS OF AMERICA

The National Council of the Boy Scouts of America supports more than 300 councils that provide quality youth programs in communities across the nation.

> "The Boy Scouts of America relies on dedicated volunteers to promote its mission of preparing young people to make ethical and moral choices over their lifetime by instilling in them the values of the Scout Oath and Law. Today, more than 1.2 million adults provide leadership and mentoring to Cub Scout packs, Boy Scout troops, and Venturing crews. Scout volunteers serve in many capacities.... Together, these volunteers gave more than 288 million hours of service in 2002 to ensure that the youth of America have access to and benefit from Scouting programs in their communities.

Through the work of these many volunteers, the Boy Scouts of America remains the foremost youth program of character development and values-based leadership training in America. To these volunteers we would like to say thank you for your dedication to Scouting. And, to adults who are not currently Scout volunteers, we invite you to become a volunteer and share in the positive experiences Scouting provides" [Boy Scouts of America].

To learn more about volunteer opportunities with the Boy Scouts, go to their website: www.scouting.org.

CATHOLIC NETWORK OF VOLUNTEER SERVICE (CNVS)

"Catholic Network of Volunteer Service, a non-profit organization established in 1963, has as its mission to be a bridge between people thinking about volunteering and member programs, over 230 of which offer volunteer opportunities [these are listed on the CNVS website]. Our goal is to help women and men use their gifts in service to the Church and the world" (Catholic Network of Volunteer Service).

CNVS publishes a *Response Directory of Volunteer Opportunities*, which explains the practical details of volunteer service. It is available online as well as in a print version. Over 70,000 copies have been distributed worldwide. The indices of the directory indicate the type of placements available as well as their geographical locations, by state and country.

Interested volunteers can submit a Profile Form online; the information will be sent to all member programs. Programs that identify a potential match for the prospective volunteer will contact the individual directly. You can also query CNVS at:

Catholic Network of Volunteer Service
6930 Carroll Avenue, Suite 506
Tacoma Park, MD 20912-4423
Telephone: 800-543-5046 or 301-270-0900
E-mail: volunteer@cnvs.org
Website: www.cnvs.org

COUNCIL OF RELIGIOUS VOLUNTEER AGENCIES (CRVA)

"CRVA is a broad, faith-based coalition of North American organizations (promoters, planners, users) of voluntary service. With roots in the religious community, CRVA is an independent, non-profit association. Members [listed on the CRVA website] include local, community-based organizations using small numbers of volunteers and national agencies placing thousands of volunteers annually. Each year CRVA member organizations place thousands of volunteers within the U.S. and around the world for periods of a few days to three years" (Council of Religious Volunteer Agencies). The CRVA website can be found at: www.religiousvolunteers.org.

Delta Society

The Delta Society is a national, nonprofit organization whose mission is improving human health through service and the utilization of therapy animals. Its program, "Pet Partners," trains volunteers and screens them and their pets to partake in animal programs in hospitals, nursing homes, rehabilitation centers, schools, and other facilities. The program was established in 1990 to ensure that "both ends of the leash"—owners as well as animals—are prepared to participate in animal-assisted activity and animal-assisted therapy programs. It is the only such national registry that requires volunteer training and screening of animal/handler teams. More than 6,400 Pet Partners teams now operate in all fifty states and four other countries, helping more than 900,000 people each year.

The society website has information and resources about the human-animal-health connection as well as the prerequisites and steps required for you and your animal to volunteer to become a Pet Partner team, and the benefits you may receive. This information is available online at: www.deltasociety.org/dsa000.htm. For additional information contact:

Delta Society
580 Naches Avenue SW, Suite 101
Renton, WA 98055-2297
Tel.: 425-226-7357
Website: www.deltasociety.org

Dominican Volunteers USA (DVUSA)

Dominican Volunteers USA is a full-time service opportunity sponsored by the Catholic Order of Preachers (the Dominicans) for laypersons around the United States. After more than 30 years of regionally based programs, DVUSA was born out of a collaborative effort to strengthen and broaden Dominican-sponsored service opportunities. Now a national program, DVUSA offers enhanced ministry opportunities for laypersons to serve communities in need around the country. DVUSA expects volunteers to give ten months of service. The period begins with orientation in August and ends in June of the following year. The volunteer works full time in a ministry to the poor and the marginalized in our society, across the nation.

Volunteers work in schools, clinics, community centers, churches, and on organic farms. They serve as teachers, teachers' aides, tutors, nurses, peace and justice advocates, community organizers, caseworkers, campus and parish ministers, and environmental educators. They live in Dominican communities around the United States, both rural and urban, including the cities of Atlanta, Chicago, New Orleans, and presently in the states of California, Connecticut, Michigan, Montana, New York, New Jersey, Ohio, Texas, Washington, and Wisconsin.

During your volunteer year, DVUSA and your ministry site cover certain of your expenses. Benefits include:

- Room and board
- Health Insurance
- $100/month stipend
- $300 at end of service

"We invite persons of Christian motivation ages 21 and older to consider becoming a Dominican volunteer. A year of full time service requires flexibility, a willingness to take risks, a sense of humor, good health, and a positive, faith-filled disposition. We ask that you have two years of college or work experience, a desire to serve the poor and an interest in working in diverse and multicultural settings" (Dominican Volunteers USA).

DVUSA accepts about 20 volunteers per year, who live in intergenerational Dominican communities with a commitment to prayer, shared meals and other activities. They participate in three retreats each year, including the week-long orientation in early August. Each retreat, which brings all Dominican volunteers together, is held in any of a number of centers around the United States.

"If you would like to spend a year making a difference by actively participating in the lives of the poor, we'd like you to consider Dominican Volunteers USA. At Dominican Volunteers USA, we invite people to join with us in our mission and ministry to work toward economic, social and political justice for all" (Dominican Volunteers USA). Those interested can find further information on the DVUSA web page: www.op.org/volusa/.

ENVIRONMENTAL ALLIANCE FOR SENIOR INVOLVEMENT (EASI)

The Environmental Alliance for Senior Involvement is a national nonprofit coalition of environmental, aging, and volunteer organizations established in 1991 as the result of an agreement between the U.S. Environmental Protection Agency and the American Association of Retired Persons—as AARP was then known.

EASI's mission is to promote and utilize the environmental ethic, expertise, and commitment of older Americans, and to increase opportunities for them to play an active, visible role in caring for, protecting, and improving the environment in their communities for present and future generations. The Senior Environment Corps is EASI's national organization that links seniors across the country to achieve that mission. EASI's national partners include more than 300 national, state and local public and private organizations. For more information, visit the EASI website: www.easi.org.

EXPERIENCE CORPS

"Experience Corps offers new adventures in service for Americans over 55. Now in 12 cities, Experience Corps works to solve serious social problems, beginning with literacy. Today more than 1,300 Corps members serve as tutors and mentors to children in urban public schools and after-school programs, where they help teach children to read and develop the confidence and skills to succeed in school and in life. Research shows that Experience Corps boosts student academic performance, helps schools and youth-serving organizations become more successful, strengthens ties between these institutions and surrounding neighborhoods, and enhances the well-being of the volunteers in the process. Experience Corps is a signature program of Civic Ventures" (Experience Corps). To determine if there is an Experience Corps project in a city near you, or for further information, visit the Experience Corps website: www.experience-corps.org.

FAITH IN ACTION

Faith in Action is a national program of The Robert Wood Johnson Foundation—the nation's largest health care foundation—with direction and technical assistance provided by Wake Forest University School of Medicine. It is a national volunteer movement that brings together community organizations and religious congregations of various faiths to assist people, who are aging and/or chronically ill, with everyday activities, enabling them to maintain their independence. The organization's website contains a searchable database that lists programs by state.

"At a time when our need to reach out to each other is greatest, Faith in Action ... stands ready to help. Americans of every faith—including Baha'i, Buddhists, Catholics, Hindus, Jews, Muslims, and Protestants—are invited to work together to improve the lives of their neighbors of all ages with long-term health needs through nearly 1,000 Faith in Action programs nationwide" (Faith in Action). You can contact Faith in Action at:

Faith in Action
Wake Forest University Medical Center
Winston-Salem, NC 27157
Telephone: 877-324-8411
E-mail:info@FIAVolunteers.org
Website: www.fiavolunteers.org

FAMILY FRIENDS

Family Friends volunteers are men and women more than 55 years of age who are interested in working with children who have special needs. The basic program involves older volunteers nurturing disabled or chronically ill children. The program also focuses on daycare services for children with disabilities, children in homeless shelters, and those who attend special schools because they are too ill or infirm to go to regular public schools.

Volunteers are advocates for those many children who need a helping and loving hand. Family Friends volunteers are recruited from the community at large. There are no income guidelines for either volunteers or families. The hundreds of involved older volunteers—committed to helping children at risk of a huge variety of illnesses, whether chronic, social, or economic—are Family Friends. This is the strength of the program.

Volunteers receive extensive training (much of it online). They may also be reimbursed for reasonable expenses incurred during the year—many volunteers elect to forego any reimbursement. These arrangements can be made with the local project director. The matching process is undertaken very carefully to make certain that the family and the volunteer have a successful relationship that bonds them and enables them to learn from each other.

To find out more about the program, or whether there is a project in your area, go to the "Resources" section on their website and review the list of projects. You can telephone Family Friends at 202-479-6675. You can also contact them at:

Family Friends
300 D Street SW, Suite 801
Washington, D.C., 20024
Website: www.family-friends.org

GENERATIONS OF HOPE

Generations of Hope (formerly Hope for the Children) began in 1994 with a mission to provide secure, nurturing adoptive families and caring intergenerational communities for foster-care children when no other option for permanency is available. Generations of Hope is a licensed foster care and adoption agency located in Rantoul, Illinois. Hope Meadows, its first planned community, is housed on a now-closed military base. Generations of Hope offers salaries for stay-at-home parents, on-site staff and therapists, weekly training and one-on-one support for families, and rent subsidies for senior citizens in exchange for their volunteer work. Generations of Hope was the 2002 winner of the U.S. Department of Human Services "Adoption Excellence Award."

One of the most unusual and successful aspects of Generations of Hope is its intergenerational component. Seniors, who serve as "honorary grandparents," are required to volunteer at least six hours a week in exchange for a reduced rent of $350 or less per month. They live in spacious three-bedroom, air-conditioned apartments. Seniors spend 15,000 hours every year volunteering at Hope; 9,700 senior hours are spent directly working with children; 20 percent of Hope's funding is derived from rentals to these seniors. To apply to be a Hope Senior contact:

Generations of Hope:
1530 Fairway Drive
Rantoul, IL 61866
Telephone: 217-893-4673
E-mail: generations@soltec.net
Website: www.generationsofhope.org

GIRL SCOUTS OF AMERICA

In a message to older or retired adults, the Girl Scouts of America asks rhetorically: "Remember growing up in your neighborhood? Didn't it feel good to know there were adults around you who cared? Neighborhoods are not what they used to be. Imagine how hard it must be for today's young people, who may not have grandparents nearby to direct and guide them the way your family did. Girls in your neighborhood need that kind of special guidance. They need your wisdom about what's right and wrong and what's really important in life. They need you, just the way you are. Give some time to a girl today." To volunteer, contact your local Girl Scout Council. You can locate a council in your area at: www.girlscouts.org/councilfinder/.

GOODWILL INDUSTRIES

"For almost as long as Goodwill has been in existence, volunteers have strengthened Goodwill programs and lent their support in numerous ways. Goodwill has deep roots in the communities where it operates and has forged a wide range of partnerships with both national and local civic or nonprofit organizations in support of local community needs—opportunities for you to make a difference and strengthen the communities in which you live" (Goodwill Industries International).

If you are an officer or administrative member of a national organization with a community base, and you would like to partner your organization with Goodwill on a volunteer project, use the online locator to find a Goodwill marketing or community relations contact in your area. Or contact:

Goodwill Industries International, Inc.
9200 Rockville Pike

Bethesda, MD 20814
Telephone: 240-333-5200
E-mail: contactus@goodwill.org
Website: www.goodwill.org

THE GRAY PANTHERS

Founded in 1970 by social activist Maggie Kuhn (1905–1995) the Gray Panthers is a national organization of intergenerational activists dedicated to social change and economic justice. They have local offices throughout the U.S. "We are age and youth in action. For almost thirty years, Gray Panthers have worked to make America a better place to live for the young, the old, and everyone-in-between. Taking on our society's toughest problems—peace, health care, jobs, and housing—Gray Panthers have been effective in creating change. Whether at the local, state or federal level, Gray Panthers fight to change laws and attitudes for social justice. Gray Panthers believe that all Americans should benefit from our country's abundance" (Gray Panthers).

Today, there are more than 20,000 Gray Panthers, many of them active in one of more than 50 local networks nationwide. The focus is broad and diverse—from affordable health care, to jobs with a living wage. To join a network, call the number shown on the network web page, or send an e-mail to the person nearest you. The network web page can be found at: www.graypanthers.org/gray-panthers/network.htm. Contact information:

Gray Panthers
733 15th Street, NW, Suite 437
Washington, DC 20005
Telephone: 800-280-5362, or 202-737-6637
E-mail: info@graypanthers.org
Website: www.graypanthers.org

HABITAT FOR HUMANITY INTERNATIONAL

Founded in 1976, Habitat for Humanity International is a nonprofit, ecumenical Christian housing ministry dedicated to eliminating substandard housing and homelessness worldwide and to making adequate, affordable shelter a matter of conscience and action. Habitat invites people of all ages, from all faiths and walks of life to work together in partnership, building homes for families in need. Since 1976, Habitat has built more than 150,000 homes in more than 89 countries, including more than 50,000 across the United States.

To volunteer in your local area, you can use the search engine on the Habitat website to find information for a program near you. Volunteer opportunities exist in the United States, Canada, and a number of foreign countries. These can be found at: www.habitat.org/local/.

LEGAL COUNSEL FOR THE ELDERLY (LCE)

AARP's Legal Counsel for the Elderly is a provider of free legal services and advocacy for older people in the District of Columbia. "Volunteers are key components of LCE programs. Volunteers can be retired people, undergraduate students, law students, retired attorneys, and attorneys between jobs or careers. Because it takes a certain amount of time to orient and train volunteers, we request that no one inquire about volunteer opportunities unless he or she is willing to make a commitment of at least one day (five hours or more) per week for at least a three month period of time" (Legal Counsel for the Elderly). For more information, contact:

AARP
601 E Street, NW
Washington, DC 20049
Telephone: 202-434-2120
Fax: 202-434-6464
Web page: www.aarp.org/lce/

THE LEUKEMIA & LYMPHOMA SOCIETY

"The Leukemia & Lymphoma Society has almost one million volunteers nationwide involved in every facet of the organization's operations. Volunteers are a critical resource in helping the Society achieve its mission. Each year we set our goals higher, and in order to reach those goals, we need you!" (The Leukemia & Lymphoma Society).

Areas of volunteer activity are listed on the Society's web page at: www.leukemia.org/all_page?item_id=68873. If you are interested in volunteering, fill out the online application form on the web page, or contact your local chapter by using the link to the "Chapter Finder."

LITTLE BROTHERS—FRIENDS OF THE ELDERLY

Little Brothers—Friends of the Elderly, is a national, nonprofit organization that is part of an international organization (*Fédération Internationale des petits frères des Pauvres*—International Federation of Little Brothers of the Poor), committed to relieving isolation and loneliness among the elderly. The organization relies heavily on volunteers. "The strength of this organization rests in the hands of its volunteers—without them, our mission could not be fulfilled" (Little Brothers—Friends of the Elderly).

Little Brothers has volunteer opportunities programs and services for older adults, such as visiting, transportation to appointments, shopping, holiday parties, and other social events and vacations. For information on volunteer opportunities with Little Brothers go to: www.littlebrothers.org/html3/usa/e/volunteer_opp.shtml; for a location nearest you, go to: www.littlebrothers.org/html3/usa/e/.

MAKE-A-WISH FOUNDATION

"Become a wish-granting volunteer. We grant the wishes of children with life-threatening medical conditions to enrich the human experience with hope, strength, and joy. Volunteers are the backbone of the Make-a-Wish Foundation. Only through the hard work and commitment of more than 25,000 volunteers around the world is the Make-a-Wish Foundation able to continue granting more wishes to children.... Local chapters are always looking for volunteers to help in several areas" (Make-a-Wish Foundation). If you are interested in learning more about volunteer opportunities in your community, contact your local chapter. You can search for a local chapter at: www.wish.org/home/volunteer.htm.

MARCH OF DIMES

Since its beginning, the March of Dimes has depended on the generosity of volunteers to carry out its mission of preventing birth defects and infant mortality. "Volunteers have always been the driving force behind the foundation, giving generously of their time and talent to serve in a variety of ways.... Volunteers are vital to the success of our mission" (March of Dimes).

To learn about volunteer opportunities in your area, contact your local chapter. You can locate your local chapter quickly and easily online at: http://209.73.237.101/aboutus/chapter_lookup.asp.

MEALS ON WHEELS ASSOCIATION OF AMERICA (MOWAA)

"The Meals on Wheels Association of America represents those who provide congregate and home-delivered meal services to people in need. Our mission is to provide visionary leadership and professional training, and to develop partnerships that will ensure the provision of quality nutrition services" (Meals on Wheels).

The need for volunteers and the types of services that volunteers perform vary from program to program. If you would like to volunteer with a Meals on Wheels program in your community, the best thing to do is to contact the program directly. To locate the program nearest you, you can use the MOWAA "Search for a Program" link on its website and search by state. This web page can be found at: www.mowaa.org/search.shtml. If you do not locate a local program, be sure to scroll back to the top of the state page. There you will find the address and telephone number of the state government office responsible for programs that serve seniors. Individuals at that office should be able to assist you in locating a program near you.

NATIONAL MULTIPLE SCLEROSIS SOCIETY (NMSS)

"Volunteers at the National Multiple Sclerosis Society are integral partners in our fight against MS. Throughout the United States, volunteers contribute valuable resources (time, knowledge, skills, and leadership), infusing our organization with the energy and passion necessary to end the devastating effects of multiple sclerosis. The National MS Society strives to be known and respected for excellence in volunteerism among the country's voluntary health agencies. We envision an organization in which volunteers work as partners at all levels, an environment that embraces, values, and recognizes every contribution" (National Multiple Sclerosis Society).

The Society has four general categories of volunteer involvement:

1. Leadership
2. Administrative
3. Program
4. Fund-raising

You can explore any of these volunteering opportunities by contacting your local chapter, or telephone NMSS at: 800-344-4867. You can visit their web page at: www.nationalmssociety.org/Volunteerism.asp. For additional information, visit the NMSS website: www.nmss.org.

NATIONAL RETIREE VOLUNTEER COALITION (NRVC)

The NRVC is a program of Volunteers of America, with a goal of "transforming the skills and expertise of retirees into community leadership and service." The coalition is a nonprofit consulting organization dedicated to creating a national movement of corporate retiree volunteer leadership and service. NRVC's unique method for mobilizing retirees to lives of community leadership and service is the Corporate Retiree Volunteer Program. Under the banner of their former employer, retirees with diverse backgrounds and interests combine their skills and experience to tackle pressing community needs, such as education, youth-at-risk, community revitalization, environmental concerns, and public health. For more information, contact:

The National Retiree Volunteer Coalition
1660 Duke Street
Alexandria, VA 22314
Website: www.voa.org

NATIONAL SAFETY COUNCIL (NSC)

The National Safety Council is a congressionally chartered national organization whose mission is to educate and influence society to adopt safety, health, and environmental policies, practices, and procedures that prevent and mitigate human suffering and economic losses arising from preventable causes. The council carries out its mission on the community level through a network of chapters. To learn more about volunteer opportunities with the NSC, contact:

National Safety Council
1121 Spring Lake Drive
Itasca, IL 60143-3201
Telephone: 630-285-1121
Fax: 630-285-1315
E-mail: info@nsc.org
Website: www.nsc.org

THE NATURE CONSERVANCY

"Since 1951, we've been working with communities, businesses and people like you to protect more than 117 million acres around the world. Our mission: To preserve the plants, animals and natural communities that represent the diversity of life on Earth by protecting the lands and waters they need to survive" (The Nature Conversancy).

The Nature Conservancy works in Asia and the Pacific area, the Caribbean, Central America, South America, and North America. The conservancy is helping preserve millions of acres of lands and waters across the continent through chapters in all 50 U.S. states and programs in Canada and Mexico.

Are you interested in:

- Helping the environment?
- Working with others who share your love of nature?
- Contributing your time and skills to an organization you believe in?
- Broadening your resume and/or life experiences?

If you answered yes to any of these questions, The Nature Conservancy has opportunities for you. To view volunteer opportunities in your area, visit the conservancy's web page: http://nature.org/volunteer/, and select your state.

OASIS (THE OASIS INSTITUTE)

OASIS is a national nonprofit educational organization designed to enhance the quality of life for "mature" adults. They offer programs in the arts, humanities, wellness and volunteer service, and create opportunities for retirees and older adults to continue their personal growth and provide meaningful service to the community. "Mature adults have a lifetime of experience, wisdom and talents to share with others. OASIS offers many rewarding opportunities to volunteer in your community. Find out how you can make a difference" (OASIS). To review a variety of volunteer opportunities in a city nearest you, go to: www.oasisnet.org/volunteer/index.htm. Or for further information, visit the OASIS home page: www.oasisnet.org.

THE SALVATION ARMY

The Salvation Army seeks volunteers to support their efforts in 109 countries. "Approximately one-and-a-half million volunteers throughout the United States dramatically extend The Salvation Army's ability to serve the needy. Volunteers provide assistance in a variety of areas from social services to office work to character building activities. If you have a skill or just the heart to serve, The Salvation Army has a place for you. Volunteers bring diversity to the Army's work in age, race, social background, and approach. If you would like to volunteer, we need you and appreciate you" (Salvation Army). A Volunteer Registration Form is on their website: www.salvationarmy.org. Volunteers will be referred to the unit nearest their community and then contacted.

SAVE THE CHILDREN

"Save the Children was founded in the United States in 1932 as a nonprofit child-assistance organization to make lasting positive change in the lives of children in need. Today we work in nineteen states across the United States as well as in forty-seven other countries in the developing world to help children and families improve their health, education and economic opportunities. We also mobilize rapid life-support assistance for children and families caught in the tragedies of natural and man-made disasters" (Save the Children).

Save the Children is a member of the International Save the Children Alliance, an association of 26 independent organizations that provide child-oriented emergency response, development assistance, and advocacy of children's rights in more than 100 countries. For information on volunteer opportunities contact:

Save the Children
54 Wilton Road
Westport, CT 06880
Telephone: 203-221-4000
Fax: 203-227-5667
E-mail: info@savechildren.org
Website: www.savethechildren.org

SECOND HARVEST

Second Harvest is the largest domestic hunger relief organization in the United States. It supplies the needy with one billion pounds of food a year—for those of all ages who are hungry due to poverty or natural disasters.

"Ending hunger in America depends on the volunteer work of literally millions of Americans who know that they can make a difference. There are as many different ways to volunteer as there are individuals and communities across this country. You can help out in your community through activities such as tutoring kids, ... repackaging donated food for use at food pantries, or transporting food to charitable agencies and the hungry people who use their services" (Second Harvest).

To search for volunteer opportunities in your local community, go to their web page: secondharvest.volunteermatch.org . For further information on Second Harvest, go to: www.secondharvest.org.

SENIOR ATTORNEY VOLUNTEERS FOR THE ELDERLY (SAVE)

"Senior attorneys everywhere now have the opportunity to help the elderly poor with legal service through a new nationwide program called SAVE ... which is co-sponsored by AARP's Legal Counsel for the Elderly and the ABA's [American Bar Association] Senior Lawyers Division, Commission on Legal Problems of the Elderly, and Center for Pro Bono" (Senior Attorney Volunteers for the Elderly). The program's goal is to encourage senior lawyers to create a local SAVE program, a local network of senior attorney volunteers for the elderly. Each program provides elder law training, supervision, and malpractice insurance by the sponsoring legal services provider. For information on how to create a local SAVE program, contact:

Managing Attorney
LCE/AARP
601 E Street, NW
Washington, DC 20049
Telephone: 202-434-2164
Web page: www.abanet.org/srlawyers/save.html

SENIORNET

"SeniorNet depends on its thousands of volunteers to support our nonprofit organization and its educational programs. With a small staff and a far-reaching mission, SeniorNet could not affect the lives of so many tens of thousands of older adults without the work of our dedicated and skilled volunteers" (SeniorNet).

Volunteers provide services at SeniorNet Learning Centers. Seniors who are generally knowledgeable about computers can volunteer their time to either teach or coach various computer classes at Learning Centers nationwide. Here any senior can learn computer skills and enter the technological age. For more information on SeniorNet, or to learn more about volunteer opportunities, visit: www.seniornet.org/php/default.php?PageID=5654.

THE SMITHSONIAN INSTITUTION

If you are not quite old enough to be on exhibit in the Smithsonian, you can still find a place there by volunteering. Volunteers have provided a primary means of support for the Smithsonian Institution since its establishment in 1846. Strong volunteer partnerships are essential for the Institution to carry out its work successfully. Opportunities to volunteer include:

- Docent Programs
- Volunteer Information Specialist
- Behind-the-Scenes Volunteer
- Special Support Programs
- Seasonal Programs

For an overview of Smithsonian volunteer programs and the opportunities for participation, visit their web page at: www.si.edu/resource/faq/volunteer/, or for additional information, telephone 202-357-2700, e-mail: info@si.edu.

UNITED METHODIST VOLUNTEERS IN MISSION (UMVIM)

"The work of the church is done largely by volunteers! In 1976, a special movement was organized in the Southeast called United Methodist Volunteers in Mission (UMVIM). This 'grass roots' organization gave direction and impetus to the volunteer effort in the United Methodist Church. Since that time, thousands of volunteers have served throughout the world. For many who have chosen this form of mission, it has been a life changing experience. The Volunteers who serve Volunteers in Mission, both lay and clergy, are engaged in Christian ministry. In fulfilling the work to which God has called us, we embody the UMVIM motto 'Christian Love in Action'" (United Methodist Volunteers in Mission).

The UMVIM advises that individual volunteers, either single or as married couples, are needed for short-term projects. The usual length of service is from two months to two years. The individual volunteer is expected to cover the cost of transportation to, and personal expenses in, the place of assignment. For further information on the types of volunteer assignments available and to download an online application form, visit the General Board of Global Ministries web page at: http://gbgm-umc.org/vim/. For general information, contact:

United Methodist Volunteers In Mission
475 Riverside Drive, Suite 330
New York, NY 10115
Telephone: 212-870-3825, Ext. 7334
Fax: 212-870-3624
Website: http://gbgm-umc.org

UNITED NATIONS CHILDREN'S FUND (UNICEF)

UNICEF's mission statement: "UNICEF is mandated by the United Nations General Assembly to advocate for the protection of children's rights, to help meet their basic needs and to expand their opportunities to reach their full potential." UNICEF is committed to ensuring special protection for the most disadvantaged children—victims of war, disasters, extreme poverty, all forms of violence and exploitation and those with disabilities.

> "For more than 50 years, the U.S. Fund for UNICEF has been providing support to designated UNICEF-assisted projects, an effort that has saved and improved the lives of millions of children around the world. We couldn't have achieved this goal without help from countless volunteers who have lent their time, talent, energy, and money to the work of the U.S. Fund over the years.
>
> Our volunteers are men and women of all ages and from all walks of life. All of them have at least one thing in common, a belief that all children deserve a chance to live and grow. Your efforts will help save children's-lives" [United Nations Children's Fund].

If you have an undergraduate degree, several years of work experience, and are interested in long-term volunteer opportunities in developing countries, you may be eligible for entry into the United Nations Volunteer (UNV) program. This is a United Nations common program, which recruits volunteers for assignments throughout the United Nations system, including UNICEF. Application procedures and information are available at the UNV website. (The UNV is discussed in the following note and in further detail in the section of this book called "International Programs.")

UNICEF does not recruit volunteers directly. In the case of U.S.-based volunteer work, opportunities are offered through the U.S. Fund for UNICEF. If you live near a UNICEF chapter, you can assist UNICEF'S local efforts by doing data entry, preparing mailings, or doing research. Flexible hours are ideal for students, retirees and/or seniors. Chapters are located in Atlanta, Boston, Chicago, Houston, and Los Angeles. The addresses and telephones of these offices can be found at: www.unicefusa.org/chapters/volunteer.html. For information on all volunteer opportunities throughout the United States, contact:

United States Fund for UNICEF
333 East 38th Street, 6th Floor
New York, NY 10016
Telephone: 1-800-4UNICEF
E-mail: webmaster @ unicefusa.org
Website: www.unicefusa.org

UNITED NATIONS VOLUNTEERS (UNV)

"The first place to look for volunteer opportunities is in your community. You could join one of your country's national volunteer organizations or offer your professional services free of charge. Check our World Volunteer Web country profiles [www.unv.org/volunteers/options/home_country/index.htm] to find names of organizations near your home" (United Nations Volunteers).

To review a list of agencies in Canada, go to the web page: www.worldvolunteerweb.org/dynamic/cfapps/national_profiles/nation.cfm?CountryID=can. To review a list of agencies in the United States, go to the web page: www.worldvolunteerweb.org/dynamic/cfapps/national_profiles/nation.cfm?CountryID= usa. Be advised that these are only lists of contacts, including some URLs; there are no hyperlinks to the agencies and organizations listed. For further information on all UNV volunteer options visit: www.unv.org/volunteers/options/ index.htm. Here you will find information about how to apply with UNV.

UNITED WAY OF AMERICA

United Way is a philanthropic organization providing support for community programs. Contact the United Way to find local chapters linking people with resources, such as dental and health services for low-income people, or to volunteer for service programs in the community. Their website has a search engine for all national chapters. You can also contact them at:

United Way of America
701 North Fairfax Street
Alexandria, VA 22314-2045
Phone: 800-892-2757 or 703-836-7100
Website: http://national.unitedway.org

VETERANS OF FOREIGN WARS (VFW)

The VFW is the nation's oldest major organization serving veterans and their communities. The more than 2.6 million members of the VFW and its auxiliaries have a rich tradition of enhancing the lives of millions through its community service programs and special projects. A commitment to volunteerism is a cornerstone of the VFW, with a particular focus on programs that build stronger communities by promoting education, civic pride, civic responsibility, and an appreciation for America's history and traditions.

The VFW shares the traditions of volunteering to build better communities and is associated with numerous national affiliations. "The benevolence of the Veterans of Foreign Wars and its Ladies Auxiliary goes well beyond the realm of veterans helping veterans. Supporting the community is a tradition of both the VFW and its Ladies Auxiliary with volunteering efforts centering on programs that benefit education and health services, enhance military morale, develop civic pride and improve the community. Last year, [2002] the Veterans of Foreign Wars and its partner, the Ladies Auxiliary, donated more than 13 million hours of community service and contributed more than 63 million [dollars] toward community service projects. Whether raising money for the March of Dimes or providing scholarships to our nation's youth, the VFW is there, partners in the community and in the schools—honoring the dead by helping the living" (Veterans of Foreign Wars). Learn more by visiting the VFW website: www.vfw.org, or by contacting the nearest VFW post.

VOLUNTEERS IN MEDICINE INSTITUTE (VIMI)

"Interested in volunteering? Retired physicians, nurses, dentists, social workers, pharmacists and others—you can make a difference! Medical professionals who volunteer their time and skills often feel they get more out of the experience than they give. Here's why: The patient-focused environment at VIMI Clinics is rarely found in today's fast-paced, cost-conscious primary care practices. Our patients have had little or no access to health care. They need care and show their appreciation to those who volunteer to provide it" (Volunteers in Medicine Institute). The volunteer defines the time that he or she is able to commit. To find a VIMI clinic in your area, go to: www.vimi.org/contact.htm#clinic; for more information on volunteering with VIMI, go to: www.vimi.org/volunteer.htm.

VOLUNTEERS OF AMERICA (VOA)

Volunteers of America is a national, nonprofit, spiritually-based organization providing local human service programs and opportunities for individual community involvement. Specific programs include housing, assisted living, meals-on-wheels, transportation, and health care services. In 2002, Volunteers of America Elderly Service programs assisted about 182,000 seniors nationwide.

VOA programs serve individuals and families in some 300 communities across the country, and volunteers have an important role in the success of these programs. Volunteers actively engage in many of the services, delivering meals to the elderly in their homes, reading mail to residents of nursing homes, and providing other services that make a real difference in people's lives.

Volunteers of America engages more than 41,000 volunteers nationwide each year. To find the local office nearest you, and learn how you can help, go to the VOA Location Directory at: www.voa.org/ext_locations.cfm. For further information on VOA, go to their website: www.voa.org.

Young Men's Christian Association (YMCA)

The YMCA is a membership organization providing physical fitness and health programs. Local YMCAs nationwide design "Active Older Adult" programs to meet the needs of older members, provide volunteer opportunities for retirees and senior citizens and offer intergenerational programs. The organization is not only for young men and Christians; anyone is welcome.

"At the YMCA, your time and talent go a long way. Every hour you spend as a YMCA volunteer translates into the caring attention a child or teen needs to grow up healthy and resilient. It translates into support for families so they can be successful and strong. Into healthier lives for people of all ages, backgrounds, abilities and incomes. Into a safer, more viable community that's a good place to live and work" (Young Men's Christian Association). Visit or call your local YMCA for more information. You can also contact them at:

YMCA
101 North Wacker Drive, 14th Floor
Chicago, IL 60606
Telephone: 800-872-9622 or 312-977-0031
Website: www.ymca.net/index.isp

Young Women's Christian Association (YWCA)

"The strength of the YWCA movement rests in the spirit and energy of our dedicated volunteers who contribute both time and talent to the over 300 YWCAs throughout the country." YWCA volunteers engage in all types of activities, including mentoring, membership on the board of directors, fundraising and program assistance." If you are interested in learning more about the volunteer opportunities that exist at a YWCA near you, visit the "Find Your YWCA" section of their website: www.ywca.org.

9. International Programs

"One is not born into the world to do everything, but to do something."
—HENRY DAVID THOREAU

Introduction

The World Wide Volunteer organization has affirmed: "Volunteers play a key role, locally and globally—for individuals, families, communities and society at large. Volunteering is defined as a non-obligatory, non-wage activity that individuals carry out for the well-being of their neighbors, community or society at large. It takes many forms, from traditional customs of mutual self-help to community responses in times of crisis and joint effort for relief and conflict resolution. The contribution of volunteers to the world economy is estimated to represent as much as 8 to 14 percent of global GNP" (World Wide Volunteer).

Volunteering for a worldwide project is not to be regarded as a casual jaunt. Prospective volunteers are strongly advised to do their homework and choose from those reputable organizations that have been operating for several decades and have a track record. Examine their annual reports. Communicate with their staff and ask how contributions are used by the host communities. If volunteers aren't careful, they might find themselves in a setting where their efforts are virtually wasted and the situation is wretched—if not dangerous!

When it comes to selecting a reputable and respected program, Joseph Collins and his co-authors, Stefano DeZerega and Zahara Heckscher, have literally written the book—*How to Live Your Dream of Volunteering Overseas* (Collins, et al., 2002). Their recommendations are based on years of research and personal experience as volunteers in countries around the world. Based on their research, the top programs include Cross-Cultural Solutions and Global Volunteers. Both are short-term volunteer vacation programs that are somewhat expensive, but very well rated. Each will be discussed in this section.

There is an increasing trend that identifies travelers of all ages who want to spend their time doing more than sightseeing, buying souvenirs, and sitting on beaches. So-called "volunteer vacations" are becoming more and more popular as the number of destinations and projects continue to rise. While they are often referred to as "volunteer vacations," these are NOT free vacations. Many volunteers are surprised to learn that they have to foot some or all of their own bills. Finances are a major factor driving decisions regarding international service placement programs. However, as prospective volunteers research the situation, they come to understand the financial considerations. Since many of the service trips are to economically challenged areas—often Third World countries—rather than pay volunteers to travel to them and financially support them while they stay there for a period of time, the sponsoring agencies can use that money in the community, where it may be desperately needed. Sponsoring agencies typically do not use the term "volunteer vacation," because it can give some people the idea that the service work is incidental to the "vacation." (Source: Volunteer News, "Volunteer vacations becoming trendy," 2004.)

In most cases, volunteer assignments are not purely physical tasks. Volunteers often serve in schools or hospitals, bridging cultures instead of rivers. There's more human interaction and cultivation of relationships. You're going to make connections and have experiences in foreign cultures.

International Organizations

American Jewish World Service

"The Jewish Volunteer Corps (JVC) places professional Jewish women and men on volunteer consulting projects with local non-governmental organizations in the developing world. Volunteers come from a variety of backgrounds and through the JVC partnership, provide humanitarian aid, in the form of technical assistance and training. Their work touches people's lives and makes a profound impact on local communities. JVC volunteers are motivated Jewish men and women from young professionals to retirees who share a passion for adventure and a commitment to make the world a better place. As computer specialists, small business consultants, public health professionals, teacher trainers, agriculturalists and others, JVC volunteers help improve the quality of life of people in need" (American Jewish World Service). JVC placement opportunities are available around the globe. To learn more, visit their web page at: www.ajws.org.

CATHOLIC NETWORK OF VOLUNTEER SERVICE (CNVS)

In addition to volunteer opportunities in the U.S., CNVS has many opportunities in foreign countries. The reader is referred to the previous discussion of CNVS in the "National Programs" section of this book.

CROSS-CULTURAL SOLUTIONS

One of the most highly rated organizations, Cross-Cultural Solutions is a nonprofit international volunteer organization that operates programs in Brazil, China, Costa Rica, Ghana, Guatemala, India, Peru, Russia, Tanzania, and Thailand. Volunteers are required to pay a fee; the website discusses the rationale for this. The program is open to anyone. For additional information contact:

Cross-Cultural Solutions
2 Clinton Place
New Rochelle, NY 10801
800-380-4777
Website: www.crossculturalsolutions.org

EARTH ELDERS

"Earth Elders is an international network connecting people of all ages who care about aging, elders, and the earth. It explores ways to strengthen elders' presence and connect the generations within communities. The mission of Earth Elders is to honor aging, elders and Earth: A call for mid-life and older persons to become conscious and caring 21st century elders—wise, compassionate, keepers of Earth and holders of a vision for future generations living in harmony with nature. We embrace this work as a sacred trust" (Earth Elders).

Earth elders is a part of Second Journey, a tax-exempt nonprofit corporation formed to "create educational experiences that explore and celebrate what it means to give one's gifts in the second half of life—experiences that promote mindfulness, service and community." For information about either organization, contact:

Second Journey/Earth Elders
P.O. Box 16671
Chapel Hill, NC 27516-6671
Telephone: 919-933-7878
E-mail: info@earthelders.org
E-mail: secondjourney@att.net
Website: www.earthelders.org
Website: www.secondjourney.org

Earthwatch Institute

Another organization with an eminent history is Earthwatch Institute, which 33 years ago pioneered the concept of volunteers contributing to projects and going along to help. The first expeditions occurred in July 1971.

The Institute is a private, nonprofit environmental agency—a scientific field research and education organization—that sponsors international cultural and environmental research and also enables the public to participate in its world-wide scientific research and environmental protection programs, on short-term expeditions, to promote the understanding and action necessary for a sustainable environment.

> "Earthwatch Institute is the world's oldest, largest, and most respected organization directly involving the public in scientific field research. This year, Earthwatch will support more than 130 expeditions in 45 countries, and will send some 4,000 members of the public into the field to work side-by-side with leading scientists.
>
> These teams of volunteers will collect data under the scientists' direction and work as full-fledged expedition members, sharing the costs of the research among them. Earthwatch invented this form of participant funding in 1972, and through it has involved more than 50,000 people in field research.
>
> We invite you to join any expedition listed on our web site. You need no special education or skills. We will teach you everything you need to know. Make a difference this year and select an expedition by month, region, or subject!" [Earthwatch Institute].

Earthwatch volunteers can greatly increase the data-gathering capacity of field research projects. What are some tasks volunteers can complete? In the past, volunteers have been successfully utilized to:

- Gather ethnographic and public health data.
- Record and document indigenous music, dance, oral folk traditions, and architecture.
- Monitor water quality in lakes, streams, wetlands and agricultural areas.
- Observe, capture, measure, band, and then release migratory birds.
- Survey flora and fauna. Collect and prepare plant specimens. Track and count animals, and observe and document their behavior.
- Study the applications of indigenous knowledge on sustainable agriculture and development.
- Teach appropriate technologies and construct solar ovens.
- Study threatened marine ecosystems, such as mangrove swamps, and estuaries. Study the causes and effects of, and efforts to mitigate, the destruction of coral reefs.
- Photograph, and record the sounds of, marine mammals.
- Participate in underwater archae-

ology. Excavate and map land-based archaeological sites.
- Conduct basic research in geology, volcanology, paleontology, geomorphology, glaciology and hydrology.

- Share the many other tasks associated with professional scientific field research. (Source: Earthwatch Institute)

In addition, on numerous occasions, Earthwatch volunteers with specific professional expertise—from computer programming to electronics to construction to public health—have made substantial contributions. Volunteers can select expedition opportunities by team, month, region, or their special interest. For further information on Earthwatch, visit their home page: www.earthwatch.org; to explore your volunteer interest: www.earthwatch.org/expedselect.html.

GEEKCORPS

Geekcorps is a U.S.-based, non-profit organization that places international technical volunteers in developing nations all over the world. The volunteer time period for some projects is four months, including training, although other placements may run for as short as one month. Geekcorps pays for airfare, accommodations, insurance and a monthly living stipend. Volunteers' only out-of-pocket expenses come from medical exams (one conducted within twelve months of an assignment is required) and any incidentals or personal purchases. The organization does not cover fixed expenses relating to the volunteer's permanent residence, loan payments, or other personal expenses that a volunteer might incur while on a project. They advise: "We do what we can to make it virtually no-cost" to a Geekcorps volunteer.

No age requirements are indicated. If you are an older technical volunteer (a "senior geek"), there may be an opportunity for you. For full details about the program, the types of experience needed, and an application, go to the Geekcorps home page: www.geekcorps.org.

GLOBAL VOLUNTEER NETWORK (GVN)

Global Volunteer Network is a private, non-profit, non-government organization based in Wellington, New Zealand, offering international volunteer opportunities. The network was launched in December 2000 by Colin Salisbury, its founder and current Executive Director. "Our vision is to support the work of local community organizations in developing countries through the placement of international volunteers" (Global Volunteer Network).

GVN places volunteers in community projects in China, Ecuador, Ghana, Nepal, New Zealand, Romania, Russia, Thailand, and Uganda. Volunteers have the opportunity to participate in a variety of educational, environmental, and community aid programs. Examples of the exciting and rewarding activities available to volunteers include teaching English, environmental work, AIDS education, and assisting in orphanages. If you would like to know more, you can contact GVN at:

Global Volunteer Network Ltd.
PO Box 2231
Wellington, New Zealand
E-mail: affiliates@volunteer.org.nz
Website: www.volunteer.org.nz

GLOBAL VOLUNTEERS

One of the most highly rated international organizations, Global Volunteers was founded in 1984, with the principal purpose of providing Americans with the opportunity to work with and learn from local people in communities worldwide. It is a private, nonprofit corporation that organizes and sends volunteer teams from North America to some 100 host communities on six continents year-round. The teams participate in short-term volunteer experiences to contribute their skills to work on human and economic development projects. Contact Information:

Global Volunteers
375 East Little Canada Road
St. Paul, MN 55117
Telephone: 800-487-1074
E-mail: mgran@globalvolunteers.org
Website: www.globalvolunteers.org

GREENPEACE INTERNATIONAL

Their stated mission: "Greenpeace is an independent, campaigning organization that uses non-violent, creative confrontation to expose global environmental problems, and force solutions for a green and peaceful future. Greenpeace's goal is to ensure the ability of the Earth to nurture life in all its diversity" (Greenpeace)—in short, to protect the environment peacefully.

If you would like to volunteer as an activist, you need to contact your local Greenpeace office and inquire there as to what opportunities they may have for you. You can find contact information for all of their offices worldwide at: www.greenpeace.org/international_en/contact/index-int. Volunteer information is available at: www.greenpeace.org/international_en/volunteer/.

The older volunteer who may not be up to "creative confrontation"—climbing trees and engaging in perching protests at precarious heights for long durations, or launching remonstrative and bilious blockades of ships-at-sea from a heaving dinghy—can take action instead as a "cyberactivist." Go to Greenpeace's Cyberactivist Center to sign up for their newsletter. They will send you free information about what you can do to help win their campaigns for the environment.

HABITAT FOR HUMANITY INTERNATIONAL

As previously noted in the section on national programs, Habitat was founded in 1976 as a nonprofit, ecumenical housing ministry, dedicated to eliminating substandard housing and homelessness worldwide and to making adequate, affordable shelter a matter of conscience and action. Habitat invites people from all faiths and walks of life to work together in partnership, building houses for families in need. Habitat has said:

> "The need for decent, affordable housing around the world is staggering. An estimated 25 percent of the world's population, some 1.5 billion people, live in substandard housing or have no home at all. Families are trapped in a daily struggle to survive amid horrible, often inhuman, living conditions. Habitat for Humanity International is building around the world, dedicated to the ideal that all people deserve a simple, decent place to live on terms they can afford to pay. Working in partnership with volunteers, churches and synagogues, organizations and the new homeowner families, Habitat for Humanity is building houses and building lives" [Habitat for Humanity].

To volunteer in a foreign country, you can use the search engine on the Habitat website. The search will yield overviews of, and links to, Habitat affiliates in 90 countries around the world. Visit the Habitat search engine at: www.habitat.org/intl/.

IDEALIST (ACTION WITHOUT BORDERS)

To find international volunteer opportunities in 165 countries, go to "Advanced Searches" in the sidebar on the right side of the Idealist home page: www.idealist.org. Click on "Volunteer Opportunities." The advanced search screen you will derive allows you to pinpoint a volunteer position by country, area of focus, keyword, skills needed, languages needed, time availability, or any combination of those criteria.

INTERNATIONAL EXECUTIVE SERVICE CORPS (IESC)

International Executive Service Corps is one of several federally supported initiatives. A part of the USA Freedom Corps, IESC endeavors to match volunteers with nonprofit organizations that are working to implement U.S. initiatives throughout the world. Their objective is to give Americans with appropriate technical expertise the opportunity to serve for flexible periods of time, such as weeks, months, or longer; and deliver skilled volunteers to developing countries and emerging economies to promote health and prosperity in a cost-efficient manner. IESC is the largest not-for-profit business development organization of its kind in the world.

"Our volunteers serve as American ambassadors of good will, transferring knowledge and expertise to create sustainable development. By helping people in the less developed world improve their lives, they ensure that globalization is truly global" (International Executive Service Corps). To learn more about IESC, go to: www.iesc.org, or the web page: www.usafreedomcorps.gov/for_volunteers/.

ISLAMIC RELIEF

"Islamic Relief benefits more than one million refugees worldwide. This effort requires a strong volunteer base both locally, and abroad. Volunteers form the heart of Islamic Relief, and without them our activities are minimal. Your support has been fundamental, and now you can get directly involved" (Islamic Relief). For further information, log on to: www.irw.org. It lists ten ways to get involved.

PROJECT HOPE

"Project HOPE's mission is to achieve sustainable advances in health care around the world by implementing health education programs, conducting health policy research, and providing humanitarian assistance in areas of need; thereby contributing to human dignity, promoting international understanding, and enhancing social and economic development. Volunteers have been at the heart of Project HOPE's work since the days the S.S. HOPE first sailed. We are able to bring medical education and health care training to counterparts in the developing world through the efforts of volunteers—physicians, nurses, surgeons, biomedical engineers, allied health care workers, and others who give their time and talents to travel overseas for short-term and long-term training assignments" (Project Hope).

More than 5,000 health care professionals have donated their services in this manner to HOPE's programs during its 44-year history. If you are interested in volunteer opportunities, go to: www.projecthope.org/employment.htm. There you will find an online application form.

SAVE THE CHILDREN

"Save the Children was founded in the United States in 1932 as a nonprofit child-assistance organization to make lasting positive change in the lives of children in need. Today we work in 19 states across the United States as well as in 47 other countries in the developing world to help children and families improve their health, education and economic opportunities" (Save the Children).

Save the Children is a member of the International Save the Children Alliance, an association of 26 independent organizations that provide child-oriented emergency response, development assistance, and advocacy of children's rights in more than 100 countries. For information on international volunteer opportunities contact:

Save the Children
54 Wilton Road
Westport, CT 06880
Telephone: 203-221-4000
E-mail: info@savechildren.org
Website: www.savethechildren.org

UNITED NATIONS VOLUNTEERS (UNV)

The United Nations Volunteers program was founded in 1970 by the United Nations General Assembly. Since then, this unique multilateral program has attracted the service of some 30,000 highly motivated men and women worldwide as part of its work to promote global volunteerism.

Rendering assistance to developing nations, UNV places emphasis on cooperation with community-based initiatives. UN Volunteers are closely involved in the communities they serve, working in direct contact with the people. In 2001, there were more than 5,400 UN Volunteer assignments. Together the UN Volunteers represented 159 nationalities and worked in 140 countries. For tens of millions of people around the world, volunteering is an expression of support for a principle that strikes to the heart of the United Nations system: that by working together, we can make the world a better place for everyone.

"The United Nations Volunteers programme is the UN organization that supports human development globally by promoting volunteerism and by mobilizing volunteers ... and operates amidst growing recognition that volunteerism makes important contributions, economically and socially, to more cohesive societies by building trust and reciprocity among citizens" (United Nations Volunteers).

The UNV web page—www.worldvolunteerweb.org/dynamic/cfapps national_profiles/index.htm—provides a wealth of volunteer content organized by region: the Americas, Europe, Africa, Asia, and Oceania. Clicking on a region will yield a list of all countries in that region. Clicking on the link for each country will bring up a list of volunteer agencies in that nation.

For further information on the UNV volunteer programs, go to the UNV websites: www.unv.org, or www.worldvolunteerweb.org. You can explore volunteer options with UNV on their web page: www.unv.org/volunteers/options/ index.htm. These options include organizations in your own country, abroad, or virtual volunteering. Here you will find information about how to apply with UNV.

Voluntary Service Overseas (VSO)

VSO is by far the largest independent agency in the world providing international volunteers. Since 1958, VSO has sent out more than 29,000 volunteers to work in Africa, Asia, the Caribbean, the Pacific region and, more recently, Eastern Europe.

"VSO is an international development charity that works through volunteers. Our vision is a world without poverty in which people work together to fulfill their potential. We bring people together to share skills, creativity and learning to build a fairer world. VSO welcomes volunteers from an ever increasing range of countries, backgrounds and ages. National agencies in Canada, Kenya, the Netherlands and the Philippines recruit volunteers from many different countries worldwide and this international approach allows us to combine and learn from a rich variety of perspectives" (Voluntary Service Overseas).

If you would like to share your knowledge, experience and skills, wish to broaden your horizons and make new friends while thriving in a different culture, you may have what it takes to be a VSO volunteer. You can learn more about VSO and volunteering with the organization by visiting: www.vso.org.uk/volunteering/index.htm.

Volunteer Canada

"Canada's Source For Information on Volunteering." The Canadian voluntary and nonprofit sector is made up of more than 180,000 organizations, 6.5 million volunteers and 1.3 million paid staff. On this extensive website, you can find general information about volunteerism in Canada, a directory of organizations, volunteer centers, national organizations, and provincial organizations in Canada, older adult volunteerism, virtual volunteering, and the benefits of volunteering. To explore the many resources for volunteerism in Canada, go to: www.volunteer.ca/index-eng.php.

WorldTeach

WorldTeach is a non-profit, non-governmental organization, based at the Center for International Development at Harvard University, which provides opportunities for individuals to make a meaningful contribution to international education by living and working as volunteer teachers in developing countries. The organization was founded by a group of Harvard students in 1986, in response to the need for educational assistance in developing countries. It also addressed a growing interest among people in the U.S. and elsewhere to serve, teach and learn as volunteers overseas.

Since its inception, WorldTeach has placed thousands of volunteer educators in communities throughout Africa, Asia, Eastern Europe, and Latin America. They work in a variety of settings. No prior teaching or foreign language experience is required; WorldTeach provides extensive teaching and language training in-country. To learn more about their program requirements go to their web page at: www.worldteach.org/requirements.html.

WorldTeach advises: "Although we do not have specific professional requirements, we seek applicants who show a commitment to teaching, international development, public service and cultural understanding. The most successful volunteers possess a high level of enthusiasm, flexibility, commitment and dedication to the communities in which they are placed." To review their rather formidable application process, go to their web page at: www.worldteach.org/applications.html.

WORLD WIDE VOLUNTEER

For the volunteer interested primarily in international opportunities, a suggested starting place would be World Wide Volunteer. Their website offers an extensive online library of information resources, including links to several international volunteer organizations and opportunities. Several of these organizations are discussed in this section. To search for volunteer opportunities worldwide, go to their website. The site has an easy-to-use search engine; it can be found at: www.worldwidevolunteer.org. From the list of eight categories, select "Volunteer Organizations." Should you like to make a more specific search, enter a keyword(s).

10. Clearinghouses

"He who does nothing for others does nothing for himself."

—Goethe

Opportunities Everywhere

Many of the organizations we have discussed in previous sections, e.g., The Peace Corps and VISTA, also serve as clearinghouses for volunteers. There are a number of organizations that act primarily as such to coordinate recruitment and volunteer assignments for both national and international organizations. The following represent the principal entities.

Charity Village

Charity Village proclaims that it is "Canada's supersite for the nonprofit sector—3,000 pages of news, jobs, information and resources for executives, staffers, donors, and volunteers. If philanthropy and volunteerism are part of your world, this is your place." Those interested in volunteer opportunities in Canada can go to: www.charityvillage.com/applicant/volunteer.asp?fn=searchform. The Charity Village home page can be found at: www.charityvillage.com. Volunteer Canada, discussed in a following entry, is another resource for volunteerism in Canada.

Idealist (Action Without Borders)

Action Without Borders, Inc., is the name of the nonprofit organization that maintains the Idealist web site. They state: "Action Without Borders connects people, organizations and resources to help build a world where all people can live free and dignified lives."

To find volunteer opportunities, go to the Advanced Searches (located in the sidebar on the right side of the Idealist home page (www.idealist.org), and click on "Volunteer Opportunities." The advanced search screen you will derive allows you to pinpoint a volunteer position by country, state, city, area of focus, keyword, skills needed, languages needed, time availability, or any combination of these.

THE NATIONAL RETIREE VOLUNTEER COALITION (NRVC)

A program of the Volunteers of America, "NRVC offers consultation, program development and training to corporations, universities, healthcare systems, governmental institutions and any other employer interested in innovative, expansive retiree volunteer programs" (National Retiree Volunteer Coalition).

Working with private companies, universities, and local governments, the NRVC has established a wide variety of volunteer programs across the country. For additional information, contact:

The National Retiree Volunteer Coalition
1660 Duke Street
Alexandria, VA 22314
Website: www.voa.org

NETWORK FOR GOOD (VOLUNTEERMATCH)

"Network for Good is a nonprofit organization dedicated to using the Web to help people get more involved in their communities—from volunteering and donating money, to speaking out on issues you care about" (Network for Good). Network for Good helps you find a volunteer opportunity that's right for you. You can "connect with a cause." To find a volunteer opportunity, go to the web page: www.networkforgood.org/volunteer/. Using the search tool on the sidebar on the left of the web page, you can find volunteer opportunities that match your interests and geographic location, or search for an organization by name. (The search is powered by VolunteerMatch.)

To search for opportunities for older volunteers:

• Indicate your area of interest—domestic or international.
• Enter your zip code.
• Select the distance you are willing to travel—from 5 miles to statewide; (there is also an international option and a "Virtual" option).
• Indicate your area of interest; these include: Everything; animals and the environment; civic and community; education and research;health and human services religion; and international."
• Select the option "Seniors Welcome."
• Click "Search."

The search will yield all volunteer opportunities that meet the criteria you have entered. Once you locate a volunteer opportunity you like, simply click the hyperlink "I Like This Opportunity" and enter the information requested for each selection. The organization you have selected will contact you directly to provide details about the volunteer opportunity in which you have shown an interest. It's that easy! To explore the wealth of information on the Network for Good website, go to their home page: www.networkforgood.org.

NON-PROFIT CAREER NETWORK: VOLUNTEER SECTION

The website of the Non-Profit Career Network states:

> To begin to solve the nation's poverty and troubled cities, we can't just give the needy a place to live or money for food. We know that this would not be a solution. A true solution is to give all people hope, dreams, and dignity. People from every walk of life can help. From every class, every nationality, every religion—we ALL can be and NEED to be a part of the solution. Many people have already begun; many organizations are bringing people together to work on solutions for a large number of different problems. But they cannot do it alone—they need EVERYBODY. The feeling you will receive from a helping experience will far outweigh any monetary reward on earth. Each one of us has something to offer, but it is up to you to get involved. You will never be sorry you did.

A list of links to more than 100 non-profit organizations around the U.S. that need volunteers is included. Simply scroll down the list and click on the name of the organization's name that might be of special interest to you. The web page can be found at: www.nonprofitcareer.com/volunteer/volunteer.htm.

POINTS OF LIGHT FOUNDATION

The Foundation, in partnership with the Volunteer Center National Network, seeks to engage more people more effectively in volunteer service. "Due to a dramatic increase in the number of 'older adults' today, we recognize the importance of effectively engaging these adults in volunteer service to help address serious community issues. These are more experienced volunteers who can make a meaningful and significant impact on their communities" (Points of Light Foundation).

Based in Washington, D.C., the Foundation works in communities throughout the U.S. to promote volunteering and community service through its network of more than 500 volunteer centers. The partnership coordinates nationwide activities to provide citizens with volunteer opportunities and resources, and reaches millions of people in thousands of communities to help recruit, train, deploy, and monitor volunteers to deliver solutions that address community problems. Through a variety of programs and services, the partnership encourages people from all walks of life—youth, and older adults—to volunteer.

In addition to the many volunteer opportunities open to older persons through federal programs, community level agencies and organizations welcome the talents of the elderly. Many communities have Volunteer Centers that offer information about the types of volunteer opportunities available and the agencies and organizations that are seeking assistance. Volunteer Centers refer an estimated 800,000 new volunteers each year who assist a wide variety of community organizations, providing services to such populations as the elderly, youth, people with AIDS, and the homeless. 1-800-VOLUNTEER.org provides volunteers with a direct connection to local opportunities that match interests, skills, and the common desire to "make a difference." It has gained a national reputation as "America's Address for Volunteering."

To locate the Volunteer Center in your community, go to the Points of Light home page: www.pointsoflight.org. Scroll down to the hyperlink "Find Your Local Volunteer Center" and enter your zip code, or search by state. You can also go to the website of Volunteer Center National Network at: www.1-800-volunteer.org/index.jsp. Click on the link at the top of the page: "Find a Volunteer Center" and enter the data requested. For additional information contact:

Points of Light Foundation
1400 I Street, NW, Suite 800
Washington, DC 20005
Telephone: 800-750-7653
E-mail: info@pointsoflight.org
Website: www.pointsoflight.org

USA Freedom Corps Volunteer Network

"The USA Freedom Corps Volunteer Network is the most comprehensive clearinghouse of volunteer opportunities ever available. For the first time in history, Americans can enter geographic information about where they want to get involved ... and areas of interest ranging from education to the environment, to access volunteer opportunities offered by a range of partner organizations across the country or around the world" (USA Freedom Corps).

To find volunteer opportunities go to the web page at: www.usafreedomcorps.gov/for_volunteers/index.asp. Enter demographic information, such as zip code or state, and your area of interest—select from the list or type in an issue, organization, or a specific category—so you can access service opportunities near your home or office, across the country or overseas. (There are advanced options also.) Click on "Find Opportunities Now." Results will be returned in six groupings:

• One-time events for those with limited time
• Ongoing programs such as tutoring or mentoring
• Full-time service such as Teach For America or programs through AmeriCorps
	• Volunteer networks such as Points of Light or United Way agencies
	• International service opportunities such as Peace Corps
	• Volunteer opportunities you can do from your home or computer (virtual volunteering).

VOLUNTEER.GOV/GOV/

Volunteer.Gov/Gov/ consolidates volunteer opportunities available in the public sector. This online service lets prospective volunteers match their interests and abilities with available opportunities nationwide through searches based on activity, location of opportunity, effective date of the opportunity, the sponsoring partner, and by keyword search. In the future, Volunteer.Gov/Gov will expand to include other channels for volunteer service to all levels of government.

"A Proud Partner of the USA Freedom Corps Network. We are building communities of service and need the help of people like you—the fundamental builders of civil society—volunteers! We extend an invitation for you to enter this one-stop portal with access to public sector volunteer positions that fit your skills and interests. Even if you are not initially successful in finding the right opportunity—do visit us again to explore the wide variety of publicly sponsored opportunities to serve—some right next door and others across the land" (Volunteer.Gov). For more information or to search for volunteer opportunities, go to: www.volunteer.gov/gov/. (If you enter only www.volunteer.gov, you will go to the USA Freedom Corps website.)

VOLUNTEERAMERICA

VolunteerAmerica connects individuals, families and groups with volunteer opportunities and volunteer vacations on public lands all across America. These include national forests, national parks, state parks, and national wildlife refuges. Opportunities exist among all public land management agencies as well as with nonprofit organizations that provide services on public lands.

"Volunteer programs have something for almost everyone—retirees, professionals, homemakers, students and young people, as well as service clubs and organizations. If you like people and care about our country's natural resources, then public agencies and service organizations need your time and talents.... Retirees or others with skills to share often find that a volunteer position provides them with a nice change of pace" (VolunteerAmerica, website).

Depending on the nature of the volunteer project and the availability of funds, some volunteer positions provide items such as housing, a uniform, a subsistence allowance, and work related transportation.

To search for volunteer opportunities, go to the VolunteerAmerica website. In the upper left corner of the home page—"Select a State"—enter the state you are interested in; click "Submit." The results will include listings for the several categories noted above. Be advised that you may not receive a listing for every state and also that most of the links on the left sidebar appear to be dead. For further information, contact:

VolunteerAmerica
P.O. Box 847
Minden, NV 89423
E-mail: volunteer@volunteeramerica.net
Website: www.volunteeramerica.net

VOLUNTEERMATCH

Describing VolunteerMatch, Cheryl Asmus says: "Too often, volunteer opportunities and activities are not well known to older people in a community. The Internet carries a Web site, called VolunteerMatch, which helps individuals find volunteer opportunities posted by organizations. This free site allows prospective volunteers to search thousands of one-time and ongoing opportunities by zip code, city, category and date. Volunteer sign-up is automatic with e-mail" (Asmus, "Volunteering When Retired," 2001).

VolunteerMatch—motto, "Get out. Do good"—is the nonprofit, online service that matches prospective volunteers with service opportunities in their communities and links to community service organizations throughout the United States. VolunteerMatch posts listings of national volunteer opportunities that can be viewed by state, agency, or type of service. Their lists include nearly 30,000 volunteer opportunities, and present direct links to service opportunities at more than 26,000 large national organizations. Links for virtual volunteering are also included.

You can search for a volunteer opportunity based on where you live and the type of organization you're interested in helping. Go to the VolunteerMatch home page: www.volunteermatch.org; enter your ZIP code; refine your search by the distance you can travel, by category/interest, by keyword, and by volunteer age (click on the hyperlink "Great for Seniors"). Click on "Search." Your search results will automatically be sorted by date, but you can re-sort the list at any time by changing the search criteria. Look in "Help" (www.volunteermatch.org/help/volunteer.jsp) for more detailed information about searching and search results, and creating a "Personalized Volunteer Account."

11. Virtual Volunteering

"People don't care how much you know, unless they know how much you care."

—ANONYMOUS

The Brave New World of Volunteerism

The World Wide Web has given impetus to a whole new form of volunteering—"virtual" volunteering. Virtual volunteering? Yes, there is such a thing. It is just one of the many profound affects Internet technology and the electronic age has had on our society and changed it in ways that could not have been imagined just two or three decades ago. The ability to communicate instantly online anywhere in the world has created a truly innovative and unique opportunity to serve others—anywhere in the world. The volunteers are real persons; the real service they provide is done electronically. Virtual volunteering allows anyone with Internet access to contribute time and expertise in innumerable ways.

Also known as online volunteering, cyberservice, cybervolunteering, telementoring, teletutoring, and by various other names, virtual volunteering allows organizations and agencies to expand the benefits of their volunteer programs by allowing more individuals to participate and by utilizing these volunteers in many new areas. Virtual volunteering is giving cyberspace a heart, and giving true meaning to the concept of online communities. "Volunteering is a social phenomenon, and has always been an instrument of social cohesion and inclusion, and a key contributor to building social capital. As such, it must be considered both within its specific context and the framework of individual societies where it is carried out. The Information Society does not represent an exception to this rule" (World Wide Volunteer, "Volunteerism & ICTs," 2001).

156

Not only are organizations all over the world taking full advantage of their websites by recruiting volunteers and listing opportunities, they have become clearinghouses for anyone who wants to lend a virtual hand. The current estimate of nearly 700 million worldwide Internet users is expected to rise to more than one billion by the end of 2005. This represents an ever-growing pool of WWW users who may embrace this new way of volunteering. "[T]he Internet has forever changed the face of volunteering by enabling an unprecedented opportunity for volunteers from around the globe and nonprofits to come together to do good" (Tyler, "E-Volunteering," 2003).

Virtual volunteering will never replace the traditional concept of "in person" volunteering; it is not a substitute for direct human contact. However, scores of volunteers are helping individuals and organizations anywhere in the world simply by communicating over the Internet; by volunteering from home or from "virtually" any remote location simply by using a computer and the WWW to donate time and expertise to nonprofit organizations, schools, government agencies, and other entities that utilize volunteer services.

What the innovative use of technology has done has been to augment the quantity and quality of such service and attract individuals who, for various reasons, might not have otherwise been able to participate. Rather, virtual volunteering presents enhanced access to community, national, and international resources and provides an increased number of ways for individuals to support such services, and the agencies that provide them. For some, service online will be the preferred way of volunteering; for others, it will be an additional way of contributing their time and talents.

Many persons now actively search for volunteer opportunities they can complete via their home or office computers. The primary purpose of this book is to assist them in their search. This sort of volunteering might be well-suited to you if you have personal preferences, family or social obligations, limited time, no transportation to a distant site, or a physical disability which precludes you from getting about freely and traveling to, and volunteering, at a site. Virtual volunteering offers these persons many flexible options and eliminates many of the barriers that might have prevented them from past participation. Such barriers as conflicting work schedules, transportation accessibility, and time and distance need no longer be impediments.

Virtual volunteering has emphasized recruiting disabled volunteers to assist others in need. On its website, VolunteerMatch notes that "the 49 million disabled Americans are an untapped resource.... People with disabilities volunteer for the same reasons as anyone else: they want to contribute their time and energy to improving the quality of life. They want challenging, rewarding service projects that address the needs of a community" (VolunteerMatch).

The Virtual Volunteering Project was launched in 1996 to encourage and assist in the development of volunteer activities that can be completed off-site via the Internet. It quickly went from a cutting-edge idea to a nationally recognized resource and is an excellent place for the prospective virtual volunteer to start. The Project's website can be found at: www.serviceleader.org/old/vv/vvabout.html.

What Is "Virtual Volunteering?"

Virtual volunteering refers to those activities which individuals conduct on their own, or on behalf of host agencies, in whole or in part, utilizing a computer and the Internet. If you have a computer, or convenient access to one, and the *fundamental* skills—you do not have to be a "senior cybergeek"—you can become a virtual volunteer. If you do not have a computer or Internet access at home, many local libraries and community centers—including a growing number of senior centers—as well as virtually all colleges and universities provide access to the World Wide Web.

Virtual volunteering is similar to telecommuting; however, instead of being online employees, participants are online volunteers who are utilized by many organizations to supplement their on-site programs. Virtual volunteering does not mean that volunteers work exclusively via the Internet. Many programs find that a combination of on-site and online tasks for volunteers works to their mutual advantage and for the maximum benefit of the clients they serve.

The concept of individuals volunteering without being physically present at the host organization's work site is not new. Telephone and mail contacts have been used by home-based volunteers for many years to help with fundraising and other activities. The advent of the revolutionary advances in information and communications technology has, however, introduced an expanded version of this type of volunteering that has come to be known as virtual volunteering. Although Internet-assisted volunteering has existed since the mid–90s, easily accessible systems to support it have been widely available only since around 2000.

Benefits for Virtual Volunteers

There are many benefits to be derived by those who volunteer online. There is usually more flexibility in the use of their time, and a greater degree of independence in utilizing it. They can derive an understanding of the many issues and challenges that face communities in America and those of populations of developing nations. They can reap the personal rewards of a lifetime of skills, experience, and education by sharing them with others. They can assume new roles and responsibilities in new opportunities. Virtual volunteering is another way for people from various walks of life, all over the nation and the world, to connect with each other and be part of the Global Village. Online volunteers can make a world of difference—literally!

In an undated online article in which he reports the results of linking two generations over the Internet, Martin Kimeldorf says:

> As the gap widens between young and old America, we will find ourselves contending with either generational conflict or reaping the benefits of inter-generational communion. Volunteer program managers who creatively address this looming social challenge will help make the 21st century a more hospitable epoch. Luckily, tentacles of the Internet reach into every nook and cranny of our society, including schools and nursing homes. E-mail has become an everyday exchange. We can now easily use this electronic web to connect people across time and space, and also across generations.... In this fashion, we leap over the traditional hurdles most intergenerational programs face [Kimeldorf, "Wiring Friendships Across Time, Space, and Age"].

Benefits for Organizations

As we have noted, virtual volunteering is off-site volunteering, completed via the WWW. This type of volunteering enables organizations to reach volunteers who may prefer to work on their computers from their homes or offices, and allows the agencies to benefit from the additional talent and resources of a larger pool of volunteers. It allows the participation of persons who might find on-site volunteering difficult or impossible because of a disability, mobility issue, home obligation, or work schedule. Volunteering online allows individuals an opportunity to contribute, according to their own schedules, and participate in a growing community of virtual volunteers. The concept offers organizations the opportunity to include volunteers of all abilities in their programs of client service.

Most organizations that utilize on-site volunteers actively solicit and utilize online volunteers also; relatively few of these function solely via the Internet. Often a combination of on-site and online assignments for volunteers works to the best advantage for everyone involved—volunteers, staff, and clients.

The Assignments of an Online Volunteer

As might be expected, virtual volunteering—which by definition depends on the use of computers and the Internet—focuses on Internet and computer-related skills—basic to advanced. However, there are many roles and opportunities for the virtual volunteer with varying levels of computer skills. The retiree or senior need not be an expert; a basic understanding will usually suffice.

The Virtual Volunteering Project at the University of Texas encourages volunteer activities that can be delivered over the Web. Among other features, their website, (www.ServiceLeader.org) includes information for involving people with disabilities in online volunteering; the site's index allows users to find organizations in their own area that might be of interest. Virtual volunteer assignments can have different levels of "virtuality." The project has defined two categories of online volunteering: technical assistance, and direct contact with clients.

TECHNICAL ASSISTANCE

Technical assistance assignments utilize the expertise of volunteers to support paid staff or other volunteers. Here are just a few examples of what a virtual volunteer can do to provide technical assistance:

- Accounting or bookkeeping.
- Assist in the organization's advocacy efforts.
- Computer programming.
- Conduct online research for information relating to the organization and its mission.
- Conduct surveys.
- Data entry, management, and analysis.
- Design and edit an agency's publications and website.
- Design and manage databases.
- Grant and proposal writing.
- Office support activities including administrative and clerical, including word processing.
- Provide professional consulting expertise.
- Technology support.
- Translation.
- Website design and development. (Those with an interest and basic skills in this area are referred to the discussion of InterConnnection.)
- Writing, authoring, or editing agency publications; design and production, including graphics.

DIRECT CLIENT CONTACT

Most organizations realize the potential of involving volunteers in virtual technical assistance. However, a more challenging task presents itself in the creation of direct client links between a virtual volunteer and a recipient of services that might include:

• Clerical support for a person with a disability, e.g., typing forms, letters.
• Communications—newsletters, e-mail—to clients.
• Create online distance learning opportunities for other volunteers and/or clients.
• Online "visitations" with someone of any age who is homebound, a patient in a hospital or hospice, a resident of a nursing home, or a prisoner. These can be done as an adjunct to on-site, in-person visits by volunteers. These could also include follow-up contacts.
• Participate with other volunteers and/or clients in identifying needed services; initiating and maintaining those services.
• Provide online mentoring and tutoring via e-mail or instant messaging. Recipients might include students, adult learners, or the incarcerated.
• Respond to e-mail or telephone inquiries—including support hotlines. Provide advice or instructions under agency protocols.
• Supervise or moderate an agency-sponsored online chat room or newsgroup.
• Supervise any of the above activities via the Internet and provide guidance, or request staff guidance, as necessary. (Source: Ellis and Cravens, *The Virtual Volunteering Guidebook.*)

Recruiting and Utilizing Virtual Volunteers

There are a number of reasons to involve volunteers via online technologies, as well as to use the Internet for recruitment of on-site volunteers:

• Potential volunteers who may not be readily reached by traditional off-line means—mailings, telephone—may be reached online. Individuals who may not see volunteer opportunities advertised in newspapers or on bulletin boards, but who would be willing to volunteer, may be more easily reached online.
• Individuals who prefer not to volunteer on-site may be willing to do so via their own computers at home or at their office.
• Presenting requirements and options to prospective volunteers online allows them to assess the organization and their own credentials and interests before initiating a contact with an agency.
• An online inquiry may be preferable to many prospective volunteers who may find it more convenient than writing a letter or sending an e-mail, making a telephone call; or a personal visit.

"Online volunteering provides organizations with new volunteers, new and additional talent and skills, and a more diverse volunteer-base. It also helps promote organizations and their mission to a much broader audience" (Net Aid). For those organizations working with developing countries, virtual volunteers provide a vital resource. They are able to connect with, and utilize, a diverse multitude of individuals from all around the globe—persons who might never be able to leave their homes, families, or jobs to travel abroad to these nations, yet who still want to contribute their efforts to make a difference.

Online volunteers can provide the skills and expertise that agencies and organizations may not have ready access to and which they may desperately need to supplement the efforts of their volunteers in the field. The result is that they can utilize the additional talents and resources of more volunteers to apply their own efforts and resources more effectively in serving a greater number of recipients.

Virtual volunteer opportunities can include virtually any other services that can be done through computer networks. A recent study by Canadian researchers Vic Murray and Yvonne Harrison suggests that many more kinds of volunteer tasks could be reorganized to accommodate virtual volunteers (Murray and Harrison, "Virtual Volunteering," 2002).

Are You Ready to Be a Virtual Volunteer?

Virtual volunteering can sound so easy that individuals frequently sign up for assignments before considering the degree of time and commitment that will be expected of them by the organization recruiting them. It has become so convenient to commit to volunteering via the Internet that many individuals readily do so before adequately considering their actions and their implications. They fail to explore their expectations and what will be expected of them.

Be advised that there is nothing virtual about the commitment you are making, nor the deadlines you will be assigned. The organizations with which you may become affiliated will be relying on you to do your best to complete all assignments efficiently, completely, and in a timely manner. Their obligations become your obligations. The decision may be far more easy than the reality.

What You Will Need to Become a Virtual Volunteer

Anyone who has the time and the desire to contribute; regular, reliable access to a computer and the Internet; and the skills and experience that would be of value to a volunteer hosting organization is an ideal candidate for virtual volunteering. As you can see, the requirements to become a virtual volunteer are minimal: a computer, an Internet connection, an e-mail account, word-processing software, and a repertoire of basic computer knowledge and skills—and dedication!

Questions to Consider Before You Become a Virtual Volunteer

A key to success and mutual satisfaction in virtual volunteering lies in choosing the organizations and the assignments that are appropriate to the volunteer's skills, interests, and availability. All prospective volunteers—virtual or otherwise—should carefully explore their motives and identify their expectations before they make a commitment. It is quite easy to sign up to become a virtual volunteer and accept an assignment, but you must assure yourself that you will be able to complete it to your, and your host organization's, satisfaction. You may be willing, but there are a number of questions to consider to determine if you are able and ready, and if the experience is right for you. Your answers to these questions may also guide you in your final decision.

- Why do you want to volunteer? What motivates you?
- What can you bring to the experience? What can you give? What benefits could an organization derive from your efforts?
- What types of services and assistance would you like to provide?
- What kind of organizations or programs would you like to help?
- How many organizations or programs could you feasibly commit to?
- Do you want to volunteer for something that uses the skills and experience you may have presently, or are you willing to attempt something completely new and different? Are you willing to learn?
- What are your skills? What do you do best? What do you like to do? These can be professional skills, hobbies or any other talents. Virtually every skill is needed by someone, somewhere. Take an honest inventory.
- Do you have the *basic* computer skills that will be required? If not, are you willing to learn? (For the "newbies" or those who, may wish to improve their skills, a number of online computer/Internet tutorials are listed in Appendix 3.)
- Do you have dependable Internet access? (A must!)
- Most, if not all, of your communications during a virtual assignment will be via e-mail. Are you proficient in its use?
- Is the computer system, software, and all peripheral hardware you will be using adequate to meet your needs?

- Would it be necessary to purchase any new hardware or software? Can you afford it?
- Are you sure you are capable of producing high-quality results?
- Do you have the required writing skills; can you communicate well?
- Are you self-motivated?
- Are you prompt and reliable?
- Will you be reasonably accessible?
- What is your availability for assignments? Do you prefer to work during a particular time of day? For a certain number of days, weeks, or months?
- Will you have the time to complete each assignment? (These typically last around three months.)
- Do you have a mind for details?
- Are you an organized person?
- Can you manage your time; are you able to set your own schedule?
- Can you manage your priorities?
- Do you occasionally over-extend yourself?
- Can you meet deadlines? (Your assignments may be virtual, but your deadlines will not be.)
- Will you be able to see an assignment through to completion? (An organization cannot be left with unfinished assignments and unmet needs.)
- Do you have a desire to learn and a willingness to be flexible about new ideas and methods?
- Will you be able and willing to accept the priorities and goals of the host agency in undertaking each assignment? Are you a "team player?"
- Can you work effectively without direct supervision? (Virtual assignments are best suited to those individuals who enjoy working on their own, with ready access to consultation as needed, or occasional supervision.)
- Do you expect regular praise and encouragement for your efforts? (Many organizations still need work in this area.)
- Is this the proper time for you to take on a volunteering project?
- Are you convinced that you can allocate sufficient time and effort for the undertaking? (If you are feeling overwhelmed by other responsibilities, it may not be a good time to volunteer, on- or offline. You may wish to defer you decision.)
- If you have volunteered in the past, on- or offline, what did you like and dislike about those experiences? Were you satisfied? Were your efforts effective?
- What benefits do you hope to derive from your efforts? What are your personal expectations? What do you hope to gain?
- Do you have a clear definition of what you expect from the experience?
- Do you have a clear definition of what will be expected of you?
- What would you NOT want to do as a volunteer?

Answering these questions may help you make a final decision to volunteer and to identify the assignments most suitable for you. If you have answered "no" to any of the above questions, or have some difficulty or uncertainty answering some of them, perhaps you are not quite ready to become a virtual volunteer. After considering both the time and skills you could bring to the endeavor, will you be able to satisfy the needs of the host organization in an effective way? If you believe you cannot, you may be more hindrance than help. It is essential that you be honest in your self-appraisal—for your sake and theirs, and ultimately for those desperate unknowns who could benefit from your efforts.

The Future of Virtual Volunteering

Susan Ellis, president of Energize Inc., says "One of the unique characteristics of [virtual] volunteers has always been that they are private citizens and, as such, can cross official jurisdiction boundaries and even national borders in ways that paid representatives of organizations and governments cannot.... . [T]his freedom allows activists to work together regardless of formal diplomatic ties, on every conceivable cause, whether environmental issues, AIDS, or the digital divide. The Internet or, more specifically, the World Wide Web, has provided citizen activists with a powerful and relatively inexpensive tool beyond anyone's expectations as little as a decade ago." Ellis goes on to say, "The Web is human-made and therefore has as much potential for destruction as for construction. Hate sites, calls to violence and terrorism, purposeful misinformation, and exploitation of the vulnerable are all in abundance online. Ironically, volunteers are supporters of some of these, too, since volunteering is a methodology to get something done, and therefore is adopted by all sides of a cause. Volunteers have been building the Web while other volunteers have used it as a tool to further their causes. Commercial interests, especially pornography and shopping for bargains, exist side-by-side with civic involvement. It's a fascinating mix-and who knows what will come next?" (Ellis, "Online Power for Volunteer Action," 2003).

It appears that while the potential for virtual volunteering might be great, it has not yet become a common feature of volunteering. That is changing. As a result of the gradually increasing pressures on volunteer supply and demand, the concept of virtual volunteering is becoming more attractive, allowing whole new groups of potential volunteers to do so. With a computer and an Internet connection, you can now help your favorite cause—without leaving home. You can stay put and do good—in your pajamas!

Organizations That Need Virtual Volunteers

AARP

"See what you can do from virtually anywhere! The Virtual Section [of the AARP website] showcases opportunities that let you volunteer without having to be physically present at a specific location. That usually means volunteering using a computer, Internet connection, phone, and/or fax" (AARP). The AARP link—aarp.volunteermatch.org/aarp/index.html—will take you to VolunteerMatch.

INTERCONNECTION

InterConnection supports many non-profit and non-governmental organizations in developing countries. That support is in the form of its website assistance program, which provides these organizations with high quality, affordable Internet services, primarily website development, at no cost or low cost.

InterConnection's Virtual Volunteer Program matches web-savvy volunteers from all over the world with non-profit organizations in developing countries who need assistance in creating individualized, professional websites. Volunteers need not be technical experts.

"The accessibility of this innovative program is the key to its tremendous success. Since all of the volunteers' work is done online, it provides an opportunity for them to help developing communities without leaving home. By capitalizing on the skills and charity of volunteers with tech experience, the Virtual Volunteer program provides both a rewarding experience and a service that is in great demand by non-profits" (InterConnection).

If you have the degree of computer skills described on the InterConnection website, you can apply online to become a virtual volunteer. Browse their "Virtual Volunteer Project Board" to identify a project that matches your skill level and interests. Complete and submit the online application. If your application is accepted, InterConnection will e-mail you the project's contact information. It is the volunteer's responsibility to make the initial contact. This must be done before a website design assignment can be made. All donated websites become the property of the recipient organization. For complete information on the program, go to the InterConnection website: www.interconnection.org.

NETAID

NetAid is a joint initiative of the United Nations Development Program (UNDP) and Cisco Systems. The United Nations Volunteers Program (UNV) provides and manages the online volunteering section of NetAid. The NetAid website has links to a great deal of information on what online volunteering entails, how you can determine if you are ready to volunteer online, and a searchable database of organizations and opportunities. If you are interested in being an online volunteer, to help an agency that supports humanitarian efforts in developing countries, NetAid should be your first stop.

On the NetAid website, you can search for online volunteering opportunities in two ways: by the kinds of assignments available; or, by the nature of the work done by the organization. (Whichever way you choose, you are advised to review your answers to the questions presented in the preceding discussion when selecting an assignment.)

You may find it necessary to do several different kinds of searches, narrowing or expanding your search criteria (skills, interests, and availability) a number of times so that you can find a range of opportunities of interest to you. There are thousands of organizations on NetAid, representing many, many different geographic areas and types of assignments. New organizations and opportunities are added daily. To conduct a search, register, and submit an online application form, go to the NetAid web page for volunteers: www.netaid.org/ov/volunteers/volunteer_4.pt, and follow the instructions.

The information you submit is sent directly to the organization that posted the volunteering opportunity. NetAid does not review applications by volunteers, and you are advised that submission of an application does not guarantee that you will be considered or placed as an online volunteer. The volunteer web page will advise you what to do in this event.

SENIORNET

SeniorNet is a national nonprofit organization that provides adults 50 and older access to and education about computer technology and the Internet. The program involves many volunteer "CyberHosts" and discussion/community leaders. It has also established learning centers throughout the country that could help older people become proficient on the computer and eventually become virtual volunteers. To learn more about volunteer opportunities with SeniorNet, go to their website: www.seniornet.org.

SERVICE CORPS OF RETIRED EXECUTIVES (SCORE)

A resource partner with the U.S. Small Business Administration, dedicated to aiding in the formation, growth and success of small business nationwide, SCORE offers e-mail counseling at no cost (for U.S. citizens and resident aliens only). Its huge searchable databank helps users find the SCORE member whose expertise best addresses their business needs. The expertise of members is highly varied and specialized. The SCORE website also has a database for finding local SCORE affiliates and information on becoming a volunteer member; this can be found at: www.score.org.

UNITED NATIONS VOLUNTEERS (UNV)

On May 17, 2004, in Bonn Germany, UNV honored ten individuals from different countries as outstanding "Online Volunteers of the Year" for their exceptional contributions to non-governmental organizations in developing countries. The honorees served in a variety of ways—editing and publishing a newsletter, helping people with disabilities, and translating resource materials. UNV affirmed: "Online volunteers can make a difference from their computers at home, work, university or community technology centres."

The Online Volunteers of the Year are just ten of the more than 15,000 people who have signed up with UNV's Online Volunteer service since its launch in 2000. Volunteers using this service have helped more than 400 organizations working in 60 countries. To learn more go to the UNV website: www.unv.org/volunteers/.

USA FREEDOM CORPS

USA Freedom Corps has been discussed in detail in a previous section. To learn more about online volunteering opportunities, go to the USA Freedom Corps web page "Find Volunteer Opportunities" at : www.usafreedomcorps.gov/for_volunteers/find_opps.asp. After you have provided the necessary information, click on the option at the bottom of the page: "From Home (Virtual)." Go to step 3, click on the link "Find Opportunities Now." Your results will depend on the search criteria you have defined.

VOLUNTEERMATCH (IMPACT ONLINE)

The VolunteerMatch virtual volunteer website—www.volunteermatch.org/virtual/—allows nonprofit organizations to post their volunteer opportunities online, which potential volunteers can then search by zip code and type of assignment, in an array of categories. Each category listed is a hyperlink which also notes the current number of volunteer opportunities posted on the linked page. To search for virtual volunteer opportunities, click on your preferred category. The VolunteerMatch categories include:

- Advocacy and Human Rights
- Animals
- Arts and Culture
- Children and Youth
- Community (Discussed in the "National" section.)
- Computers and Technology
- Crisis Support
- Disabled
- Education and Literacy
- Emergency and Safety
- Employment
- Environment
- Gay, Lesbian, Bisexual
- Health and Medicine
- Homeless and Housing

- Hunger
- Immigrants and Refugees
- International
- Justice and Legal
- Media and Broadcasting
- Politics

- Race and Ethnicity
- Religion
- Seniors
- Sports and Recreation
- Women
- Uncategorized

PART IV

Appendices

1. A Profile of Older Americans: 2003

This appendix excerpts a publication of the U.S. government's Administration on Aging. Pages 4, 5, 7, 8, and 10 through 15 of this document have been omitted from this appendix. Much of the material that has been excluded is not directly relevant to the topic of the book. Should the reader wish to review the text of the omitted pages, the full report can be downloaded from the URL shown in the sources listed at the back of this book.

*Highlights**

- The older population (65+) numbered 35.6 million in 2002, an increase of 3.3 million or 10.2% since 1992.
- The number of Americans aged 45–64—who will reach 65 over the next two decades—increased by 38% during this decade.
- About one in every eight, or 12.3 percent, of the population is an older American.
- Over 2.0 million persons celebrated their 65th birthday in 2002.
- Persons reaching age 65 have an average life expectancy of an additional 18.1 years (19.4 years for females and 16.4 years for males).
- Older women outnumber older men at 20.8 million older women to 14.8 million older men.
- Older men were much more likely to be married than older women—73% of men vs. 41% of women (Figure 2). Almost half of all older women in 2002 were widows (46%).

• About 31 percent (10.5 million) of noninstitutionalized older persons live alone (7.9 million women, 2.6 million men).
• Half of older women age 75+ live alone.
• Almost 400,000 grandparents aged 65 or more had the primary responsibility for their grandchildren who lived with them.
• By the year 2030, the older population will more than double to 71.5 million.
• The 85+ population is projected to increase from 4.6 million in 2002 to 9.6 million in 2030.
• Members of minority groups are projected to represent 26.4 percent of the older population in 2030, up from 16.4 percent in 2000.
• The median income of older persons in 2002 was $19,436 for males and $11,406 for females. Median money income of all households headed by older people (after adjusting for inflation) fell by -1.4% from 2001 to 2002; however, this difference was not statistically significant.
• The Social Security Administration reported that the major sources of income for older people was:

  ◦ Social Security (reported by 91 percent of older persons),
  ◦ Income from assets (reported by 58 percent),
  ◦ Public and private pensions (reported by 40 percent), and
  ◦ Earnings (reported by 22 percent).

• About 3.6 million older persons lived below the poverty level in 2002. The poverty rate for older persons was 10.4% in 2002 which is not statistically different from the rate in 2001. Another 2.2 million or 6.4% of the elderly were classified as "near-poor" (income between the poverty level and 125% of this level).

The Older Population

The older population—persons 65 years or older—numbered 35.6 million in 2002 (the most recent year for which data are available). They represented 12.3% of the U.S. population, about one in every eight Americans. The number of older Americans increased by 3.3 million or 10.2% since 1992, compared to an increase of 13.5% for the under-65 population. However, the number of Americans aged 45–64—who will reach 65 over the next two decades—increased by 38% during this period.

In 2002, there were 20.8 million older women and 14.8 million older men, or a sex ratio of 141 women for every 100 men. The female to male sex ratio increases with age, ranging from 116 for the 65–69 age group to a high of 230 for persons 85 and over.

Since 1900, the percentage of Americans 65+ has tripled (from 4.1% in 1900 to 12.3% in 2002), and the number has increased eleven times (from 3.1 million to 35.6 million). The older population itself is getting older. In 2002, the 65–74 age group (18.3 million) was eight times larger than in 1900, but the 75–84 group (12.7 million) was more than 16 times larger and the 85+ group (4.6 million) was almost 38 times larger.

In 2001, persons reaching age 65 had an average life expectancy of an additional 18.1 years (19.4 years for females and 16.4 years for males).

A child born in 2001 could expect to live 77.2 years, about 30 years longer than a child born in 1900. Much of this increase occurred because of reduced death rates for children and young adults. However, the past two decades have also seen reduced death rates for the population aged 65–84, especially for men— by 29.0% for men aged 65–74 and by 22.5% for men aged 75–84. Life expectancy at age 65 increased by only 2.5 years between 1900 and 1960, but has increased by 3.8 years from 1960 to 2001.

Over 2.0 million persons celebrated their 65th birthday in 2002. In the same year, about 1.8 million persons 65 or older died. Census estimates showed an annual net increase of approximately 249,000.

There were 50,364 persons aged 100 or more in 2002 (0.02% of the total population). This is a 35% increase from the 1990 figure of 37,306.

(Data for this section were compiled primarily from Internet releases of the U.S. Bureau of the Census and the National Center for Health Statistics.)

Future Growth

The older population will continue to grow significantly in the future (*see Figure 1*). This growth slowed somewhat during the 1990's because of the relatively small number of babies born during the Great Depression of the 1930's. But the older population will burgeon between the years 2010 and 2030 when the "baby boom" generation reaches age 65.

By 2030, there will be about 71.5 million older persons, more than twice their number in 2000. People 65+ represented 12.4% of the population in the year 2000 but are expected to grow to be 20% of the population by 2030. The 85+ population is projected to increase from 4.6 million in 2002 to 9.6 million in 2030.

Minority populations are projected to represent 26.4% of the elderly population in 2030, up from 17.2% in 2002. Between 2000 and 2030, the white** population 65+ is projected to increase by 77% compared with 223% for older minorities, including Hispanics (342%), African-Americans** (164%), American Indians, Eskimos, and Aleuts** (207%), and Asians and Pacific Islanders** (302%).

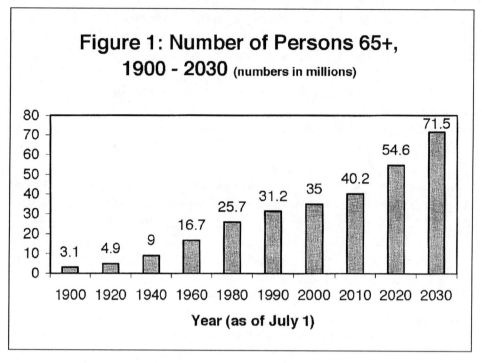

Figure 1: Number of Persons 65+, 1900 - 2030 (numbers in millions)

Note: Increments in years are uneven.
(Sources: Projections of the Population by Age are taken from the January 2004 Census Internet Release. Historical data are taken from "65+ in the United States," Current Population Reports, Special Studies, P23-190 Data for 2000 are from the 2000 Census and 2002 data are taken from the Census estimates for 2002.)

Racial and Ethnic Composition

In 2002, 17.24% of persons 65+ were minorities—8.1% were African-Americans,** 2.7% were Asian or Pacific Islander,** and less than 1% were American Indian or Native Alaskan.** Persons of Hispanic origin (who may be of any race) represented 5.5% of the older population. In addition, 0.5% of persons 65+ identified themselves as being of two or more races.

Only 6.7% of minority race and Hispanic populations were 65+ in 2002 (8.2% of African-Americans,** 8.18% of Asians and Pacific Islanders,** 6.6% of American Indians and Native Alaskans,** 5.1% of Hispanics), compared with 15.0% of whites.**

(Data for this section were compiled from Internet releases of the Census 2002 Estimates.)

Geographic Distribution

In 2002, about half (52%) of persons 65+ lived in nine states. California had over 3.7 million; Florida 2.9 million; New York 2.5 million; Texas 2.2 million; and Pennsylvania 1.9 million. Ohio, Illinois, Michigan, and New Jersey each had well over 1 million (Figure 6).

Person 65+ constituted approximately 14% or more of the total population in 9 states in 2002 (Figure 6): Florida (17.1%); Pennsylvania (15.5%); West Virginia (15.3%); North Dakota (14.8%); Iowa (14.7%); Rhode Island (14.2%); Maine (14.4); South Dakota (14.2); and Arkansas (13.9%). In nine states, the 65+ population increased by 20% or more between 1992 and 2002 (Figure 6): Nevada (63.8%); Alaska (53.6%); Arizona (35.2%); New Mexico (28.4%); Colorado (24.3%); Hawaii (24.0%); Delaware (24.0%); Utah (23.7%) and South Carolina (20.7%). The ten jurisdictions with the highest poverty rates for elderly over the period 2000-2002 were the District of Columbia (18.8%); Mississippi (17.9%); Alabama (15.2%); Tennessee (14.6%); North Carolina (14.0%); Arkansas (15.2%); New Mexico (13.8%); Texas (13.7%); Louisiana (13.2%); and Kentucky (12.4%).

Most persons 65+ lived in metropolitan areas in 2002 (77.4%). About 50% of older persons lived in the suburbs, 27.4% lived in central cities, and 22.6% lived in nonmetropolitan areas.

The elderly are less likely to change residence than other age groups. In the five year period from 1995 to 2000, 22.8% of older persons had moved (compared to 47.7% of persons under 65). Most older movers (59.7%) stayed in the same county while only 18.8% (of the movers) moved to another state. The 85+ segment of the older population had a much higher rate of moving. During this period, 32.3% of the 85+ population moved, 61.1% of them within the same county.

(Data for this section and for Figure 4 were compiled primarily from the Census Population Estimates for 2002 as well as other Internet releases of the U.S. Bureau of the Census including tables from the March 2002 Current Population Survey and "Internal Migration of the Older Population: 1995 to 2000," Census 2000 Special Report, CENSR-10, August 2003.)

Figure 6: The 65+ Population by State 2002

Numbers	Number of Persons	Percent of All Ages	Percent Increase 1992–2002	Percent Below Poverty 2000–2002
US Total (50 States + DC)	35,601,911	12.3%	10.2%	10.2
Alabama	588,542	13.1%	9.6%	15.2
Alaska	39,200	6.1%	53.6%	6.3
Arizona	701,243	12.9%	35.2%	7.5
Arkansas	376,387	13.9%	5.6%	15.2
California	3,716,836	10.6%	13.8%	8.4
Colorado	434,472	9.6%	24.3%	8.2
Connecticut	472,314	13.6%	3.7%	6.5
Delaware	105,488	13.1%	24.0%	6.5
District of Columbia	68,534	12.0%	-11.1%	18.8
Florida	2,854,838	17.1%	15.2%	10.0
Georgia	813,652	9.5%	19.3%	12.6
Hawaii	166,910	13.4%	24.0%	8.1
Idaho	151,141	11.3%	19.3%	6.6
Illinois	1,499,249	11.9%	2.2%	8.6
Indiana	757,451	12.3%	5.8%	8.9
Iowa	432,785	14.7%	0.4%	8.4
Kansas	355,094	13.1%	1.7%	7.9
Kentucky	509,476	12.4%	7.0%	12.4
Louisiana	520,446	11.6%	8.4%	13.2
Maine	186,383	14.4%	10.8%	11.2
Maryland	616,699	11.3%	14.1%	11.1
Massachusetts	863,695	13.4%	2.9%	10.6
Michigan	1,231,920	12.3%	6.8%	9.3
Minnesota	601,741	12.0%	7.4%	9.0
Mississippi	346,251	12.1%	6.1%	17.9
Missouri	757,197	13.3%	3.5%	6.8
Montana	122,806	13.5%	11.8%	9.6
Nebraska	232,134	13.4%	2.8%	9.2
Nevada	240,255	11.1%	63.8%	8.0
New Hampshire	152,577	12.0%	16.9%	6.8
New Jersey	1,121,197	13.1%	5.9%	8.4
New Mexico	221,454	11.9%	28.4%	13.8
New York	2,473,510	12.9%	4.0%	11.8
North Carolina	998,391	12.0%	17.9%	14.0
North Dakota	94,076	14.8%	1.6%	11.5
Ohio	1,513,372	13.3%	4.2%	7.5
Oklahoma	460,459	13.2%	6.1%	11.6
Oregon	443,968	12.6%	8.5%	6.0
Pennsylvania	1,908,962	15.5%	1.8%	8.4
Rhode Island	152,286	14.2%	-0.6%	11.4
South Carolina	503,256	12.3%	20.7%	14.2

South Dakota	108,322	14.2%	4.4%	10.3
Tennessee	719,177	12.4%	12.7%	14.6
Texas	2,152,896	9.9%	19.3%	13.7
Utah	199,041	8.6%	23.7%	10.1
Vermont	79,241	12.9%	16.6%	10.5
Virginia	817,441	11.2%	17.4%	9.8
Washington	677,532	11.2%	13.0%	7.9
West Virginia	275,974	15.3%	1.0%	10.6
Wisconsin	706,418	13.0%	5.9%	8.0
Wyoming	59,222	11.9%	19.4%	7.9
Puerto Rico	449,176	11.6%		

Population data is from the Census Bureau Population Estimates and poverty data is from the Current Population Survey, 2001, 2002, and 2003 Annual Social and Economic Supplements.

Notes

*Principal sources of data for the Profile are the U.S. Bureau of the Census, the National Center on Health Statistics, and the Bureau of Labor Statistics. The Profile incorporates the latest data available but not all items are updated on an annual basis.

**Excludes persons of Hispanic origin.

***Calculated on the basis of the official poverty definitions for the years 2000-2002

****Census 2000 figure

*****2000 figure

A *Profile of Older Americans: 2003* was prepared by the Administration on Aging (AoA), U.S. Department of Health and Human Services. The annual Profile of Older Americans was originally developed and researched by Donald G. Fowles, AoA. Saadia Greenberg, AoA, developed the 2003 edition.

AoA serves as an advocate for the elderly within the federal government and is working to encourage and coordinate a responsive system of family and community based services throughout the nation. AoA helps states develop comprehensive service systems which are administered by 56 State and Territorial Units on Aging, 655 Area Agencies on Aging, 226 Native American and Hawaiian organizations, and more than 29,000 local service providers.

2. Volunteering in the United States: 2003

This appendix excerpts a publication of the U.S. Department of Labor. The extensive statistical tables 1–7 of this publication have not been included here. The full text of the report can be found online at the URL for the U.S. Department of Labor, which is included in the sources listed at the back of this book.

Volunteering in the United States, 2003

Both the number of volunteers and the volunteer rate rose over the year ended in September 2003, the Bureau of Labor Statistics of the U.S. Department of Labor reported today. About 63.8 million people did volunteer work at some point from September 2002 to September 2003, up from 59.8 million for the similar period ended in September 2002. The volunteer rate grew to 28.8 percent, up from 27.4 percent.

These data on volunteering were collected through a supplement to the September 2003 Current Population Survey (CPS). Volunteers are defined as persons who did unpaid work (except for expenses) through or for an organization. The CPS is a monthly survey of about 60,000 households that obtains information on employment and unemployment among the nation's civilian noninstitutional population age 16 and over. For more information about the volunteer supplement, see the Technical Note.

CHANGES IN VOLUNTEER RATES

About 25.1 percent of men and 32.2 percent of women did volunteer work in the year ended in September 2003, increases of 1.5 and 1.2 percentage points from 2002, respectively. For teenagers, the volunteer rate jumped by 2.6 percentage points to 29.5 percent. In contrast, the volunteer rate for the group most likely to volunteer, 35- to 44-year olds, was little changed at 34.7 percent. (See tables A and 1.)

The volunteer rate for whites rose from 29.2 percent for the year ended in September 2002 to 30.6 percent for the year ended in September 2003, while the rates for blacks and Hispanics were little changed. About 18.7 percent of Asians performed some sort of volunteer work through or for an organization over the year ended in September 2003. (Data for Asians were not tabulated in 2002.)

Among persons 25 years of age and over, the volunteer rates for those with at least some college education or a bachelor's degree or better rose over the year, while the rates for those whose education had not gone beyond high school graduation remained about the same.

VOLUNTEERING AMONG DEMOGRAPHIC GROUPS

Almost 64 million persons, or 28.8 percent of the civilian noninstitutional population age 16 and over, volunteered through or for organizations at some point from September 2002 to September 2003. Women volunteered at a higher rate than did men, a relationship that held across age groups, education levels, and other major characteristics. (See table 1.)

By age, 35- to 44-year olds were the most likely to volunteer, closely followed by 45- to 54-year olds. Their volunteer rates were 34.7 percent and 32.7 percent, respectively. Teenagers also had a relatively high volunteer rate, 29.5 percent, perhaps reflecting an emphasis on volunteer activities in schools. Volunteer rates were lowest among persons age 65 years and over (23.7 percent) and among those in their early twenties (19.7 percent). Within the 65 years and over group, volunteer rates decreased as age increased.

Parents with children under age 18 were more likely to volunteer than persons with no children of that age, with volunteer rates of 37.5 percent and 25.0 percent, respectively. Volunteer rates were higher among married persons (34.0 percent) than among never-married persons (22.8 percent) and persons of other marital statuses (22.5 percent).

Whites volunteered at a higher rate (30.6 percent) than did blacks (20.0 percent) and Asians (18.7 percent). Among individuals of Hispanic or Latino ethnicity, 15.7 percent volunteered.

Overall, 31.2 percent of all employed persons had volunteered during the year ended in September 2003. By comparison, the volunteer rates of persons who were unemployed (26.7 percent) or not in the labor force (24.6 percent) were lower. Among the employed, part-time workers were more likely than full-time workers to have participated in volunteer activities—38.4 percent and 29.6 percent, respectively.

Table A. Volunteers by selected characteristics, September 2002 and 2003

(Numbers in thousands)

Characteristic	September 2002r			September 2003		
	Number	Percent of population	Median annual hours	Number	Percent of population	Median annual hours
Sex						
Total, both sexes	59,783	27.4	52	63,791	28.8	52
Men	24,706	23.6	52	26,805	25.1	52
Women	35,076	31.0	50	36,987	32.2	52
Age						
Total, 16 years and over	59,783	27.4	52	63,791	28.8	52
16 to 24 years	7,742	21.9	40	8,671	24.1	40
25 to 34 years	9,574	24.8	33	10,337	26.5	36
35 to 44 years	14,971	34.1	52	15,165	34.7	50
45 to 54 years	12,477	31.3	52	13,302	32.7	52
55 to 64 years	7,331	27.5	60	8,170	29.2	60
65 years and over	7,687	22.7	96	8,146	23.7	88
Race and Hispanic or Latino ethnicity						
White[1]	52,591	29.2	52	55,572	30.6	52
Black or African American[1]	4,896	19.1	52	5,145	20.0	52
Asian[1]	(2)	(2)	(2)	1,735	18.7	40
Hispanic or Latino ethnicity	4,059	15.5	40	4,364	15.7	40
Educational attainment[3]						
Less than a high school diploma	2,806	10.1	48	2,793	9.9	48
High school graduate, no college[4]	12,542	21.2	49	12,882	21.7	48
Less than a bachelor's degree[5]	15,066	32.8	52	15,966	34.1	52
College graduates	21,627	43.3	60	23,481	45.6	60
Employment status						
Civilian labor force	42,773	29.3	48	45,499	30.9	48
Employed	40,742	29.5	48	43,138	31.2	48
Full time[6]	32,210	28.3	46	33,599	29.6	48
Part time[7]	8,532	35.4	52	9,539	38.4	52
Unemployed	2,031	25.1	50	2,361	26.7	48
Not in the labor force	17,010	23.7	72	18,293	24.6	66

[1] Beginning in 2003, persons who selected this race group only; persons who selected more than one race group are not included. Prior to 2003, persons who reported more than one race group were included in the group they identified as the main race.

[2] Data for Asians were not tabulated in 2002.

[3] Data refer to persons 25 years and over.

[4] Includes high school diploma or equivalent.

[5] Includes the categories, some college, no degree; and associate degree.

[6] Usually work 35 hours or more a week at all jobs.

[7] Usually work less than 35 hours a week at all jobs.

r = revised. Estimates for 2002 have been revised to reflect the use of Census 2000-based population controls. See the Technical Note for additional information.

NOTE: Estimates for the above race groups (white, black or African American, and Asian) do not sum to totals because data are not presented for all races. In addition, persons whose ethnicity is identified as Hispanic or Latino may be of any race and, therefore, are classified by ethnicity as well as by race.

Total Annual Hours Spent Volunteering

Volunteers spent a median of 52 hours on volunteer activities during the period from September 2002 to September 2003, unchanged from the previous survey period. The median number of hours men and women spent volunteering was the same (52 hours). (See table 2.)

Among the age groups, volunteers age 65 and over devoted the most time— a median of 88 hours—to volunteer activities. Those age 25 to 34 years spent the least time, volunteering a median of 36 hours during the year.

Number and Type of Organizations

Most volunteers were involved with one or two organizations—69.2 percent and 19.2 percent, respectively. Individuals with higher educational attainment were more likely to volunteer for multiple organizations than were individuals with less education. (See table 3.)

The main organization—the organization for which the volunteer worked the most hours during the year—was either religious (34.6 percent of all volunteers) or educational/youth-service related (27.4 percent). Another 11.8 percent of volunteers performed activities mainly for social or community service organizations, and 8.2 percent volunteered the most hours for hospitals or other health organizations. This distribution is largely the same as in the prior year. (See table 4.)

Older volunteers were more likely to work mainly for religious organizations than were their younger counterparts. For example, 46.5 percent of volunteers age 65 and over performed volunteer activities mainly through or for a religious organization, compared with 29.1 percent of volunteers age 16 to 24 years. Younger individuals were more likely to volunteer for educational or youth service organizations.

Among volunteers with children under 18 years, 47.2 percent of mothers and 36.1 percent of fathers volunteered mainly for an educational/youth-service related organization, such as a school or little league. Parents were more than twice as likely to volunteer for such organizations as persons with no children of that age. Conversely, volunteers with no children under 18 were about twice as likely as parents to volunteer for some other types of organizations, such as social or community service organizations.

Volunteer Activities for Main Organization

The activities of volunteers varied. Among the more commonly reported (volunteers could report more than one activity) were fundraising or selling items to raise money (28.8 percent); coaching, refereeing, tutoring, or teaching (28.6 percent); collecting, preparing, distributing, or serving food (24.9 percent);

providing information, which would include being an usher, greeter, or minister (22.0 percent); and engaging in general labor (21.8 percent). (See table 5.)

Some demographic groups were more likely to engage in certain activities than were others. For example, parents of children under 18 were much more likely to coach, referee, tutor, or teach than were persons with no children of that age. College graduates were more than four times as likely as those with less than a high school diploma to provide professional or management assistance.

The volunteer activity categories were redesigned for 2003 to be more consistent conceptually and to provide better information about the types of volunteer activities performed. The redesign eliminated a "catch-all" category used in 2002 that received over two-fifths of all responses to the question on the type of volunteer activities performed. As a result of the redesign, the 2003 data on volunteer activities performed are not comparable with the data for 2002.

HOW VOLUNTEERS BECAME INVOLVED WITH MAIN ORGANIZATION

Two in five volunteers became involved with the main organization for which they did volunteer work on their own initiative; that is, they approached the organization. Almost 44 percent were asked to become a volunteer, most often by someone in the organization. (See table 6.)

REASONS FOR NOT VOLUNTEERING

Among those who had volunteered at some point in the past, the most common reason given for not volunteering in the year ended September 2003 was lack of time (44.7 percent), followed by health or medical problems (14.7 percent) and family responsibilities or childcare problems (9.5 percent). Lack of time was the most common reason for all groups except those age 65 and over and for those with less than a high school diploma, or who were not in the labor force— both of which contained a relatively high proportion of older persons. For each of these three groups, health or medical problems was the primary reason for not volunteering.

Changes in Volunteer Estimates

Estimates shown in this release for the years ended September 2002 and September 2003 are based on Census 2000 population controls. For this reason, the estimates for the year ended September 2002 appearing in this release may differ from those published earlier, which were based on population controls derived from the 1990 census. For further information on these changes, see the Technical Note.

Technical Note

The data in this release were collected through a supplement to the September 2003 Current Population Survey (CPS). The CPS—a monthly survey of about 60,000 households conducted by the U.S. Census Bureau for the Bureau of Labor Statistics—focuses on obtaining information on employment and unemployment among the nation's civilian noninstitutional population age 16 and over. The purpose of this supplement to the CPS was to obtain information on the incidence of volunteering and the characteristics of volunteers in the United States.

The 2002 data in this release have been revised to reflect Census 2000-based population controls and thus may differ from previously published estimates which were based on population controls that were derived from the 1990 census. Sample results from the CPS are weighted up to independent estimates of the population by sex, age, race, and Hispanic or Latino/non-Hispanic ethnicity. The weights, or population controls, are developed using counts of the civilian noninstitutional population derived from the decennial census and are updated using information from administrative records.

Information in this release will be made available to sensory-impaired individuals upon request. Voice phone: 202-691-5200; TDD message referral phone number: 1-800-877-8339.

RELIABILITY OF THE ESTIMATES

Statistics based on the CPS are subject to both sampling and nonsampling error. When a sample, rather than the entire population, is surveyed, there is a chance that the sample estimates may differ from the "true" population values they represent. The exact difference, or *sampling error*, varies depending on the particular sample selected, and this variability is measured by the standard error of the estimate. There is about a 90-percent chance, or level of confidence, that an estimate based on a sample will differ by no more than 1.6 standard errors from the "true" population value because of sampling error. BLS analyses are generally conducted at the 90-percent level of confidence.

The CPS data also are affected by *nonsampling error*. Nonsampling error can occur for many reasons, including the failure to sample a segment of the population, inability to obtain information for all respondents in the sample, inability or unwillingness of respondents to provide correct information, and errors made in the collection or processing of the data.

For a full discussion of the reliability of data from the CPS and for information on estimating standard errors, see the "Explanatory Notes and Estimates of Error" section of *Employment and Earnings*.

Volunteer Questions and Concepts

In the September 2003 supplement, questions on volunteer activities were asked of all households. Efforts were made to have household members answer the volunteer questions for themselves. (Generally, one member of the household answers all the questions in the CPS.) Self response was considered important for the volunteer supplement because research indicated that self respondents could more easily answer questions on the characteristics of the volunteer activity. About three-quarters of the responses were self reports.

The survey was introduced as follows: "This month, we are interested in volunteer activities, that is, activities for which people are not paid, except perhaps expenses. We only want you to include volunteer activities that you did through or for an organization, even if you only did them once in a while."

Following this introduction, respondents were asked the first supplement question: "Since September 1st of last year, have you done any volunteer activities through or for an organization?"

If respondents did not answer "yes" to the first question, they were asked the following question: "Sometimes people don't think of activities they do infrequently or activities they do for children's schools or youth organizations as volunteer activities. Since September 1st of last year, have you done any of these types of volunteer activities?"

Respondents were considered volunteers if they answered "yes" to either of these questions.

Respondents thus classified as volunteers were asked further questions about the number and type of organizations for which they volunteered, total hours spent volunteering, how they became involved with the main organization for which they volunteered, and the type of activities they performed for the main organization.

In a redesigned question, non-volunteers were asked if they had ever volunteered. If they responded "yes," they were asked for the reason that they had not volunteered during the previous year.

The volunteer activity categories also were redesigned for 2003 to be more consistent conceptually and to provide better information about the types of volunteer activities performed. This redesign eliminated a "catch-all" category used in 2002 that received over two-fifths of all responses to the question on the type of volunteer activities performed.

The reference period for the questions on volunteering was about 1 year, from September 1, 2002, through the survey week in September 2003. The reference period for other characteristics, such as labor force status, educational attainment, and marital status, refer to the survey reference week in September 2003. It is possible that these characteristics were different at the time volunteer activities were performed.

DEFINITIONS

Volunteers are persons who performed unpaid volunteer activities at any point from September 1, 2002, through the survey period in September 2003. The count of volunteers only includes persons who volunteered through or for an organization; the figures do not include persons who volunteered in a more informal manner. For example, a woman who teaches acting to children through a local theater would be considered a volunteer. A woman who, on her own, organizes softball games for the children in her neighborhood would not be counted as a volunteer for the purpose of this survey.

Organizations are associations, societies, or groups of people who share a common interest. Examples include churches, youth groups, and civic organizations. For the purpose of this study, organizations are classified into eight major categories, including religious, youth, and social or community service organizations. (See table 4.)

The *main organization* is the organization for which the volunteer worked the most hours during the year. If a respondent volunteered for only one organization, it was considered the main organization, even if exact hours were not obtained.

In order to identify the type of main organization, respondents had to provide information about the organization and, for those who volunteered for more than one organization, annual hours worked for each. Some respondents did not provide the information necessary to determine the type of main organization. For these respondents, the follow-up questions on activities and how they became involved with the main organization asked them to report on the organization for which they think they spent the most time volunteering.

3. Internet Tutorials

In March of 2004, the Pew Internet & American Life Project "Older Americans and the Internet" reported that

> 22% of Americans 65 and older use the Internet. The percent of seniors who go online has jumped by 47% between 2000 and 2004. In a February 2004 survey, 22% of Americans age 65 or older reported having access to the Internet, up from 15% in 2000. That translates to about 8 million Americans age 65 or older who use the Internet. By contrast, 58% of Americans age 50–64, 75% of 30–49 year-olds, and 77% of 18–29 year-olds currently go online. There is a burgeoning group of Americans who are slightly younger than retirees and who are vastly more attached to the online world. This "silver tsunami" identified in the Pew Internet Project's 2001 "Wired Seniors" report has gained momentum. As Internet users in their 50s get older and retire, they are unlikely to give up their wired ways and therefore will transform the wired senior stereotype [Fox, "Older Americans and the Internet," 2004].

Since most of the opportunities for volunteering listed in this book are on the Internet, the reader may need a course in the basics of WWW browsing. There are many online resources; a select number of these are listed in this appendix. A short course in basic computer skills may be advisable before attempting to browse the WWW. Such courses are also online and are frequently available from local community colleges, senior centers, and public libraries, at little or no cost to seniors.

AARP
Website: www.aarp.org/computers/.
The "Computers and Technology Section" of the AARP site is a comprehensive guide to the world of computing and the Web. Start at the "Learn the Internet" tutorials page for tips on basic and intermediate browsing.

Basics of Computing
Website: http://members.aol.com/shobansen3/index.html.

Computer help for those over 50, this home-grown site is dedicated to "every elderly person in the world who needs a little help using computers and Windows."

California State University Hayward Library
Website: www.library.csuhayward.edu/search_the_internet.htm.

A comprehensive collection of search tools and tutorials.

Computers Made Easy (For Senior Citizens)
Website: www.csuchico.edu/csu/seniors/computing.html.

Computers Made Easy is a nonprofit website designed to help seniors understand how computers work and locate some resources for improving their computing skills. The site links to many free Internet tutorials and other instructional sites, along with information about organizations, research techniques and other resources.

Internet 101
Website: www.internet101.org.

For those who want to know just the basics. The website describes itself as a "guide that will provide you with enough knowledge to have fun on the Internet, yet will not bore you with too many details—a set of instructions—for people who don't like to read instructions!"

Internet for Beginners
Website: www.netforbeginners.about.com/od/internet101.

The "Internet Beginner's Handbook," tips and tutorials for new users. An excellent online resource on using the Internet. The site also includes links to many articles and related resources.

Internet Tutorials from SUNY-Albany
Website: http://library.albany.edu/internet.

A comprehensive resource for all levels, but especially beginners. Topics include: how to connect to the Internet, basic guide to the Internet, and understanding the World Wide Web.

Learn the Net
Website: www.learnthenet.com/english/index.html.

Learn the Net is Internet for beginners. This site has an array of do-it-yourself resources such as tutorials on e-mail, newsgroups, Web publishing, Internet research, and many other topics.

Site-Seeing on the Internet
Website: www.pueblo.gsa.gov/cic_text/computers/site-seeing/.

This publication from the Federal Trade Commission and the National Association of Attorneys General may serve as a primer or refresher on the Internet. The full text of this eight-page document is online. It is in the public domain and can be downloaded, copied, and distributed freely.

Third Age
Website: www.thirdage.com/learning/tech/booster/.

The Third Age Learning Center provides free online classes that you can take at your own pace. Topics include: browser basics, how to search the Web, using bookmarks/favorites, and how to download and save web pages. This site also provides a Computer Section that lists articles related to computer skills and web pointers.

Web Teacher
Website: www.webteacher.org.

An outstanding tutorial and reference site for beginners and intermediate users. Clear and easy to navigate, it includes a Web Primer and a Web Tutorial covering all the basics: getting started, browsers, e-mail, newsgroups, and much more. Start the tutorial with "Web Basics and learn how to navigate the WWW.

Internet Glossary

You don't have to be a computer expert to book a trip into cyberspace, but it certainly helps to know a few words of cyber-speak. Before long, you'll sound like a native and get around like an experienced traveler.

BOOKMARK—an online function that lets you access your favorite websites quickly.

BROWSER—special software that allows you to navigate several areas of the Internet and access and view a website.

BULLETIN BOARD/NEWSGROUP—places to leave an electronic message or share news that anyone can read and respond to. Marketers or others can get your e-mail address from bulletin boards and newsgroups.

CHAT ROOM—a place for people to converse online by typing messages to each other. (Once you're in a chat room, others can contact you by e-mail.)

CHATTING—a way for a group of people to converse online in real time by typing messages to each other.

COOKIE—when you visit a site, a notation may be fed to a file known as a "cookie" in your computer for future reference. If you revisit the site, the "cookie" file allows the website to identify you as a "return" guest—and offer you products tailored to your interests or tastes. You can set your online preferences to limit or let you know about "cookies" that a website places on your computer.

CYBERSPACE—another name for the Internet.

DOWNLOAD—the transfer of files or software from a remote computer to your computer.

E-MAIL—computer-to-computer messages between one or more individuals via the Internet.

FILTER—software you can buy that lets you block access to websites and content that you may find unsuitable.

INTERNET—the universal network that allows computers to talk to other computers in words, text, graphics, and sound, anywhere in the world.

ISP (Internet Service Provider)—a service that allows you to connect to the Internet.

JUNK E-MAIL—unsolicited commercial e-mail; also known as "spam." Usually junk e-mail doesn't contain the recipient's address on the "To" line. Instead, the addressee is a made-up name, such as "friend@public.com." Or the address on the "To" line is identical to the one on the "From" line.

KEYWORD—a word you enter into a search engine to begin the search for specific information or websites.

LINK—highlighted words on a website that allow you to connect to other parts of the same website (web pages) or to other websites. Also known as a "hyperlink."

LISTSERV—an online mailing list that allows individuals or organizations to send e-mail to groups of people at one time.

MODEM—an internal or external device that connects your computer to the Internet at various speeds. It can utilize a telephone or cable line.

ONLINE SERVICE—an ISP with added information, entertainment and shopping features.

PASSWORD—a personal code you use to access your account with your ISP.

PRIVACY POLICY—a statement on a website describing what information about you is collected by the site, and how it is used. Ideally, the policy is posted prominently and offers you options about the use of your personal information. These options are called opt-in and opt-out. An opt-in choice means the website won't use your information unless you specifically say it's okay. An opt-out choice means the website can use the information unless you specifically direct it not to.

SCREEN NAME—the name you call yourself when you communicate online. You may want to abbreviate your name or make up a name. Your ISP may allow you to use several screen names.

SEARCH ENGINE—a browser function that lets you search for information and websites. Using a search engine is like accessing the main card file in a library, only easier. A few keywords can lead you almost anywhere on the Internet. You can find a search function on many websites to look for specific information on that particular site.

URL (Uniform Resource Locator)—the address that lets you locate a particular site. For example, www.aoa.gov is the website for the Administration on Aging. All government URLs end in .gov. Nonprofit organizations and trade associations end in .org. For example, www.aarp.org is the URL for the AARP. Commercial companies generally end in .com, although additional suffixes or domains are being developed as the Internet grows.

VIRUS—a file maliciously planted in your computer that can damage files and disrupt your system. A "worm" can be equally dangerous.

WEB PAGE—A sub-site on a website that is reached by clicking on a link.

WEBSITE—An Internet destination where you can examine and/or download information. Linked together, they make up the World Wide Web.

PDF (Portable Document Format)—some online publications that you may wish to download and save are long and have complex formatting (e.g., graphics) which makes them more difficult to convert to the standard ".html" file format which your browser usually displays. As a result, websites may offer these publications in Adobe Portable Document Format (PDF). Many government websites are in PDF format. You can download the current version of Adobe Acrobat software from a number of different websites—frequently the site you have retrieved; just click on the link. It is free, it installs quickly and easily, and is very simple to use. There is no obligation, and no personal questions are asked. Adobe Acrobat can be downloaded at: www.adobe.com/products/acrobat/.

Sources

AARP. Website. www.aarp.org.

_____. February 2003. "Taking the Lead in Community Service." www.aarp.org/connections/feb2003/comm-service.html.

_____. November 2003. "Multicultural Study 2003: Time and Money: An In-Depth Look at 45+ Volunteers and Donors." www.research.aarp.org/general/multic_2003.html.

_____. No date. *AARP Connections.* www.aarp.org/connections/archives.html.

_____. No date. "Serve Your Community." www.aarp.org/serve/.

_____. No date. "Volunteer." www.aarp.org/volunteer/.

_____. No date. "Volunteer Match." http://aarp.volunteermatch.org/aarp/index.html.

Administration on Aging. Website. www.aoa.gov.

_____. 2003. *A Profile of Older Americans: 2003.* www.aoa.gov/Statistics/2003/2003profile.pdf.

_____. 2004. "Older Americans Month 2004." www.aoa.gov/press/oam/oam.asp.

AIG SunAmerica. April 30, 2002. "Re-Visioning Retirement Study." www.re-visioningretirement.com.

_____. April 30, 2002. "The History of Retirement." www.re-visioningretirement.com/History/history.html

America Reads. Web page. www.ed.gov/inits/americareads/index.html.

American Cancer Society. Website. www.cancer.org.

American Heart Association. Website. www.americanheart.org.

American Jewish World Service. Website. www.ajws.org.

American Red Cross. Website. www.redcross.org.

American Society on Aging. July-August 2003. "Reimagining Work: The Next Chapter." www.asaging.org/at/at-244/IF_Reimagining_Work.cfm.

AmeriCorps. Website. www.americorps.org.

_____. VISTA. Website.www.americorps.org/vista/.

Amnesty International USA. Website. www.amnestyusa.org.

Armas, Genaro C. June 14, 2004. "An Explosive Growth Among Hispanics." www.newsday.com/news/politics/wire/sns-ap-census-population,0,4797374.story.

Arthritis Foundation. Website. www.arthritis.org.

Ask a Friend Campaign. Website. www.volunteerfriends.org.

Asmus, Cheryl. February 2001. "Volunteering When Retired." www.ext.colostate.edu/pubs/columnha/ha0102.html.

Berger, Sandy. September 10, 2002. "Reinvent Retirement Completely." www.aarp.org/computers-features/Articles/a2002-09-10-ct-reinvent.html.

Big Brothers Big Sisters. Website. www.bbbsa.org.

Boy Scouts of America. Website. www.scouting.org.

Bridgeland, John. May 26, 2003. "Why Serve?" www.businessweek.com/adsections/2003/pdf/0526volunteerism.pdf.

Bureau of Prisons. Website. www.bop.gov.

_____. Volunteer Management Branch. Web page. www.bop.gov/ievpg/ccdvmb.html.

Business Week. May 26, 2003."Volunteerism: What Makes America Great." www.businessweek.com/adsections/2003/pdf/0526volunteerism.pdf.

Canadian Ministry of Citizenship and Immigration. "Volunteering." www.gov.on.ca/mczcr/english/citdiv/voluntar.

Caspari, Rachel, and Sang-Hee Lee. July 13, 2004. "Older Age Becomes Common Late in Human Evolution." *Proceedings of the National Academy of Sciences*, 101(28). www.pnas.org.

Catholic Network of Volunteer Service. Website. www.cnvs.org.

The Center for Information & Research on Civic Learning & Engagement. September 19, 2002. "The Civic and Political Health of the Nation: A Generational Portrait." www.puaf.umd.edu/CIRCLE/research/products/Civic_and_Political_Health.pdf.

Charity Village. Website. www.charityvillage.com.

Citizen Corps. Website. www.citizencorps.gov.

Civic Ventures. August 2002. "The New Face of Retirement: An Ongoing Survey of American Attitudes on Aging." Full report: www.civicventures.org/site/action/work_in_prog/survey_8_02/Fi6678b-final.pdf. Summary: www.civicventures.org/site/action/work_in_prog/survey_8_02/survey_analysis.pdf.

Clinton, Bill. September 1998. "America's Voluntary Spirit." In "United States: A Nation of Volunteers," *U. S. Society & Values*. www.usta.gov/journals/journals.htm.

CNN. January 20, 2004. "Transcript of State of the Union Address." http://www.cnn.com/2004/ALLPOLITICS/01/20/sotu.transcript.7/

Collins, Joseph, Stefano DeZerega, and Zahara Heckscher. 2002. *How to Live Your Dream of Volunteering Overseas*. Penguin USA.

Corporation for National and Community Service. Website. www.cns.gov.

_____. November 2003. "Thanksgiving Volunteer Drive Urges Seniors to Pledge Their Time and Experience." www.nationalservice.org/news/pr/111203.html.

Council of Religious Volunteer Agencies. Website. www.religiousvolunteers.org.

Cross-Cultural Solutions. Website. www.crossculturalsolutions.org.

Delta Society. Website. www.deltasociety.org.

Dennis, Helen. February 16, 2002. "Ten Trends That Will Change Retirement." www.asaging.org/at/at-216/trends.html.

de Tocqueville, Alexis. 1889. *Democracy in America*. http://xroads.virginia.edu/~HYPER/DETOC/home.html

Dominican Volunteers USA. Web page. www.op.org/volsusa/.

Duka, Walt, and Trish Nicholson. December 2002. "Retirees Rocking Old Roles." www.aarp.org/bulletin/yourlife/Articles/a2003-06-26-retireesrocking.html#poll.

Earth Elders. Website. www.earthelders.org.

Earthwatch Institute. Website. www.earthwatch.org.

Eldercare Locator. Website. www.eldercare.gov.

Ellis, Susan J. September 1998. "Volunteerism and the Government Sector." In "The United States: A Nation of Volunteers." usinfo.state.gov/journals/itsv/0998/ijse/ijse0998.htm.

_____. September 1998. "Volunteerism on the Global Scene." In "The United States: A Nation of Volunteers." usinfo.state.gov/journals/itsv/0998/ijse/ijse0998.htm.

_____. 2003. "Online Power for Volunteer Action." www.worldwidevolunteer.org/en/library/documents_show_text.cfm?document_id=979.

Ellis, Susan J., and Jayne Cravens. Web page. *The Virtual Volunteering Guidebook*. www.energizeine.com/download/vvguide.pdf.

Ellis, Susan J., and Katherine H. Noyes. 1978. *By the People: A History of Americans as Volunteers*. Energize Books. www.energizeinc.com/art.html.

Environmental Alliance for Senior Involvement. Website. www.easi.org.

Environmental Protection Agency. Website. www.epa.gov.

_____. Aging Initiative. www.epa.gov/aging/.

_____. Volunteer Monitoring Program. www.epa.gov/owow/monitoring/volunteer/epasvmp.html.

Experience Corps. Website. www.experiencecorps.org.

Faith in Action. Website. www.fiavolunteers.org.

Family Friends. Website. www.family-friends.org.

Farrell, Christopher. Web page. "The Not-So-High Cost of Aging." http://www.businessweek.com/bwdaily/dnflash/jul2004/nf20040715_7326_db013.htm.

FirstGov for Seniors. Website. www.seniors.gov.

_____. February 10, 2003. "President Calls for Senior Volunteers." www.seniors.gov/articles/0203/volunteer.htm.

Foster Grandparent Program. Web page. www.seniorcorps.org/joining/fgp/index.html.

Fourinfo.com. Web page. "Volunteerism, The Volunteer's Rights and Responsibilities." www.fourinfo.com/volunteer/.

Freedman, Marc. 2002. "Prime Time: How Baby Boomers Will Revolutionize Retirement and Transform America." *Public Affairs*, March.

Geekcorps. Website. www.geekcorps.org.

Generations of Hope. Website. www.generationsofhope.org.

Girl Scouts of America. Website. www.girlscouts.org.

Global Computing. Website. www.globalcomputing.com/states.html.

Global Volunteer Network. Website. www.volunteer.org.nz.

Global Volunteers. Website. http //www.globalvolunteers.org.

Goodwill Industries International. Website. www.goodwill.org.

The Gray Panthers. Website. www.graypanthers.org.

Greater San Francisco Bay Area Combined Federal Campaign. "Volunteerism at Any Age." www.cfcsfbay.org/volunteerism.htm.

Greenpeace International. Website. www.greenpeace.org.

Habitat for Humanity International. Website. www.habitat.org.

Hadley, M. L. 1998. "Themes and challenges for future service and research." In M. Maunsell (Ed.), *Designing Meaningful New Volunteer Roles for Retired Persons*.

Harris Interactive. May 2002. "Re-visioning Retirement." A summary of the research report can be found at: www.re-visioningretirement.com./PDF/press_release.pdf.

Hawthorne, Lillian. September 17, 1999. "The Rest of Our Years, the Best of Our Years." www.seniorworld.com/articles/a19990917171400.html.

Henchman, Joseph. Website. 1963. "President Kennedy's speech at American University." members.aol.com/jdhenchman/papers/kennedy.html.

Idealist. Website. www.idealist.org.

Independent Sector. June 2000. "America's Senior Volunteers." Summary: www.independentsector.org/programs/research/senior_volunteers_in_america.html. Full report: www.independentsector.org/pdfs/SeniorVolun.pdf.

_____. November 2001. "Giving and Volunteering in the United States 2001." www.independentsector.org/PDFs/GV01keyfind.pdf.

_____. November 4, 2003. "Experience at Work: Volunteering and Giving Among Americans 50 and Over." www.independentsector.org/media/experiencePR.html.

_____. 2004. "Value of Volunteer Time." www.independentsector.org/programs/research/volunteer_time.html.

_____. No date. "Ten Tips on Volunteering Wisely." www.networkforgood.org/volunteer/volunteertips.html.

International Executive Service Corps. Website. www.iesc.org.

InterConnection. Website. www.interconnection.org.

Islamic Relief. Website. www.irw.org.

Johnson, Richard P. 1999. *Creating a Successful Retirement: Finding Peace and Purpose*. Liguori Publications, Liguori, MO.

Kausler, Donald H. August 10, 2003. "The Graying of America: Volunteering Increases Longevity for Senior Citizens." www.naplesnews.com/03/08/neapolitan/d956953a.htm.

Kerry, John. May 19, 2003. "A New Era of National Service." www.johnkerry.com/pressroom/speeches/spc_2003_0519.html.

_____. No date. "Compact with the Greatest Generation." www/johnkerry.com/issues/seniors/.

Keyser, Cheryl M. 2003. "The Importance of Civic Engagement to Older Americans." www.ncoa.org/attachments/Innovationsfinal.pdf.

Keyser, Mark. 2003. "Reimagining Work: The Next Chapter." *Aging Today*, July-August. www.asaging.org/at/at-244/IF_Reimagining_Work.cfm.

Kimeldorf, Martin. "Wiring Friendships Across Time, Space, and Age: An Evaluation of Intergenerational Friendships Created Online." http://e-voluneerism.com/quarterly/01fall/kimeldorf.php.

Kleyman, Paul. 2002. "Study Shows How Older-Volunteer Force in U.S. Could Double." *Aging Today*, January-February. www.asaging.org/publications/dbase/ AT/AT.24_1. Kleyman.pdf.

Knechtel, Robert. "Productive Aging in the 21st Century." www.go60.com/go60work.htm.

Kotlikoff, Laurence J., and Scott Burns. March 2004. *The Coming Generational Storm: What You Need to Know About America's Economic Future*. The MIT Press. http://mitpress. mit.edu/catalog/item/default.asp?sid=67984DA8-6F51-46EA- B837-87D378DD70EE& ttype=2&tid=10055.

Landry, Roger F. 2003. "Facts on Aging Are Brighter: Seniors Can Positively Impact Their Aging Process." www.go60.com/go60active.htm.

Lawson, Willow. "Aging's Changing Face." http://www.psychologytoday.com/htdocs/prod/PTOArticle/PTO-20030826-000004.asp

Legal Counsel for the Elderly. Web page. www.aarp.org/lce/.

The Leukemia & Lymphoma Society. Website. www.leukemia.org.

Little Brothers—Friends of the Elderly. Website. www.littlebrothers.org.

Long Term Care Ombudsman. Web page. www.aoa.gov/prof/aoaprog/elder_rights/LTCombudsman/ltc_ombudsman.asp.

The MacArthur Foundation. October 28, 2003. "A New Perspective on Growing Old." www.macfound.org/anniv/fostering_new_knowledge/network_on_successful_aging. htm.

Make-A-Wish Foundation. Website. www.wish.org.

March of Dimes. Website. http://209.73.237.101/.

McCool, Grant. October 14, 2003. "Clark Proposes New Civilian Volunteer Corp."

www.reuters.com/newsArticle.jhtml;jsessionid=LVCALJSJ4A5AWCRBAE0CFEY?type=
politicsNews&storyID=3613325.

Meals On Wheels Association of America. Website. www.mowaa.org.

Medical Reserve Corps. Website. www.medicalreservecorps.gov.

Merrill, Mary V. December 2000. "In Search of a Contemporary Definition of Volunteerism."
www.merrillassociates.net/topicofthemonth.php?topic=200012

Moen, Phyllis. August 6, 1999. "Senior Volunteering Connected to Well-being."
www.news.cornell.edu/releases/Aug99/volunteering.seniors.ssl.html.

_____. October 15, 2002. "Retired Seniors Gain Lots from Volunteering." www.hon.ch/
News/HSN/509017.html.

Morrow-Howell, Nancy. September 2000. "Productive Engagement of Older Adults: Effects
on Well-being." Summary: www.longerlife.org/white_papers/nmh_productive_
engagement_summary.pdf. Full report: gwbweb.wustl.edu/csd/Publications/2000/
reportmhowell.pdf.

Morrow-Howell, Nancy, James Hinterlong, and Michael Sherraden (Editors). 2001. *Productive Aging: Concepts and Challenges.* Johns Hopkins University Press, Baltimore, MD.

Morrow-Howell, Nancy, Jim Hinterlong, Philip A. Rozario, and Fengyan Tang. May 1, 2003.
"Effects of Volunteering on the Well-Being of Older Adults." *The Journals of Gerontology Series B: Psychological Sciences and Social Sciences* 58(3) (May 1): S137–45.
psychsoc.gerontologyjournals.org/cgi/content/abstract/58/3/S137.

Murray, Vic, and Yvonne Harrison. 2002. "Virtual Volunteering: Current Status and Future
Prospects." www.worldwidevolunteer.org/documents/Murray-SR2-English-Web.pdf.

Musick, Marc A., A. Regula Herzog, and James S. House. May 1999. "Volunteering and Mortality Among Older Adults." *Journals of Gerontology Series B: Psychological Sciences and
Social Sciences*, 54(3): S173–S180. Abstract: http://psychsoc.gerontologyjournals.org/
search.dtl.

National CASA Association. May 1999. "Recruiting Minority Volunteers." www.casanet.org/
program-management/diversity/recrmin.htm.

The National Council on the Aging. Website. www.ncoa.org.

_____. March 29, 2000. "Myths and Realities of Aging." http://206.112.84.147/content.cfm?
sectionID=105&detail=43.

_____. May 9, 2000. "National Study Says Retirement Not Determined by Work Status or
Age." www.ncoa.org/content.cfm?sectionID=105&detail=42.

_____. 2002. "Volunteerism." www.ncoa.org/content.cfm?sectionID=185&detail=182.

_____. April 5, 2002. "American Perceptions of Aging in the 21st Century." www.ncoa.org/
attachments/study_aging.pdf.

_____. 2003. "The Importance of Civic Engagement to Older Americans." *Innovations: The
Journal of the National Council on the Aging,* Summer 2003. Full report: www.experi-
encecorps.org/images/pdf/Innovations_2003.pdf.

_____. November 7, 2003. "Wisdom Works: Building Better Communities." www.ncoa.org/
content.cfm?sectionID=65&detail=461#release.

_____. April 23, 2004. "Boomers Want to Revitalize Communities But Need New Volunteer
Opportunities." www.ncoa.org/content.cfm?sectionID=65&detail=586.

National Forest Service. "Senior, Youth, and Volunteer Programs." www.fs.fed.us/people/
programs/index.htm.

_____. "Volunteering in the National Forests." www.fs.fed.us/people/programs/volunteer.htm.

National Institute on Aging. Website. www.nia.nih.gov.

_____. September 2002. *Aging Under the Microscope: A Biological Quest.* www.niapublications.org/
pubs/microscope/index.asp.

National Multiple Sclerosis Society. Website. www.nmss.org.

National Oceanic and Atmospheric Administration. Website. www.noaa.gov.

National Park Service. Website. www.nps.gov.

_____. Volunteers-In-Parks Program. www.nps.gov/volunteer/index.htm.

Natural Resources Conservation Service. Website. www.nrcs.usda.gov.

_____. NRCS Earth Team Volunteers. www.nrcs.usda.gov/feature/volunteers/.

National Retiree Volunteer Coalition. Website. www.voa.org.

National Safety Council. Website. www.nsc.org.

National Senior Service Corps. Website. www.seniorcorps.org.

The Nature Conservancy. "Volunteer." http://nature.org/volunteer/

NetAid. Website. www.netaid.org.

Network for Good. Website. www.networkforgood.org.

Nonprofit Career Network. Website. www.nonprofitcareer.com.

Nunn, Michele. "Building Social Capital." www.businessweek.com/adsections/2003/pdf/0526volunteerism.pdf.

OASIS. Website. www.oasisnet.org.

_____. 2003. "Volunteers Find Fulfilling Ways to Serve Their Communities." *Outlook*, Summer. www.oasisnet.org/about/OutlookSummer2003.pdf.

O'Connell, Brian. September 1998. "America's Voluntary Spirit." In "United States: A Nation of Volunteers." *U. S. Society & Values*. www.usta.gov/journals/journals.htm.

Online Volunteering. www.onlinevolunteering.org

Park, J. M. 1983. *Meaning Well Is Not Enough: Perspectives on Volunteering*, Groupwork Today.

PBS. "Aging in the Hispanic Community." www.pbs.org/americanfamily/aging.html

Peace Corps. Website. www.peacecorps.gov.

_____. Web page. "Older Volunteers." www.peacecorps.gov/diversity/older/index.cfm.

Pennsylvania Department of Aging. Website. www.aging.state.pa.us/aging/site/default.asp.

Pennsylvania Senior Environmental Corps. Web page. www.dep.state.pa.us/hosting/pasec/.

Points of Light Foundation. Website. www.pointsoflight.org.

Project HOPE. Website. www.projecthope.org.

Putnam, Robert D. 2000. *Bowling Alone: The Collapse and Revival of American Community*. Simon & Schuster.

ReFirement. "What is Refirement?" www.refirement.com.

Retired and Senior Volunteer Program. Web page. www.seniorcorps.org/joining/rsvp/index.html.

Rowe, John W., and Robert L. 1998. Kahn. *Successful Aging*. Pantheon Books.

The Salvation Army. Website. www.salvationarmy.org.

Scheibel, James. "Seniors: A Vital Resource." http://usinfo.state.gov/journal/itsV/0699/ijse/volblrb.htm

Save the Children. Website. www.savethechildren.org.

Second Harvest. Website. www.secondharvest.org.

Senior Attorney Volunteers for the Elderly (SAVE) www.abanet.org/srlawyers/save.html.

Senior Citizens Guide. "Volunteering: Helping Others ... And Yourself!" www.seniorcitizensguide.com/articles/activities/volunteering.htm.

Senior Companion Program. Web page. www.seniorcorps.org/joining/scp/index.html.

Senior Corps. Website. www.seniorcorps.org.

_____. Joining Senior Corps. www.seniorcorps.org/joining/scp/index.html.

Senior Journal. January 30, 2002. "Which Corps Should You Join?" www.seniorjournal.com/NEWS/SeniorCorps/01-30-02WhichCorps.htm.

_____. January 31, 2002. "President Bush's Speech on Senior Corps." www.seniorjournal.com/NEWS/SeniorCorps/01-31-02SenCrps.htm.

_____. June 2003. "Senior Corps Seeks 100,000 Volunteers." www.seniorjournal.com/NEWS/SeniorCorps/3-06-25seeks.htm.

Senior Medicare Patrol. Web page. www.aoa.gov/smp/.

SeniorNet. Website. www.seniornet.org.

Seniors Research Group. March 10, 1999. "Volunteerism Improves Seniors' Satisfaction with Life." www.srgvoice.com/images2/pdf/variety-oct99.pdf.

The Service Corps of Retired Executives (SCORE). Website. www.score.org.

ServiceLeader. Website. www.serviceleader.org.

Shapiro, Peter, Ed. 1994. "National Senior Service: A History of National Service in America." www.academy.umd.edu/publications/NationalService/senior_service.htm.

Smith, M.P. 1989. "Taking Volunteerism into the 21st Century: Some Conclusions from the American Red Cross." *Journal of Volunteer Administration*, 8(1), 3–10.

The Smithsonian Institution. Website. www.si.edu.

Sokolowski, Gloria J. "Volunteerism: A Precious National Resource." www.seniorcitizens-guide.com/articles/activities/volunteerism.htm.

State and Local Government on the Net Directory. Website. www.statelocalgov.net/index.cfm.

Stewart, Jocelyn Y. May 17, 2000. "Retired No Longer Means No Work." www.detnews.com/2000/nation/0005/17/a15-58011.htm.

Streisand, Betsy. June 14, 2004. "Today's Retirement Journey." www.usnews.com/usnews/biztech/articles/040614/14intro.htm.

Too Young to Retire. "Top Ten Ways To Reinvent Retirement." http://2young2retire.com/tenways.html.

Tyler, Randy. 2003. "E-Volunteering: A Means to Build Better Tomorrows for Children, Youth and Families." www.worldwidevolunteer.org/en/library/documents_show_text.cfm?document_id=938.

United Methodist Volunteers in Mission. Website. http://gbgm-umc.org/vim/.

The United Nations. April 12, 2002. "Statement by USA at the Second World Assembly on Ageing." www.un.org/ageing/coverage/usaE.htm.

The United Nations Children's Fund. Website. www.unicefusa.org.

The United Nations Volunteers. Website. www.unv.org/volunteers/.

U.S. Army Corps of Engineers. Website. www.usace.army.mil.

_____. No date. Volunteer Clearinghouse. www.orn.usace.army.mil/volunteer/.

U.S. Bureau of Land Management. Website. www.blm.gov.

_____. Volunteer Opportunities. www.blm.gov/volunteer/opportunities/index.html.

U.S. Census Bureau. Website. www.census.gov.

_____. April 20, 2004. "Older Americans Month." www.census.gov/Press-Release/www/releases/archives/facts_for_features_special_editions/001746.html.

_____. June 14, 2004. "Hispanic and Asian Americans Increasing Faster Than Overall Population." www.census.gov/Press-Release/www/releases/archives/race/001839.html.

U.S. Department of Labor. Website. www.bls.gov.

_____. Bureau of Labor Statistics. December 17, 2003. *Volunteering in the United States, 2003.* www.bls.gov/news.release/volun.nr0.htm.

U.S. Environmental Protection Agency. Volunteer Monitoring Program. www.epa.gov/owow/monitoring/volunteer/epasvmp.html.

U.S. Fish and Wildlife Service. September 1999. "Conserving the Nature of America." www.pueblo.gsa.gov/cic_text/misc/conserv/conserve.txt.

_____. No date. Volunteers. http://volunteers.fws.gov.

U.S. Forest Service. Website. www.fs.fed.us.

U.S. Information Agency. 1998. "The United States as a Nation of Volunteers." usinfo.state.gov/journals/itsv/0998/ijse/ijse0998.htm.

U.S. Park Service. Website. www.nps.gov.

USA Freedom Corps. Website. www.freedomcorps.gov.

_____. January 30, 2003. "President Bush Celebrates USA Freedom Corps' One-Year Anniversary." www.freedomcorps.gov/about_usafc/whats_new/announcements/20030130-2.asp.

_____. No date. Volunteer Network. www.usafreedomcorps.gov/for_volunteers/index.asp. or www.usafreedomcorps.gov/for_volunteers/find_opps.asp.

United Way of America. Website. http://national.unitedway.org.

University of Missouri, Kansas City, Center on Aging Studies Without Walls. Web page. "Volunteerism." http://iml.umkc.edu/casww/

Veterans of Foreign Wars. Website. www.vfw.org.

VISTA. Web page. www.americorps.org/vista/.

Voluntary Service Overseas. Website. www.vso.org.uk.

VolunteerAmerica. Website. www.volunteeramerica.net.

Volunteer Canada. Website. www.volunteer.ca.

Volunteer Centre of Toronto. 2002. "Ready & Able: Including Volunteers with Disabilities." www.e-volunteering.org/specialneeds/sn_viewforum.asp?pagetext=198.

Volunteer Friends. Website. www.volunteerfriends.org.

_____. 2003. "Volunteer: Ask a Friend." www.volunteerfriends.org.

Volunteer.Gov/Gov/. Website. www.volunteer.gov/gov/.

VolunteerMatch. Website. www.volunteermatch.org.

_____. "Virtual Volunteering." www.volunteermatch.org/virtual/.

VolunteerMatch/Network for Good. Website. www.networkforgood.org.

Volunteer News. May 25, 2004. "Volunteer Vacations Becoming Trendy." www.worldvolunteerweb.org/dynamic/cfapps/news/news2.cfm?ArticlesID=532.

Volunteer Today. Website. www.volunteertoday.com/GOVT/stategovt.html.

Volunteering for the Coast. Web page. www.csc.noaa.gov/techniques/volunteer/.

Volunteers in Medicine Institute. Web page. www.vimi.org/volunteer.htm.

Volunteers for Prosperity. Website. May 21, 2003. "President's Speech." vfp.gov/presspeach.htm.

_____. 2003. "Fact Sheet." vfp.gov/fact.htm.

Volunteers in Service to America. Website. www.americorps.org/vista/.

Volunteers of America. Website. www.voa.org.

The White House. "National Volunteer Week, 2004. Presidential Proclamation." usinfo.state.gov/usa/volunteer/proc041704.htm.

_____. January 29, 2001. White House Office of Faith-Based and Community Initiatives. http://www.whitehouse.gov/government/fbci/.

Williams, Candy. "Volunteering: Helping Others ... And Yourself!" www.seniorcitizensguide.com/articles/activities/volunteering.htm.

Wooden, Ruth. March 2002. "Recasting Retirement: New Perspectives on Aging and Civic Engagement." www.asaging.org/at/at-233/Recasting_Retirement.html

Woolston, Chris. "Seniors and Volunteering: A Whole New Life." www.buildingbetterhealth.com/topic/volunteer.

World Wide Volunteer. Website. www.worldwidevolunteer.org.

_____. 2001. "Volunteerism & ICTs." www.worldwidevolunteer.org/en/icts_and_vol/index.cfm.

WorldTeach. Website. www.worldteach.org.

Young Men's Christian Association. Web page. www.ymca.net/index.jsp.

Young, Richard. "Volunteerism: Benefits, Incidence, Organizational Models, and Participation in the Public Sector." www.iopa.sc.edu/publication/volunteerism%20/FINAL.pdf.

Young Women's Christian Association. Web page. www.ywca.org/html/B6.asp.

Index

AARP 117, 166, 193; *Connections* 117; "Multicultural Study 2003" 27, 37
Action Without Borders *see* Idealist 145
Administration on Aging 101
age, in the origins of civilization 46
aging: defined 40; negative stereotypes 43; redefined 42; socioeconomic implications 47
Aging Under the Microscope 41
AIG SunAmerica 49, 52
America Reads 101
American Cancer Society 117
American Heart Association 118
American Jewish World Service 140
American presidents, reflections on volunteerism 29
American Red Cross 119
AmeriCorps 94
Amnesty International USA 119
Arthritis Foundation 120
Ask a Friend 97

baby boomers 20, 78
Big Brothers Big Sisters 120
Boy Scouts of America 120
brave new world of volunteerism 156
Bureau of Labor Statistics 19, 36

Bureau of Land Management 108
Bureau of Prisons 102
Bush, George W. 31, 39, 91

calls to action 29
Canada, government 115; *see also* Volunteer Canada
Caspari, Rachel 46
Catholic Network of Volunteer Service 121, 141
Center for Information and Research on Civic Learning and Engagement 53
Charity Village 150
Citizen Corps 89
Civic Ventures 66
Corporation for National and Community Service 91
Council of Religious Volunteer Agencies 121
Cross-Cultural Solutions 140

Delta Society 122
Democracy in America 27
Dennis, Helen 14, 56
Department of Labor definition of volunteer 10
de Tocqueville, Alexis 27
Dominican Volunteers USA 122
Dychtwald, Ken 50

Earth Elders 141
Earthwatch Institute 142
Environmental Alliance

for Senior Involvement 123
Environmental Protection Agency 103
Experience Corps 124

faith-based initiatives 92
Faith in Action 124
Family Friends 124
federal government programs 85
Foster Grandparent Program 95
Freedman, Marc 15, 53, 80

Geekcorps 143
Generations of Hope 125
Girl Scouts of America 126
Global Volunteer Network 143
Global Volunteers 144
Goodwill Industries 126
Gray Panthers 127
Greenpeace International 144

Habitat for Humanity International 127, 145
Hawthorne, Lillian 45
helping others helping society 79

Idealist 145, 150
Independent Sector 11, 26, 145
InterConnection 166
International Executive Service Corps 145

international organizations
140
Islamic Relief 146

Jewish Volunteer Corps *see*
American Jewish World
Service
Johnson, Richard 56

Kausler, Donald 78
Kerry, John 32
Keyser, Cheryl M. 16
Knechtel, Robert 45
Kotlikoff, Laurence J. 47

Landry, Roger 44
Learn and Serve America 94
Lee, Sang-Hee 46
Legal Counsel for the Elderly
128
Leukemia & Lymphoma Soci-
ety 128
Little Brothers—Friends of
the Elderly 128
local government 115
Long Term Care Ombuds-
man 87

MacArthur Foundation 42
Make-a-Wish Foundation
129
March of Dimes 129
Meals on Wheels Association
of America 129
Medical Reserve Corps 90
Merrill, Mary 9; four tenets
of volunteerism 10
minorities and volunteerism
35; AARP study 37, 61
Moen, Phyllis 77
Morrow-Howell, Nancy 54,
76
"Multicultural Study 2003"
37
Musick, Marc A. 78

National Council on the
Aging 16
The National Multiple Scle-
rosis Society 130
National Oceanic and
Atmospheric Administra-
tion 109
National Park Service 110
national parks and forests 110
National Retiree Volunteer
Coalition 130, 151

National Safety Council 131
National Senior Services
Corps 94
Natural Resources Conserva-
tion Service 106
The Nature Conservancy
131
NetAid 166
Network for Good 151
Non-Profit Career Network
152
Nunn, Michelle 13, 28

OASIS 131
O'Connell, Brian 28
Older Americans Act pro-
grams 87
Older Americans Month 39

Peace Corps 99
Points of Light Foundation
152
Project HOPE 146
Putnam, Robert 60

ReFirement 57
Retired & Senior Volunteer
Program 97
retirees and seniors as volunteers 17; number who vol-
unteer 63
retirement: defined 48; four
phases of 49; history of in
America 49; preparing for
57; redefining 50; top ten
ways to reinvent 57; vol-
unteering in 58
rights and responsibilities of
a volunteer 22

The Salvation Army 132
Save the Children 132, 146
Scheibel, James 48
Second Harvest 133
Senior Attorney Volunteers
for the Elderly 133
Senior Companion Program
96
Senior Corps 94
Senior Medicare Patrol 101
SeniorNet 133, 167
Seniors: as social capital 59;
how seniors learn about
volunteer opportunities
71; number of 63
Service Corps of Retired
Executives 98, 167

The Smithsonian Institution
134
socioeconomic implications
of an aging society in the
present 47
state government: programs
113; websites 114
state parks and forests 113

United Methodist Volunteers
In Mission 134
United Nations Children's
Fund (UNICEF) 135
United Nations Volunteers
136, 147, 168
United Way 136
U.S. Army Corps of Engineers
107
U.S. Bureau of Land Manage-
ment 108
U.S. Fish and Wildlife Service
104
USA Freedom Corps 88, 168
USA Freedom Corps Volun-
teer Network 89, 153

Veterans of Foreign Wars
136
virtual volunteers and volunteering 156; assignments
159; benefits for organizations 159; benefits for volunteers 158; defined 158;
future of 165; organiza-
tions that need 166; questions to consider 163;
recruiting and utilizing
161
VISTA *see* Volunteers in
Service to America
Voluntary Service Overseas
148
volunteer(s): activities 19,
69; deciding to 14; definition of 11; monetary value
of 68; number of retirees
and seniors who volunteer
65; opportunities at na-
tional and state parks and
forests 110; reasons people
volunteer 13; reasons seniors do not volunteer 81;
rights and responsibilities
of 22; ten tips 23; type of
work 69; U.S. Department
of Labor definition 10;
value of volunteers' con-

tributions 68; virtual 156; where to begin 21; why retirees and seniors volunteer 13

Volunteer Canada 148

Volunteer Match 155, 168; *see also* Network for Good

VolunteerAmerica 154

volunteering: benefits of 11, 73; helping society 79; and longevity 78; minorities and 35; in the national forests 112; in retirement 58; ten tips on wise volun-

teering 23; in the U.S. 63; virtual 156

Volunteering for the Coast 110

Volunteering in the United States, 2003 66

volunteerism: in America today 33; American presidents and 29; brave new world of 156; changing face of 15; four tenets of 10; history in America 26; minorities 35

Volunteers for Prosperity 91

Volunteers in Medicine Institute 137

Volunteers in Service to America 100

Volunteers of America 137

Wisdom Works 15

Wooden, Ruth 55

World Wide Volunteer 149

WorldTeach 148

Young Men's Christian Association 138

Young Women's Christian Association 138